Slipstream

Slipstream
A DAUGHTER REMEMBERS

RACHEL MANLEY

Alfred A. Knopf Canada

PUBLISHED BY ALFRED A. KNOPF CANADA

Grateful acknowledgment is made to Mary F. Smith, for her kind
permission to quote an unpublished poem by M.G. Smith, and to
George Campbell, for his kind permission to quote his poem "A Cloud"
from *First Poems* (Garland Publishing: New York and London), 1981.
Copyright © 1945, 1981. Originally published in a different format
and order in Kingston, Jamaica, in 1945. All rights reserved.

Canadian Cataloguing in Publication Data

Manley, Rachel
Slipstream : a daughter remembers

ISBN 0-676-97279-9

1. Manley, Michael, 1924– .   2. Manley, Michael, 1924– — Family.
3. Manley, Rachel.   4. Prime ministers — Jamaica — Biography.
5. Fathers and daughters — Jamaica.   I. Title.

F1887.M26M36 2000   972.9206'092   C00-930376-6

First Edition

Visit Random House of Canada Limited's Website: www.randomhouse.ca

Printed and bound in the United States of America

10 9 8 7 6 5 4 3 2 1

— Michael Manley's last letter to his daughter Rachel.
February 1996.

For Joseph
In memory of our father

ONE

MY FATHER DIED ON A THURSDAY. It's strange how casually we say the names of the days, or refer to a month and a date: Thursday, March the sixth. We say it with the ease of walking down a familiar sidewalk. A date is, after all, a public thing, and belongs to everyone. We make of it what we will. We do not shudder with the premonition that we may be walking over a grave, or trespassing on a future anniversary.

At the moment of his death, shortly before midnight, my father was looking at a picture on the far wall. It was drawn by his mother. The simple line drawing, red chalk on an aqua page, showed a nude woman cupping her hand to her left breast as though indicating what was in her heart. It was a gentle gesture, coy for my grandmother's bold work, a gesture a woman might make when thinking of her child. It had been a gift to my father, and always hung in his bedroom. He died looking at that picture, and I was looking at him. I was holding his hand. There we were, my late grandmother, my father and me. It occurs to me now how profound yet intricate are the bonds that link the generations; how a family marks its own landscape like a mountain range, but the shape that others see was formed by some gradual, unrelenting continental drift.

Cancer colonizes. It subdues. It imposes an entirely foreign culture. It wins by dividing the body against itself, by disrupting the lines of communication within. We turn against the piece of us that hurts. A lifetime's natural harmony is ripped apart. We become a battlefield in which we are fighting ourselves.

My father's cancer had lived with him so long that, to a certain extent, each had learned to accommodate the other. Between each attack and countering line of defence, they had learned to compromise — for space, for food, for time awake or asleep, for margins between one thing and another. "You are nowhere without me," my father would remind his occupant. It was, after all, *his* cancer. It was learning from a master.

For it seemed as if the cancer had taken on its host's characteristics. Like my father, it had audacity. It had a great and powerful foe, but it was an intelligent enemy. It knew exactly how far to push. It knew when to lie low and lull him into a false sense of security. Let him make his mistakes, wait too long for the next test. Let him work too hard, lower his resistance, develop pneumonia so that surgery was delayed. Let him feel well enough to go to his appointments, distracting the doctors with his charisma and bravado. In the meantime it quietly amassed its soldiers, spreading subversion to further cells. When it had weakened the walls, it challenged the foundations of the house it was intent on destroying; it occupied his very bones.

In his final days, my father was like a night watchman fighting the defenceless oblivion of sleep. He feared that, if he relented, he might never wake up. He appeared to spend his time juggling the perimeters of his situation in his head, always watchful, assessing and balancing, as though he suspected that some crucial but invisible piece of information out there could make all the difference to the outcome.

He was still fighting the system.

Two mornings before his death, he may have sensed that the central spool from which his life had unwound for over seventy-two years was spinning faster and faster. He may have sensed an oncoming midnight by which his span must be complete. I was struck by something he said that was quite out of character.

"Remorse, come."

The dry, wind-wounded words rasped like pumice, yet I had the feeling they were spoken in challenge.

Remorse, come? What did he mean? Regret? Repentance?

Repent. I found this word repeating itself in my head. He hung his eyes on me, as I unwittingly returned his stare till it surprised me, embarrassed me, when I bounced back from my thoughts. We must all have seemed so self-righteous, choreographing his limited life, telling him how much to take of this or that, when to be moved, what he could and couldn't do. Even his sickroom must have seemed smug, with its interminable timetable and hospital rules, as if some disobedience had sent him in there for discipline and reform.

Remorse, come.

Did he address remorse as though in combat, as though he were a boxer taunting an opponent in the ring? Or was the enormity of his tribulation a thought he could entertain only in a moment of dark humour?

"What is it you regret, Dad?" I asked. I moved to the side of the bed, feeling self-conscious, the corners of my mouth tugged by the invisible needs of my conscience. I felt we had all let him down. I knew he was going to die. Yet he had come so close so many times before and surprised us. I felt a moment of hope, but it was only an outline, like lightening at the edge of deep cloud.

"What, dear?" He looked as though I had woken him from an unremembered nightmare. I wondered if it was the effect of a newly prescribed tranquillizer, combined with his morphine.

"Do you want to talk about anything, Dad?"

He seemed puzzled, as though he was going to ask me something, then appeared to change his mind. "Never mind," he said irritably.

I took his hand in mine and leaned over the bed, so close that it seemed the bone in his forehead ached as he lifted his eyes to me. His skin always felt cool and appropriate. I had the feeling that he wished he hadn't opened his mouth, that he felt he must keep me in sight lest I run away with his thoughts, and God only knew what I'd do with them. Did he dread my annoying habit of taking over his room, my tendency to lecture? How had I grown so old and set in my ways, like his late aunts, beige and determined, whose later years one remembered more for the certainty of their pronouncements than for the frailty of their steps?

I returned his hand fondly to its twin on his stomach and, retreating, looked at it with characteristic sentimentality, my own hands still holding the shape of his. I wanted to remember each moment.

"Are you sure you wouldn't like to talk to someone?" I asked him. It seemed unlikely, but maybe his use of the word *remorse* revealed a subconscious need for something spiritual.

I had already heard about his preoccupation with remorse from Vita, the take-charge, possessive morning nurse. We owed her so much gratitude for all that she saved the rest of us from doing, and for much that she diagnosed before anyone else. Beautiful in an upright, precise way (she could have been chiselled and fixed perpendicular to the prow of a ship), she had phoned me with satisfaction to tell me it was time for a priest.

"So what if he speaks of remorse?" my brother Joseph had said when I told him. "He's only babbling. It's all the medication. What's to regret? He's had a spectacular life. Maybe you just hope he's sorry!"

We were not a religious family, despite the fact that
Jamaica is a predominantly Christian country and that my
grandmother's father was a Methodist minister once sent to
Jamaica from England. I suppose my grandparents were of an
age whose intellectuals questioned existing assumptions.
Although my grandfather quoted the Bible, and my grandmother wrestled with its themes in her art, and was very
superstitious about how to avoid the wrath of the Lord, their
belief systems were not formally inspired by religion. During
the last six months of his illness, when my father was confined to his bed, there had never been talk of a priest. While
this omission caused the afternoon nurse to lift her eyebrows
in disapproval as if her spiritual judgements were suspended
from them, Vita worked from a calm assumption that God was
not an issue one had to push; He was one of the inevitable,
recognizable milestones of this and all terminal illness. And
here it was: God had brought another wayward sheep to
heel. But I didn't know who had arranged for a bishop to come
at noon.

"Talk to?" His eyes alone moved in my direction now, his
neck already stretched as far as possible from the angle at
which he had been placed. He had to be periodically turned
in the bed. He hated lying on this side. These two hours on
his left were usually interrupted by pain. The knees of his
dead legs were bent away from him like the struts of a col-
lapsed easel; his torso was a canvas thrown clear, twisted so
far in the opposite direction that his shoulders and back lay
flat on the bed, as if defiantly going on with their own life.

His fingers began tracing the hemmed border of his sheet
over and over, with minute indulgences, as though he were
searching for an errant pin lost in the overfold of fabric. Vita,
in her initial week as his nurse, had been the first to notice
that he did this whenever he had pain.

I said, "Maybe you'd like to discuss things with someone other than us." I could feel Vita's busy approval behind me as she organized the medicines on my father's desk. "It's been a terrible ordeal for you, Dad, and I thought you might want to talk to someone used to dealing with these situations."

He was smiling at me. I felt like a fool. My father, Michael, the fixer of the universe. Michael the ultimate activist, solver of problems, creator of visions, dreamer of Sagittarian dreams, my Rock of Gibraltar; Michael, an archangel of Jewish and Christian tradition, the head of the heavenly host. Michael, my dangerous quagmire and quicksand, my umbilical rope.

"Now you're making me feel stupid," I said.

"No . . . I'm not, really . . . ," he insisted, but softly, his smile outlasting the quick, small shake of his head, which was like a moment of punctuation in a long sentence. "I'm thinking how wonderful you've all been . . . the burden on you and Joseph . . . on Glynne. You know, if I could only move forward, stop this horrible pattern . . . each day some new symptom raising its awful spectre."

He stared at the ceiling in frustration, as though his optimism had been forced to see limits there, and I regretted taking him so seriously, sometimes not taking him seriously enough. I had a familiar feeling of making my way back to the start of some perpetual race that never quite began; as if, in my relationship with my father, I had no sooner started to run than I was stopped by the sound of a second gun. I felt that, since my grandmother's death ten years before, I had lost the rules of the game.

This was my father's last room. Day after day it remained benign around us, in resolute contradiction to everything happening within. It even seemed uncommitted to the pictures that hung there. It was a long, narrow, neutral blue-grey room, an upstairs extension to the house's original plan he had conceived as a study over the patio when, shortly before he embarked on his last campaign for re-election as Jamaica's prime minister in 1989, he bought the unpretentious unit in a well-guarded suburban development. This was his final incarnation.

At first I had thought he seemed too big for the townhouse, but during the slow course of his illness the narrow structure seemed slowly to engulf us all, even him. The new custom-made furniture, contemporary and overstuffed, seemed odd after his previously spartan, uncoordinated world. Everything felt so bland here, things matching things, things that fitted together perfectly — from the clear slab of glass on legs instead of the mahogany dining table that bore our scars, to the obesity of the upholstery, which efficiently muffled the years of our common past. It was a place accountable only to the limits of this present life.

Whether his bedroom was short and wide or deep and long depended on which way my father's hospital bed was placed. It now lay east to west, between the longer walls with their windows on either side. At the far end an indeterminate L-shaped wooden contrivance, painted the same colour as the walls, joined at the corner as a doubled-winged desk. There were few drawers, and these slithered open and snapped shut like the bolt of a gun. There was little but fresh stationery inside them, stationery he would ask me to pass to him so he could make his customary lists of things to be done, which until recently he had kept folded in the left-hand pocket of his shirts or pyjamas. Now the current list lay on the bedside table under the clip of a thin, black ballpoint pen.

The room's neutrality made it easy to modify. The desk had become a nurse's station. It seemed to me that we were all taking shifts — people or objects — just passing through.

"The doctor was asking me the other day if I thought

you'd like to talk to a priest, and of course I said no, but I think someone may have arranged a visit today."

"A priest?" He let go of the edge of the sheet and pulled his hands away, as though he thought the imaginary pin might stick him.

"Or a bishop or something. Don't you want to talk to anyone?"

"Talk about what? I mean, in what sense am I to speak?" His eyes swept the room as though envisioning throngs of supporters who would readily agree with him. "I must be honest, this is not a conversation I would be continuing; it's out of left field. You know I've never walked that road." He had a way of expanding lavishly on any idea he didn't like, as though spreading the folds of a concertina, and he would shade his remarks with enough mild sarcasm to illustrate the idea's inherent folly. The experience was usually humiliating, but I accepted it today.

"Which bishop is this?"

"I don't know. But if he's a bishop he's probably an Anglican."

"But don't you see, dear? I couldn't see him and not then see an Episcopalian and a Catholic. And what about the Baptists and Rastafarians, and the Methodists? For God's sake, I think I am actually a Methodist myself. They will all want to come and see me!"

His words, as he delivered them, were still carefully arranged in thoughtful phrases, although they arrived on rasps of diminishing breath.

"But this is not about politics, Dad."

"Well, what is it about?"

I thought about that. "Your eternal soul, I suppose."

"Oh, is *that* it?" His brow relaxed from a clutch of concentration, and his head fell back on the pillows. "Cancel it," he said simply.

He was tired now. His pain, always straining against the opiate leash that controlled it, pounced at the first moment of opportunity. His face darkened and I knew he would need me now, would be glad of my company until it was time for his next pill. I knew that the freedom to think beyond his illness would abandon him, and this room would once again be his shrunken world.

The hospital bed had become a familiar frame in which to locate him. In a perverse way, I found this comforting. He was like a baby who wakes to a constant world, to the hands always there to hold over the bedrails, to the same heads hovering, the same solicitous faces, parts of a whole benevolence shining down, nurturing images that I knew endured within the frames of other people's lives — baptisms and first communions, weddings in churches and graduations — and so what if, now, fixed in a common space at last, I was the mother hovering?

In the final six months of his illness, I felt a great need to be near my father. To help him if I could. I had not been there for my grandfather as he slowly broke down. I had not been there for the sudden departure of my grandmother, for by then I had remarried and moved to Canada, though my sons, Drum and Luke, were still at school in the Caribbean. After a lifetime of chasing my father's attention like a fleeting phantasm, I needed to be with him now. When the time came for him to go, I would send him safely on to his parents. My grandmother would have wanted me to clear things up afterwards, to ensure his legacy as best I could, as she had done for my grandfather, as my father and I had tried to do for her.

"I love having you all to myself," I said. "I wish we'd been a normal family." And immediately I regretted saying it.

He continued the minute search of his sheet as if, had he stopped, either my comment or the pain might have overtaken him. "Normal." He moved his head from side to side. "Normal," and he lengthened the first syllable till it was big enough to think in. "Ah, my first-born, what *is* normal?"

His remorse. My regrets.

Between my father and me there was often misunder-standing. There always seemed to be some residue that rose like a flavour on steam, and hung over us, and whatever that essence was (and make no mistake, we loved each other), it was guided by our excessive feelings onto our surrounding walls. Despite being a sycophant, I usually ended up saying the wrong things to my father. "Suck-Up," my four paternal step-siblings called me.

He gestured to the chair, the Dubonnet-seated upright metal one that we used for bridge games or dictation or per-sonal chats. I sat down and bent my head to the bony, dis-quieted hands he released for me. He gave my hair a tousling benediction.

If Vita was disappointed by her patient's latest show of evangelic reluctance, she showed no sign of this, coming over to give him his pills and ask, in an enigmatic code rem-iniscent of lovers, if he was ready for a change. "Yes," he said, as though it meant more to them than simply that. We helped him over to his right side, Vita holding him under his arms. "I'll float through the air," and I bunched the folded fork of his knees, "with the greatest of ease . . . ," in the link of my bent arms, "the daring young man . . . ," the sheer weight of his bones completed the heave we had begun, "on the flying trapeze." He called this change to the right side his "redemption."

We rearranged the small pillows lovingly made for him by his daughter-in-law, Della, beneath his shoulders and knees, and placed a third, smaller one — assembled from a red British Airways shoe bag by my not-to-be-outdone self —

between his ankles while he continued to mutter a twist on one of his childhood cheer-everybody-up songs.

"My right turn," he quipped.

"And you the big socialist?" Vita teased him.

His spirit seemed to smooth as his body settled into the more comfortable province. "You are my shield," he said with a slight ironic gesture, waving his hand to indicate the picture window that now faced him. Despite his wish to the contrary, it was said to be made of bulletproof glass, on the advice of his security staff when he moved into this house as prime minister. Overlooking an empty lot, they felt the far side of the house was more vulnerable. From this cocoon he could see only the tops of the trees and the sky consumed by its moods.

"To heal the hurts . . . to build bridges, if one only could. To have time," he said and sighed. I got the impression he was making ponderous notes for some invisible internal audit.

More steam, more residue on our walls, more sorrow.

"How is the pain?"

"Receding. The pills are working. It comes in waves." And he suddenly gave his hoarse abbreviated laugh. "I am like poor old King Canute who cannot stop the waves!"

He looked at me for affirmation. The morphine's seconds of reprieve were ticking by. He would soon slip into his next trough of sleep.

"He just couldn't stop them," he whispered. I suppose he meant the waves.

It was hard to imagine then, but once upon a time I believed that he could.

~

Cable Hut Beach, east of Kingston, has no white sand, no immaculate duning of the shore's skin beneath a placid transparency of aqua. There are no gashed coconut boughs applauding the horizon with excited nods, no caretaking breezes to ward off the swords of the sun. No, Cable Hut Beach has none of this.

From when I was a small child I always seemed to know that there were two Jamaicas. In my mind it was a little like the difference in sand. One Jamaica was refined and whiter and appeared to have the unquestionable virtues of safety and comfort and predictability, its ultimate loyalty extraneous to our island. This Jamaica reminded me of the unblemished order of the north-coast seabed. Sedated by its reef, it looked pale blue and composed, like the eyes of some of the English people who governed us or taught me. It appeared to be a landscape of kept promises, but even though a grandmother I loved had similar pale eyes, even though I sometimes visited that shore, I always knew that neither the landscape nor its promises were meant for me. They belonged to the big hotels that kept our richest gifts for other people. The hotels fenced their beaches and declared them private, so that they were as rare and mystifying to us and other inhabitants of the southern shores as the idyllic depictions in glossy magazine advertisements must have been to foreigners.

The local fishermen ignored such distinctions. Burning tourists captured them with childlike appreciation in the gaze of their tiny Brownie cameras. To the visitors the fishermen were like pre-dawn Arawak ghosts who moved mysteriously in and out of the world as they dragged their nets impassively across the restricted sand, disappearing over the water in the pods of their canoes.

Jamaicans know their sand can be dark and dull and of the earth, shuffling like gossip in the chattering edge of the sea, leaving proof of itself with a stain of dust on those who trespass. Without the barrier of a reef, water is lustral, opaque and deep like a dark bruising, and there are all sorts of reasons beneath the sea's face that we cannot fathom. Wind and water curse each other in this elemental tenement yard, and the trees are short and ungainly, stopped in mid-life and yet not stopped enough, with their dry, wind-sawn leaves like chewed skeletons. Everything has gone on long enough, but nothing will stop. The waves seem never to have lapped in their lives; they are full of argument, like brass bands outcrashing each other, leaving a salt-white crust, like a dog's madness, in the jaws of the coast.

I remember my father taking me to Cable Hut Beach as a small child. It was most often on a Sunday. "You two need a little time together," my grandmother would say.

My father had returned from England when I was five, and had come to live with us at his parents' house in Kingston. I should explain that I was born in England; my father went to study at the London School of Economics, and had married my mother there. But she became ill when I was two and a half, and I was sent to Jamaica with my elder maternal half-sister, Anita, to visit my father's parents. When my parents' marriage subsequently ended, Anita returned, but I didn't. I'm not sure I remember life before my father's return, for I don't recall my half-sister being there or my father not being there, and in my mind the lines between my grandmother's musings and my own memories have blurred.

Sometimes we took my friends Jeannie and Lindy along to the beach, the three of us squeezing into my father's Austin Standard 8. In that case I would take sides with one of them against the outnumbered other. Beloved by grandparents who were committed to me, I was a brat who liked ganging up.

My father was always first to the water. I can still see him emerge out of the ocean like a mountain with shoulders, wet and alive, his head thrusting up from his sun-rimmed back and tossing a mane of spray from his hair. He is a big beige rock parting the sea. I have never known life to emanate so forcefully from anyone.

"Hey," he calls, and I look up, for I think he is saying my name. (He called me "Ra" which rhymed with "hey," though he didn't like this abbreviation spelled with a Y.) "Hey," and we all scramble down across the burning sand to the rim of wetness. My father is a safe mooring bobbing in the water. He seems to be his own island. (Later his hair would dry and solidify into a geographic contour, leaving the top of his head looking like frills of his mother's wet sculpting clay.) Bits of seaweed cling to him, half hanging from him, as he squeezes his eyes against the light, shouting to us to come and join him.

I was always afraid at Cable Hut. Afraid of being stranded in that salt-dry ghetto of nature that felt more like a desert than a beach. I was afraid of the bony dogs that would come begging, dragging their feet weakly across the sand, and of the man with locks on his head who always walked that beach smoking ganja and hailing his Maker as if this show of allegiance was really being made to threaten us. I feared looking across the horizon in case I saw God, like a magician with a handkerchief, pull up the edge of the world into a tidal wave that would cause the ocean to fall on me. I was afraid of the ships I saw in the aftermath of each wave, and of my flimsiness against the currents that churned like a roomful of quarrelling adults. I was afraid of everything, natural or unnatural, that I believed lurked in the depths: seaweed and the hulls of sunken ships, fish, crabs and jellyfish, barracudas and sea-eggs, the thigh bone of a friend's uncle eaten at Rackham Quay by sharks, the murdered, the suicide victims I thought might float face-down from the mental hospital, garbage, the lost finger of a rubber glove, the ghosted ripples of opaque things you feel but never quite touch.

Most of all, I was afraid of disappointing my father. So I always went to him.

How salt made water live and made me light, that is what I remember when I think of taking the terrifying steps that only faith could explain, out to the Atoll of Michael. Just two steps, or three, till the disappearance beneath me of the sea's floor, which I can barely touch while kicking away the seaweed menacing me like a circle of beggars. Over there, in a deeper lap, my father crouches waist-deep. Now comes my single act of unconditional surrender to a passage that makes no sense, to his rail of arms. Suppose he forgets to collect me, I wonder as I plunge. But then he has me on one knee inside one arm, and another child on and in the other, a third around his neck, spread like a rug across his back.

"Oh, ho, ho," he shouts over my head, and I think this is because he's proud of me, but then I see he's calling to a woman on the shore. "Here we are" — as though she, the colour of rust inside that stark black swimsuit, whoever she is, is his city, and he the explorer who sets forth on her behalf to conquer lands never dreamed of. He beckons her to come. And I am angry that he knows her; I hate her, and I hate the sea and I hate the sun, and in a flash I think I hate my father.

I am going to tell my grandmother.

This disquieting stranger arranges her hair on her head, and seeks stones to leave on her towel, which lifts like a tent flap when affronted by a gust.

My father rises and drops, rises and drops, to the heartbeat of the waves. Sometimes he can't quite move into the stomach of their curve, and misses their rhythm, and hoists me as though separating me from his seabed, out of its reach but not quite, and I am a limb of him, and the tides are pulling me down, just for a second drowning me, drowning me, and then I shoot out like a cork on a string to resettle on him. I am telling him that my eyes are full of salt, but he cannot hear me, for he is shouting over my head to the stranger.

She has crossed the sand now, and waits, hugging herself as though against the future. The waves seem to wait as well. She touches the water with her toes and gives a little cry that drifts like a piece of coral, all fragmented and hollow, over the water to us. I want him to disapprove of this reticence. But she spills herself slowly into the water and marvels at the sudden waist-high coldness, and at us, the pyramid of children laughing from the Atoll of Michael. She swims, an elegant side-to-side crawl with a dancer's sure shoulders. She comes back to us and stops in front of my father, taking me and then another child as he hands us off; we are squirming like blind puppies. "This is Thelma," he says, as though he is naming a fellow island.

We are passed from hand to hand to practise the shallow paddle of instinctive survival, and then my father takes me on his back for a swim, my arms round his neck. He moves like a submarine, lifting his head to heave in air, and disappearing beneath me again. I am his papoose. Then he delivers us all back to the beach. My friends run across the sand with the stranger.

"I don't like this sea," I tell my father. "I can't learn to swim, it's too rough. I like white sand and blue water. I don't want those waves. Make them go away, Daddy."

We sit on the damp rim of beach, where the sand has been stained by the wake of the sea's latest intention.

"Not even a king can stop the waves," he says. But I don't believe him.

"Let me tell you a story. There was an English king whose name was Canute. He wanted his subjects to know that a king is only human, and there are limits to his powers. One day he called all his fawning courtiers down to the edge of the water. He commanded the tide to cease rising, and the waves to stop. But the water kept on coming and the waves came crashing down — much bigger waves than even these — like the huge waves in Cornwall, where you were born. You used to laugh when I took you for walks along that beach. You were not a bit afraid. Anyway, the point is — he overreached. But he did it for a purpose. He did it to teach the people the limited power of a king."

I think about this. I don't remember Cornwall, but I'm sure my father can do what King Canute could not. "But you are bigger than King Canute!" I say.

He laughs and scoops me up to carry me over the scorching sand. "Better you learn to swim in the roughest seas," he chants, like the last line of a hymn.

I feel relieved and hungry. My father leaves us on the sand, on a large blanket with the stranger of the lovely name, Thelma. She is looking for driftwood, and finds the curled ear of a listening shell, forever intent on its own story. She kneels beside us, wrapped in a colourful striped towel. Dark glasses. The first person I've ever seen with dark glasses. And she has a straw basket, a real Jamaican carry-me-ackee-go-a-Linstead-Market basket, round like the hampers on a donkey, with a bowed, permanently upright handle. In there, under a red plaid cloth, are sandwiches and a flask of lemonade, and all sorts of old plastic and metal flask-caps from which to drink. And smaller shells that the lady found. I marvel. This must be a picnic, a thing my grandmother says only certain people can make. (She inexplicably blames her own inability on her sculptor's hands!)

I watch my father plunge back into the heaving sea, rolling strong and unafraid through the declension of some noun native to the vernacular of water. And I feel us moving across the morning, like a hike across the sky that leads to afternoon, when we will pack up and go all the way back to Drumblair, my grandmother's house.

When it's time to leave, my father kisses the stranger goodbye. I am glad she is going in her own car. The rest of us climb into his. We roll around in the back seat with the bends in the road, limp souvenirs of the day in sun-drenched sleep.

I do not remember when I actually learned to swim, to defy the might of that water as it defied us, to learn that it will never obey but that you can coax it to cooperate. What I do know is that before we left that day, I believed that my father had tamed the sea. It became his accomplice, hastening him on his way, buoying him up as though, when he parted the crowded sea, it recognized its leadership in him. I watched an adoring wake that streamed obligingly behind him.

He had taken over the beach. He had taken over the sea. *He* was the sea's god.

Or so it seemed to me.

TWO

AT ONE O'CLOCK THURSDAY afternoon, the soft-spoken Grenadian professor of internal medicine — a title I have never understood, for what medicine besides dermatology is not internal? — called me as promised. I had asked him to see if he thought anything more could be done for my father. He sounded as though he came to this call with difficulty, and he had obviously taken at face value the sane and practical tone in which I had asked for his opinion.

"As you requested, I have been to see your father."

By that time, I was feeling even the most trivial thought in my stomach. I noticed a familiar house lizard whose progress in size I had been watching over several months. It was apparently listening to me, poised on a lampshade in the living room of the flat I was renting while in Jamaica to be near my father. A flimsy premise, but its presence seemed a comforting sign of continuity.

"I checked his ankles, his hands, the swelling, as you said, listened to his chest and so on, my dear. It's way beyond us now. Let me tell you this, as I see it." A pause, for his own sake, I assumed. "Nothing more can be done . . . well you knew that, but nothing can be done *at all*. Pneumonia. I think we are near a conclusion, in the sense . . . ."

He was not telling me something I didn't know, but the words seemed to make it irrevocable. We were actually *at* the end, at the gateway, at the door.

"Tell me how long he's got."

Tell me how long he's got, tell me how long, how long? went the question that had always haunted me: *how long till my grandfather's gone? how long till my grandmother? how long till my father?*

"The lungs are full of fluid. It could be any time. Maybe tonight or tomorrow. I would guess no more than forty-eight hours."

Forty-eight hours. My mind lurched. How dare he predict the end of such a precious life so matter-of-factly? My mind lurched again and recovered. I am descending into a vortex, I thought. I must keep myself together; perhaps the quieter I am, the less I will feel; if it happens and I don't struggle, maybe I can pretend I don't know, maybe I won't know.

"How do you find him?"

"Oh, that is the thing, my dear. He is superb. So alert, so very much there. You say he is not ready. I must agree."

He spoke in little eruptions, the words bubbling over the edges of his thought. I could imagine his tall frame, conservatively dressed, swaying slowly, and the gentle generosity in his incline as he leaned to listen more closely, his sympathy agreeing with what I said before he was forced to disagree.

"Why, what did he say?" I asked.

"Well, we spoke of cricket a bit, but then he asked me how I thought he was doing, and I had to be honest . . . . I tried as best I could, of course, to speak to him about the time being here when one has tried everything one can; when one has run out of options. He didn't like that much, I could see him 'tuning out,' as they say, yes, but I felt I had a duty. I had promised you I'd see him. I tried to tell him how much he had done for all of us, yes? How much his life had accomplished. So very much . . . ." As he said this, I imagined him combing his memory. "I told him that all of us come to a time when we have to see the job as done." The *all of us* was said as if in admission of his own mortality — "and in this case done so magnificently" — between his words, the receiver felt clumsy in my hands — "but that the time does come."

The music of his lilting speech came comfortingly over the line. It surrounded the menace of his certainty with the distraction of fantasy and distance: a neighbour's perspective, a separate evolution of some dreaming green point in a benign, aqua sea.

"How did he take this?" Although I already knew the answer.

"I don't think well. He was polite and thanked me — always such nice manners. I don't know him that well, of course, but it wasn't what he wanted to hear, obviously, and I got the feeling . . . well, it's hard to put into words . . . ."

I could have finished the thought for him, but what was the point in saying that my father would find no use for words that led into that cul-de-sac? Death he would at any cost ignore. He would stand at the top of that street, glance only long enough to establish that it led nowhere and move straight past. For him, no hope of pearly gates, not even a Saint Peter with whom to negotiate. He didn't think in hereafters. As far as he was concerned, this was his one and only chance at life, and the terms of that chance were the luck of the dice. He had a great reverence for this world, and his life — whatever fate's terms — he treasured as a gift.

Soon after I hung up, my brother arrived. I had never before seen him arrive anywhere as though it was a destination. Usually he came in tentatively, as if not prepared to stay, even if he came for dinner. He would open up doors and windows wherever he went, to create a draft that would excuse his customary cigarette. But today he walked to the closed glass doors at the end of the room and hung his head helplessly in front of them, as though conceding defeat to a world he could not change. He sat down on the small sofa.

"Look at me," he said, but he didn't raise his head, didn't light a cigarette. I sat with him.

"You will never see me like this again," he said, and only then did he turn to look at me as though my face might reveal what he couldn't see in his own. His eyes seemed almost gouged: red and liquid, the way fierce heat can look. He started to shake as though his body sobbed without him.

I have no memory of the time we sat there, only of a sense of heaviness pouring down and hardening into an unwelcome new reality. He sat as though he had come to stay, taking a place in my life that only over these last six months had become familiar. Eventually he lit a cigarette, concentrating on the void between the untidy table and the shaking tip of a favourite black Adidas running shoe hoisted over the opposite knee. Joseph, like his father, is able to concentrate on thin air. He doesn't need to look at anything, but can fix his stare at some indifferent point between this and that, and attach his attention.

"When I was a child," he addressed the indeterminate middle distance, "I used to practise coping with death. I would sit and imagine either my mother or my father dead. And I would imagine what I was feeling and tighten the muscles of my mind against it. I would do it over and over, till I knew what it felt like and could automatically switch to the correct mode to deal with it."

I remembered how he used to harden his hands for karate by soaking them in vinegar when he was a teenager, and it made me think of my own lifelong fears, how I would both dread and yet imagine the deaths of the people I loved. I would peep dangerously over the steep ledge of imagination, intending to ponder the supposition, but my thoughts would recoil with a shudder. As well, I feared bringing on bad luck.

"Should we have . . . ?" I thought I was only thinking, and was surprised when Joseph answered.

"Don't blame anyone. Least of all yourself. It's the old story of the dike. We are just, almost arbitrarily, plugging up some holes, but we aren't able to deal with others. It's all a bit frantic and pointless now. He was doomed long ago. The doctors can see that. We don't because Dad doesn't, and because Dad doesn't want us to." He got up abruptly. I knew he was at the last twist before breaking.

I thought of the previous six months, of how tightly we had needed to hold onto each other to support our father. I waited. I wanted us to go and see him, but Joseph had come straight from there and wasn't ready to go back.

"It's horrible, Ra. He's making these choking noises. He can't seem to clear his throat. His eyes are like those little spouts that look out over the water from a submerged submarine." As he conjured up the image, he was lost for a moment in the safety of the mechanical world of logic, in the justice of its accuracy. "Checking to see if the enemy's out there, when he knows it's out there. He's just seeing how near *out there* is." He laughed. It was a grim sound in our terrible dark.

"Does he know he's going?"

"Going? Oh, you mean *dying*." He had no problem with saying the word. "Yes, he knows. Hence the paintings must be given out, and he has even taken to saying goodbye carefully each time one of us leaves the room."

A few days before, Joseph had delivered familiar pieces of art to the homes of his siblings, which he placed on tables or leaned carefully against the walls. These were my father's gifts to each of his five children.

"Don't make me go," Joseph had said.

"But who can I ask? The girls can't manage them," my father had pleaded.

And Joseph had gone; Joseph, who bore all things definable by blood on his slender, mother-strong shoulders. And he had brought them all, each one given in reflection of a time — pieces that had once adorned each child's brief home, each mother's brief but welcome reign over our father's life.

"But he does not know," I said now. "The doctor says he doesn't."

"Doesn't *accept*," he corrected me. His eyes looked out safely from behind his glasses as he replaced them, and I realized for the first time that up till then they had not been on his face, that I had been seeing his eyes naked.

We sat quietly for a while longer — two fragments of Michael — staring at the dull clutter within my present parentheses, poised as though waiting for the flash at the end of a sunset, or for that of a camera; a brief respite; proof of ourselves.

My father loved mountains. He called them "the hills." My grandmother used to say this was a sign of his affection for them. In fact, that's where he spent his last day out of bed, in late September 1996, in a home he had built in the mountains.

He had been vomiting for weeks. It was bad that day, and we kept encouraging him to sip coconut water, worried that he might become dehydrated. Though he was reluctant to leave, we convinced him to return to town. This dislocation seemed to remain an interruption in his psyche, for he waited somewhat impatiently for the day when he could go up again.

I think, in a way, he equated his sickness with his separation from the hills; recovery would be his ability to return to them. Maybe he thought of the completion of the cycle of life as reaching a mountain's permanence, his own walk towards death like the return of a peak to its range.

"I want to go up to the hills," he kept saying.

"Of course he does," said Joseph when I told him this. "But he can't. The drive would break his back. His bones are brittle, they are being eroded by the cancer. Just humour him."

In late October we sat in our father's townhouse, in the quiet living room where, even on a bright morning, the light was dim and dappled. The lone window, a stained-glass pane by the Cuban artist René Portocarrero — one that duplicated the painting used as a symbol for the eleventh youth festival in Havana in 1978 — bore the profile of a young woman's face melded with an abstract, brightly coloured flower. Here and there, transient refractions lit the walls with ghostly impressions as unpredictable as memory. The window had been a gift to my father from his friend Fidel Castro. The room seemed in meditation, a brief interim of personality within the stark space of an unextraordinary house.

Joseph was ten years younger than I. Though not the height of his father, a perpetual slump gave the impression that he was quite tall and had trouble fitting under doorways. His face had an eastern inscrutability; no matter his emotions, he offered only a limited range of expressions. This belied a capacity for inner tension as great as his father's. His outward persona had a predictability that reminded me of a healthy house plant, one which always looked the same no matter what went on around it. His features, too, had a comforting symmetry, like the shapely plant bones that lie under leaves; plant bones like those of his mother, my father's beautiful stranger on the beach, my first stepmother, Thelma. His nuance lurked in subtle, invisible vibrations whose pulses you had to know how to find. Now he hadn't once lifted his eyes from the triangular marble surface that was part of a diamond of small coffee tables, hadn't once looked over at me. Upstairs, the man who was sick in bed was waiting patiently to get better. But Jamaica was expecting him to die. Many who loved him were praying. The traditional doctors had basically given up.

By late September, the weekly PSA results — an indicator of the status of this type of illness, which Joseph tracked on an elaborate graph — had soared so high that the doctors feared the spread was getting out of hand. These results reflected the patient's deterioration with an eerie accuracy, his limbs now stark as those of a wintered tree. Nothing seemed to be working any longer. He had lost so much weight that one Monday, when he observed that he was almost five pounds lighter than he had been on the Friday, he dismissed the scale with a disgusted wave of his hand and, as though calling a halt to his own diminishment, said with new resolve to Rennie, the gardener turned guardian of my father's shrunken domain, "Take it away. Don't bother to bring it back."

As the situation worsened, I had asked my brother, "So . . . what do we do next?"

"What he wants us to do."

"Which is?"

"It's a war. Move to the next line of defence."

"Presuming there is a next line of defence. And if there isn't?"

"We'll have to invent one."

The subject of holistic medicine came up. We had heard about doctors who combined various approaches to medicine. But even the more holistic-friendly doctors we contacted offered no more than a slim hope of a brief extension of time. Joseph and I knew what we couldn't help knowing while still searching for a miracle. By now we were fuelled only by our father's inexhaustible optimism. And we had no way of knowing whether this was genuine, or whether he was feeding on what he thought might be our hope — or was, in a last act of paternal kindness, merely indulging us. I could only trust my certainty that, no matter what problems we faced, the mind and spirit of the man upstairs did not appear to be dying. The contradictions that existed between his state of mind and his state of health reminded me of running out of thread when one has misjudged the length of a hem.

"We don't know enough about all these alternatives," I said doubtfully. We were waiting to meet a highly recommended scientist.

"Then we must learn. Things are critical, so we must be both bold and flexible. As he would be for us. As he has been for everyone in the past. We owe it to him." This last, Joseph declared fanatically.

I knew he was thinking about our father in Jamaica's socially tumultuous seventies. Joseph had become close to him then, and much more involved in his politics than I ever was. Beyond politics, their conversations spanned a host of themes, including the capabilities of clunky things like cars and audio phonics and satellite dishes that didn't mean a thing to me. As far as Joseph was concerned, by the time he was old enough to notice me, I had left Jamaica and was too busy with my own life to understand my father's. He always spoke of our father as the misunderstood hero of that time. But he had never known the younger Michael I had known, had never been close to the bedrock of Drumblair from which both my father and I had grown. Maybe he did not yet realize how deep the connection ran beneath the surface of presences and absences, not only in my life but in his own.

Now Joseph looked nervous and tired. I just felt old.

Dr. Jinxy arrived a few minutes later. He limped into our lives on that Saturday morning, a diminutive figure who had flown in from somewhere or other to have this consultation. I called him Jinxy because he had a complicated name I could not pronounce, and this was how I kept remembering it. He had a doctorate in microbiology. We had heard of him through a friend I had known at university. She was now a doctor who was tolerant of science beyond the realm of traditional medicine, but she felt it was too often employed as a last resort, when the latter had failed. She had investigated reports of terminal cases going into remarkable remission when treated with a serum developed by Dr. Jinxy. The doctor had followed the trails of two patients, and was satisfied that the claims were accurate, but warned us that there was no way of knowing whether the remissions were a coincidence. We were assured by others of Dr. Jinxy's credentials, although one of the more strictly conventional doctors treating my father said to me bluntly, when I asked his opinion, "No matter how good the credentials . . . put it this way, I wouldn't be injecting *my* father with any untested substance."

We had scoured everything from the Web — Joseph searched it daily — to the knowledge of friends who had studied medicine. We were leaning towards alternative medicine more from desperation than from conviction. Dr. Jinxy was here to give shape to our hope.

He lurched in, assisted by a cane, listing and correcting as though his two short legs had been launched on separate tracks. He doffed a flamboyant felt cowboy hat, and his wide head appeared too heavy for his squat frame, which might have been borrowed from a child. His face, though smiling, looked oddly malevolent, half masked by fierce black spectacles.

He handed me some vials of cloudy liquid improbably contained in small plastic bags whose ice had long since melted, asking me to place them in our freezer. He then sat down with us and took notes, as we tried to explain our father's complicated medical history. He looked unsurprised by most of it, occasionally asking for the name of a hospital or medication, or for clarification of a date or a sequence of events. Joseph was succinctly plotting the course of the illness while I editorialized about mistakes I thought we had made, or insights into how our father and the rest of us felt. Dr. Jinxy nodded briskly as he noted Joseph's salient points, and paused to raise his head during my interruptions, his face softening into an indulgent expression that accorded respect to our pain, ceasing to write — as though the emotions, though even more familiar than the symptoms, were not noteworthy.

Dr. Jinxy explained his system. I gathered that his work was based on the premise that the only cells that keep dividing are in embryos and in cancerous tumours.

"All other living cells in organisms have blueprint . . . die after limited division." He explained that his serum consisted of embryonic cells of a specific sea creature. When the serum was introduced into the body, for reasons not fully deciphered, both the cancer cells and the embryonic cells stopped dividing. "How you say? Two pluses make minus — two minus make plus." I had the impression of a mutual standoff, a complicated espionage game in which neither side was certain of the movements of the other.

We updated the scientist as best we could: 1984, a non-malignant prostate condition; 1985, a partial thyroidectomy; 1986, a partial colectomy for diverticulitis; 1987, a total colectomy, no malignancy; 1990, treatment at a New York hospital, where he was diagnosed with prostate cancer and then pneumonia, which delayed his surgery till later that year; a gallstone that Christmas; and then the secondary tumours discovered on his most recent honeymoon, two years later.

Joseph had to return to his office, and I escorted the scientist up the stairs to see the patient. He mounted them with great difficulty. He left his cane behind, but insisted on taking his hat, which he clutched in one hand while the other prodded the wall to steady him and provide leverage. I knocked on my father's door and ushered the visitor into the middle of the room.

I was surprised to see my father sitting in a chair beside his bed. I don't think he realized at first that the new arrival represented the hope of salvation. His eyes moved towards an expectation somewhere above and beyond us, and then uncertainly back to me. I nodded and he said hello to the figure — no taller than my father was sitting down — just visible across the bed that lay between them.

They shook hands and my father indicated a chair facing him. His hands clutched the arms of his chair awkwardly, as if he was preparing to stand up, while the doctor appeared to go into reverse, shuffling backwards, still holding onto his hat, glancing over his shoulder till he reached the vacant seat. He heaved himself up into the chair, and shoved and writhed till he was perched like an enthusiastic child, his legs swinging.

"Mr. Manley," said the scientist, with a look of resignation that bespoke the lateness of the family's cry for help.

"Doctor," said my father, returning his expression. He looked alternately skeptical and alarmed as the scientist once again explained the treatment he had to offer.

"But what is this serum?" asked my father. "You don't use *human* embryos, surely?"

"Oh no. No, no," he assured him. "But I cannot disclose my serum," he said quietly. "I tell you only this. It is from sea."

On hearing this, my father seemed relieved, prepared once again to chug along towards any fate other than the one that conventional wisdom was offering.

"But . . . ," announced Dr. Jinxy, erecting a solid little finger as though checking the direction of the wind, "first I must see patient's last scan." He explained that there was a danger that the cancer might have become part of the spine's support. He had to see how far the metastases had entwined themselves into the structure of their host. His concern about the involvement of the cancer with the spinal cord brought to mind the walls of my grandmother's house, whose ivy she had resisted dismantling for fear the structure might come crashing down. I was struck by the extent to which the victim was at one with his undoing.

"If the deterioration isn't. . . ." My father left his mouth open, as though passing the rest of the riddle to the little man.

The scientist also left the "what if" unspoken. "If you agree, we begin immediately. One injection per day. You have slight fever maybe on third day and red circle on arm. This is good. Means working."

"Forgive me, but what do you mean by *working*?" My father separated the words carefully, as though reminding the scientist that the significance of each one was far greater than the import of everyday conversation.

"It will stop cancer . . . ," began Dr. Jinxy brightly, and this surprised me because up till then he had made no categorical claims about his treatment.

My father's face leapt from its mask of resignation and sickness. "Look, I am an intelligent man. Don't tell me foolishness."

"No, he doesn't mean . . . ," I interceded, one hand held up like a tentative stop sign, the other pointing like a conductor's towards Dr. Jinxy, encouraging the approaching clarification I felt had been interrupted.

". . . for little time, then body gets used to puzzle," he continued smoothly, ignoring my father's outburst. I was aching to supply the definite articles for him.

"Now, that's a whole different ball game." My father's irritation gave way to his inclination to grant second chances to second thoughts, to underdogs of any nature. By the time Dr. Jinxy was ready to leave, he seemed to have come to an inner truce between hope and his conflicting reservations. He shook the scientist's hand, and thanked him with the first sign of warmth. His attitude had noticeably softened, probably due to relief that the meeting was over, and possibly for my sake.

I walked Dr. Jinxy to the front door, where the car that had brought him now waited to take him back to the airport, for he was leaving the island that day.

"Does it really work?" I asked pointlessly as we said good-bye. I wanted to believe in him, but the visit had not gone as well as we'd hoped. Yet the patient's resistance was probably more to do with himself than with the visitor, my father being a man who could not be hoodwinked by his own yearnings, except in matters of the heart.

"Listen. When I am nine, my mother die of cancer. I spend life studying this. I keep serum for myself. In case. I don't know all answers to all questions. You call me when great doctors, great hospitals . . . you go everywhere and none of them can stop this. And you want me now" — he paused, staring at me with enormously magnified eyes — "so late . . . you say, 'Make this go away.'" He waved both hands, brandishing his hat and his cane as though clearing a room, and then he shrugged. "I am not magician. But he see something will stop." He looked up the stairs, as though towards my father. "PSA drop and then everyone will see. Buy time. How long? Can't say. Others, they give up. Send home to die. So we see. He is strong man," and he pointed to his own head. "But some time" — and he indicated a distance by open hands, as though describing the length of a baby — "you *must* let go."

He bowed his head and looked thoughtfully at his hat. Then he said — in almost perfect English, apart from his accent and two lost articles — "In journey to death, there is always designated driver." And he combined a bow with an abrupt turn, and left. I never saw him again.

By the time I returned to my father's room, he looked tired and strained.

"That was the figure of my salvation?" he asked laconically.

"Help comes in unexpected forms," I suggested.

Rennie helped him to the bathroom, and then back into bed. His frailness was most noticeable when he rose to walk, the movements consuming his sparse reserves as he mapped each one out, as if both his body and his room were a minefield.

"See those scans get sent to him," he said.

"I know he irritated you."

"Forgive me, I know you and Jo mean well, but I'm too knowledgeable, too realistic a person. I have to be sure I'm not being given placebos. Look, if the scan shows that I can take the treatment, I will try it. I promise you."

I think that was the first time I was stunned by the thought that perhaps it was we who were dragging life on for him. Suppose I was wrong, and he had had enough of the pain and the pills and the sickroom and the doctors and the tests and their gloomy results. Was he doing this only for Joseph and me?

"I've got to pull myself out of a patch of the blues." He tried to say "patch of the blues" lightly, as though in self-derision.

"Well, you're entitled."

"It's such a difficult time for everyone. I'm giving you a hard time. You all look exhausted." He looked at me sympathetically, but I knew he needed assurance that he wasn't too much trouble.

"We are with you a hundred percent, each in our own way,"
I said emphatically. "But you probably feel a lot of tension."

"Sometimes I do. Am I right that it's the pressures caused
by this cursed illness?"

He was asking me for an explanation of what he sensed
around him, a gradually widening faultline running through
his family's ranks. Sometimes it felt as if different agendas
were dividing his room. It was so like my father to be unwittingly at the centre of controversy — everyone arguing over
how to please him or help him — but he never liked it, and I
knew it was troubling him now. I thought for a moment how
to express myself without mentioning the awful inevitability
of which we were all aware.

"Everyone means well," I said, but when I saw his concentration I wished I hadn't strayed into this subject; I knew
there would be no easy way out. "A few weeks ago, when we
couldn't stop your vomiting, remember? Well, maybe we
misunderstood, but we got the impression the doctors had
given up."

My father never flinched, but nodded for me to go on.

"So Jo and I went looking for a doctor who would think
of something else for us to do, because, well, we were certain
things hadn't come to that. I mean, you're obviously not going
to die yet." I looked at him as flippantly as I could. "And I think
what happened was this: everyone loves you and wants what
is best for you, but we divided into two camps. And if you
look at who went in which direction, it makes sense. On one
side are your children, who, with your influence, have been
taught not to blindly accept the wisdom given to us by experts
. . . have been taught to question everything, to try another
door if the first one is closed, to believe that every convention
was once no more than someone's unproved theory, that rules
are to be broken, luck can be changed, miracles do happen."

I stopped as I saw him trying to reach his glass of pawpaw juice beside the bed without interrupting me. He had a look of studied patience that he used to get when his mother tried to fix emotional things that she thought needed fixing. I got up and passed the glass to him, and muttered, "Sorry, I'm going on."

"No, no," he said, "I want to hear."

"Well, I suppose on the other side of the equation are Glynne and the doctors. The traditional prognosis must have brought down a terrible shutter over Glynne's world. And you know your wife is more the practical realist. So I think, on the one hand, she is coping with terrifying information and utter desolation, and on the other, she sees us as asking too much of the doctors, and raising your hopes in a situation she has been told is hopeless."

I was furious at myself for getting drawn into such analysis, but I had done my best to be objective. It was what I believed was the truth. He looked thoughtfully across the room to his mother's picture on the wall. The silhouette held her customary position, her hand cupped at her heart as though it were a shell whose continuing echoes were memory. It must have been the hardest thing in life for him to be bound by his sentence to that room, caught between science and optimism, between stoicism and fear, between his children fiddling at hope, and the common sense that surrounded him.

"Do you understand?" I whispered.

"I think so," he said, very calmly, as though he were taking a last long look at a master plan, checking to see if everything was in place. "Now, be an angel and see if you can get those scans so he can see them and talk to my doctor."

I promised I would, and got up to go.

"Hope springs eternal," he said brightly, for my benefit, lifting his chin and his eyebrows.

Worried that I may have upset him, ever cautious lest I arouse his displeasure in regard to his wife, I hesitated at the door.

"Are you sure you understand, Dad?"

"Yes. But more im*port*antly" — he had a soft but deliberate way, so like his father's, of spitting out the syllable *port*, his upper lip lingering to witness the vowel disappearing before the *t* retrieved it, which added weight to anything that followed — "nowadays, I understand *you*."

I understand you. The echo remains.

~

When I think of my grandmother, I think of horses. Horses with big eyes and long, thin faces. I see my grandmother riding like some great revolutionary hero, her lanky torso extending from the animal's back like one of its own dimensions, a horsemaid. Her long feet are hitched casually on the stirrups, the L of her bent legs periodically goading the expanse of the animal's trunk-like stomach. She appears tall and hingey, like the instruments in a geometry set; her arms one way down to the elbow at her side, then sharply out to hold the reins; her legs the opposite, out and then down. Sometimes I get confused as to where the horse ends and she begins. Is it her forelock that is too long, hanging down into her eyes? She always had short grey hair with a part in the middle and a joyous wave on either side, and she considered that the waves, along with her ample bottom, announced her quarter of coloured blood, her legitimacy as a coloured member of the human race.

Family members are limbs of a tree; they have common timber. And so, although we were born two decades apart, I imagine that my father's journey and mine were very similar.

We were both fostered by dreams that seemed like the thoughts of an old wooden house, its doors open to welcome history. We shared more than a genetic code, for I was raised by his parents. We lived in a world larger than life. It was a world lit by perpetual energy and wonder. My grandparents were always on a joyful march towards a new order, unlatching doors that had been closed before, making possible the world they imagined.

What I missed when I was away from my father, I found at my grandparents' house, Drumblair — their home since the 1920s — in the markings he and his elder brother, Douglas, had left on the cellar walls; in the sweep of sliding descents down the ancient banister, time-shined by him a generation before me; in the sunlight that came back to call me each morning where I slept in the small cot in his room; in the Plasticine clues wedged between the boards of his low nursery table, as I followed the silent path of his youth. We would both bear witness to a rare state of being, a place vivid with passions, with people who assumed creativity and talent in all things and usually found both, and who forgave most faults if they were the spills of fullness.

My grandmother always told me the story of my arrival, and it's a funny thing but I don't remember my elder sister, Anita, in her version of the story, though I now know she was there.

" 'Bubble, bubble, toil and trouble,' " recited my grandfather, ever a realist, on the way from the airport.

"I am your grandmother," explained my grandmother.

"No, you are not," I declared, for she wasn't the small, fierce-eyed French grandmother I knew, who packed tobacco from cigarette stubs into her pipe. "You are *not* my gwanmufer." I spoke like an English girl then.

I cried so hard in the car that my grandmother said she

wondered if this was all a big mistake. My grandfather thought my behaviour quite reasonable, "considering."

My grandmother asked him to stop the car at the side of the road, beside the Kingston Harbour. She showed me a pair of island goats. I crawled onto my grandfather's lap to look through the window and saw the goats chomping on sparse, salty twigs.

"There, look at the goats. They are small and nimble and tough. They will survive anything, goats," said my grandmother.

"Goats," I repeated, comforted by the embrace of the solid being now anchoring me on his lap.

"Let's count all the goats we pass on the road, shall we?" my grandmother suggested, repossessing me, and the dream she had always had of a daughter. (My father was supposed to be June Patricia, and the nursery had been painted pink.)

"Goat, goat, goat," we shouted each time we saw one, and she said that sometimes I thought donkeys were big goats and hungry mongrels were little goats.

"When your daddy and your Uncle Douglas were small, we used to take them on long drives to the country, and if one of them felt carsick we'd get them to look for goats in the road and count them. There would be loud competitions from the back seat. They were looking for goats and more goats. They got goats on the brain! Now you are a little girl with goats on the brain."

"Do you have goats on the brain too?" I asked.

"Oh dear me, no. I am a Woman with Horses in My Hair!"

I had an odd problem with this grandmother: I didn't know what to call her. "Grandmother" was such a long name, and it didn't seem to suit her. And I couldn't exactly call her "Woman with Horses in Her Hair," so I tried to call her "Granny."

"Granny!" And she looked all around the world, trying to see this granny.

"You're my granny."

"Oh, no, call me anything but Granny."

"What did Daddy call you?" I asked this strange woman who lived in the largest house I had ever seen, with big rooms downstairs and smaller rooms upstairs, which she was always flying through.

"Mummy," she said softly, as though it was a secret. She always got dreamy when she spoke of my father. "But you have a mummy already. I want you to find me my very own name, one that will make me timeless."

Timeless.

I looked for her name everywhere — up the big stairs, between the smooth, curvy rails of the banister, on the landing where my grandparents' portraits rested, in the bathtubs standing on their dog paws, between the grooves of wood that fitted together like sections of toy train lines, between the crisp, curled edges of the shingles on the roof outside their window.

Every time I passed my grandmother on those shiny brown stairs, or by the hall table with its tray full of letters, or bending to open the cupboard door beneath the bookcase where she kept old photographs and *Studio* art magazines and my grandfather's medicinal cigarettes for his asthma — even sneaking past me to the grass-piece on her way to the little forbidden room that was her studio — I would try out her latest name.

"Grandma!"

"Go back and look again," she'd say.

On our way to visit the cows in the dairy beside the plum tree; walking between tamarind trees in the pasture where the Boy's Club played cricket, with Wog (short for "Wrath of

God"), a white mongrel I loved as one can love only a first dog, trailing along. My grandmother said my father's first dog was the size of a small horse. Its name was Biggums, and it was a mastiff that ate lots of meat. She said the breed died out during the war when they couldn't get enough meat due to rationing. I saw a picture of Biggums sitting with his huge tongue lolling out, as tall as my boyish father standing next to him. My father's next dog was a little one called Skittles, whom my father raced to finish its food. She said that, with Skittles, her son was making up for the sense of inadequacy he had felt in the presence of Biggums. I decided that Wog was a reincarnation of my father's two dogs mixed together.

"Margrand!"

"Go back and look again."

I would watch her chew her tongue on one side of her mouth as she made her grocery list, or seated in a deep chair on her side of the verandah, talking to contentious writers or brooding artists or a wise old potter with a face like a terra-cotta mask.

"Great Mama," "Marmalady," and for each one I gave a name to my grandfather: "Great Papa," "Parpaladdie." And a "Pargrand" for "Margrand."

"Nearly there," she said.

Then I heard about the Mardi Gras carnival on Shrove Tuesday. As my grandmother graced her silver-legged dressing table — which sounded as if it were made of tin, and tinkled if you dropped a pin or a button into the drawer, despite all the loose face powder she sprinkled in there every time she batted her face with her puff — I stood beside her, equal in height as she sat on the stool, stuck my finger straight at her sharp, witty nose and said, "Mardi Gras."

"That's it," she declared. "What a girl!" On the rug beside us, Wog thumped his tail.

Mardi Gras and Pardi Gras. Mardi and Pardi.

I learned from Mardi that when his parents were out, which was most of each day, my father's domain had been the top floor of Drumblair: the two back bedrooms, Douglas's vacant one and his own. (He must have missed his brother, who was often away in the country at boarding school.) This was a sacred citadel he would defend at any cost. He would entertain himself for hours on the steep roof at the front of the house — also my favourite place to play — under his parents' windows, a creaking presence above the heads of busy care-takers beneath, people who came each morning and seemed to flow through the veins of the house like its blood; the throb of their presence was the pulse of Drumblair.

My young father would plan elaborate battles. Sometimes it was his world that was at stake; the circle of green before him stretched like an ocean he yearned to cross, or a distance whose horizon he checked for the mast of a ship. The circular driveway around the lawn was the moat, keeping him in, keeping everything else out. Sometimes he was marooned like Robinson Crusoe, or he was at the Battle of Hastings. The lawn below was anything Michael wanted it to be — the map of his possibilities. He would sit in his room at the head of dozens of battalions, moving toy sol-diers like chess pieces. He could be the ally or the enemy, the invader or the defender; he was the omniscient deity. He would lead his foot soldiers and reward their bravery. He was just and caring; he was bold and judicious; "But he always had to be in charge," said his mother. "I knew that one day he'd be rearranging Jamaica!"

He must have learned to be alone, as I did. Fathers were busy men who went out and worked all day; in the evenings they deepened like shadows. Mothers were artists, creatures of spirit who disappeared at dawn to tempt form out of wood or stone; in the evenings they bloomed like flowers. Brothers went away to school, and boxed and ran races, and were taller, stronger, faster. Only during the yearly summer holiday did all these disparate elements come together as a family.

Drumblair was now my world. The two great guango trees that stood at the top of the driveway, on either side of the house, were the sheltering edges of my universe, like the presence of my grandfather on the left and my grandmother on the right. The tree on the left was the taller, and cast a long shadow over the lawn.

There were things I knew about my father's youth, for they were Drumblair rituals. In the evenings we'd be together for dinner. My grandparents and I would eat at the mahogany dining table, which had extra leaves that fitted into the middle and could make it go on growing forever. After that, before my grandfather went to ever more work in his study, we would gather in the drawing room to listen to music, music ascending the walls to the glorious wooden roof of heaven. My grandfather would conduct some symphony in the living room, from his deep red chair, in a grey three-piece suit, the chain of his fob-watch glinting each time his hands flashed their orders across his chest, putting each note in its proper place and, by the nudge of a frown, milking it of so much more than it seemed to have, inching it to perfection. And my grandmother would all at once be the soprano, the wind in the flute or the trembling edginess of a violin. There, planted in their chairs, were the pillars of our world: the woman with horses in her hair, and my father's father, the tree with the long shadow.

Although my infant memories of my father in England had faded, over time they were replaced by my grandmother's vivid stories. I don't know at which point her memories intercepted mine, but my father came into being like one of her carvings whose features I traced, day by day, through their progress in the pale new chips of wood.

My father had still been a small child when Pardi, a barrister, had been appointed a King's Counsel. Mardi said that when the little boy heard the news, he ran to the top of the Drumblair staircase and stood there shouting at the top of his voice, "My father is Norman Washington Manley, King's Counsel!" Always so generous of others' success, she noted. And soon I thought I had seen him there like my own childhood's brother, and had heard his announcement. Mardi told me how one day when he was about my age, four or five, young Michael got a spanking from Pardi. He thought it unfair, and stood behind the door with a cricket bat all afternoon, waiting for his father's return, to hit him over the head. The matter was never resolved, as Pardi came in through another door.

Mardi had a large brown mare, a former racehorse, called Gay Lady. She used to ride it around the grass-piece at the back of the house, in brown riding pants, with her big bottom rubbing down into Gay Lady's back — two big brown bottoms, if you believed how she thought of herself (and it took an act of belief, for she appeared very fair with her "good" hair, "straight" features and blue-grey eyes).

There was a game my grandmother and the horse played. Mardi would say, "Kick-kick," and Gay Lady would set off, lifting her dainty feet in a controlled trot along the flat bottomland of the pasture, till they reached the foot of the steep grade before the far fence, and then Mardi would duck, lying flat along the animal's shoulders and neck as though she were avoiding branches — or maybe she thought she was a jockey at Knutsford racetrack — and Gay Lady would not so much slow down as gather herself so they both compressed, and together they would lunge up that hill like an explosion of nature, and emerge out of the steep corner at the top and onto the straight, *de-de-up, du-du-dum, de-de-up, du-du-dum*, till the pasture became their arrangement of earth and shudder, might and flying mane, horse hoof and the occasional metallic sound when the animal's shoe hit a stone, the old mare snorting and stamp-stomping as she slowed down, leaving my grandmother stranded mid-air, leaning forward with her bottom sticking up like a chimney, all girl-like with tousled sweaty hair. She'd pat Gay Lady's neck in their private mid-life conspiracy, then return to the harmony of her back, their two bottoms quietly indulging each of their pegs with their little eases to the left and right.

Mardi used to break wild horses in the Great War. She trained them, she said sadly and madly, only to see them go off to the battlefront to certain death. Horses, she told me, need to be able to be alone. They can't share a stable. I think she thought of herself as a horse, always tossing her head or getting startled; dividing her life into distances, a trot or a canter which might or might not lead to a gallop, gathering forces for lunges or hanging on for dear life during the plunges. Mardi even had a little stomp of her foot like a horse, which we called her impatience.

My grandmother's great apocalypse featured a horse. Everyone has one apocalypse, she told me, but you can miss it if you're not paying attention. My father hadn't had his apocalypse yet. My grandfather's was in the riots of 1938, and he *was* paying attention, she said. She had been alert for hers. It was long before I was even born. She woke up in the Blue Mountains early one morning, and there, rearing up in the sky behind Lady Peak, was a huge golden horse. She could see only his mighty neck and his head and a lifted foreleg, and his mane, which rose in a transcending exuberance of rippling light, tearing open a pale sky. He stood there shimmering from the crest of a lunge, all force and muscle, the moment of creation, the spiritual with the physical, the light with the solid, the given with the taken, all taut in the erotic moment when what has arrived has not yet left, and what yields has not let go, and what demands has not yet received; what loves still loves and has not yet tired. He was there, all things met in him, the birth of day, the Horse of the Morning.

There she was, with a horse in the sky that she knew she must keep forever. She pounded him out of a log of Guatemalan redwood, right up there in the hills. She was a sculptress, and after her family and horses she loved a log of wood best. It was an exclamation, all mane and mighty neck, huge eyes and lifted foreleg. She said it reminded her of my father.

"Only the brave shall see the horses of the morning!" she told him, and gave him this carving as a lifelong challenge.

I got to know the world through the eyes of the woman with horses in her hair. We shared the two men in the world who really mattered to me. But I knew they both belonged to her.

I loved my grandfather Pardi. He and Mardi were first cousins. He was chocolate brown, and he had the nose he was supposed to have, the more substantial husband nose to Mardi's skinny, sharp one. His forehead had what Mardi called thinking lines, and a single frown that he sometimes reached into when he had to be more profound. He had deep, sad eyes that never quite smiled themselves, but sometimes met his smile halfway. Mardi said he lost his eye-smiles in the Great War; a whole generation lost their eye-smiles, she said. She used to give me the reasons for things, so I would think of his eyes as always longing for his younger brother, who had died in his arms at the Battle of the Somme. When Pardi smiled, it seemed to be a secret pulling at the inside of his top lip. Every now and then he'd suddenly laugh, and it would attack him like a sneeze, and his eyes would disappear and his whole face would be oxblood and undone.

If Pardi spilled salt at the table he would take a few grains in his fingers and throw them over his left shoulder, three times. To avert bad luck, he said. Mardi would hit the table three times and say, "Knock on wood." That was also for luck. She'd do it if she got good news, or if she sold a carving, even if she had to hit her own head, which she said was as hard as wood. I suspect that success was always a mystery to them. Maybe that was why they were both superstitious, never walked under ladders, always gave a pin with a gift of a knife, and never took back a gift for fear of a sty in the eye. They tried never to let the gods see them too happy, in case that happiness was taken away.

My grandfather was the baseline of my world, consistent, bold as an underline, a dependable touchstone. He listened, he answered; he was there like a quiet library, a steadfast reference point. "Rain, as a blessing, is incremental," he said. "Be glad. If it all came at once it would crush us." He left thoughts in my head that I could think forever.

His birthday was July the fourth, mine was the third. This, said Mardi, was a rich horoscopic bond we shared as Cancerians. She was Piscean, a good thing, for our signs had water in common. "Now your daddy, he is fire. *He* is all Sagittarian." I somehow knew, by the way she said it, that that was trouble, whatever it was.

Although my grandfather gave me wonderful thoughts, I knew all things through my grandmother. We were women of a world that was full of magic, Mardi told me — although we were not, of course, the only women in the world.

According to Mardi, there were various categories of women. For instance, there were Tupsy-Tupsy women. Tupsy-Tupsy women were always neat and tidy. Then there were Fenky-Fenky women, who had limp handshakes. La-De-Das were haughty ladies with lots of makeup, and fancy linen clothes freshly pressed to show they had someone to press them. Mus-Mus women were like nice little mice, and Silly-Billies always flirted. Terribly-Terriblys were exaggerated La-De-Das.

Mardi and I were Free Spirits, but I had touches of Fenky-Fenky, Mus-Mus and Silly-Billy. Free Spirits were intelligent women who used their intelligence. Free Spirits were often artists or teachers. Free Spirits didn't have mirrors in their handbags, and their bags didn't have to match their shoes. Free Spirits liked to wear silver instead of gold, and if they wore a brooch it was big enough to be a statement. Free Spirits often wore alpargatas and Guatemalan stoles (some didn't wear a bra, but Mardi said she was not *that* free-spirited), and they never wore girdles if their tummies got big; they did a hundred sit-ups instead. Free Spirits thought of a tummy as more like a stem than a fruit. They often had what Mardi called dicey kidneys, so they sometimes didn't have babies, she said. Mardi seemed to approve of this; she didn't like a lot of babies, and said children under the age of three weren't people. She had dicey kidneys; I assumed I must have dicey kidneys too. She certainly had a ferocious hill-and-gully surgical scar that I saw when she took off her clothes. Her kidneys must have gone dicey after her babies, since she did have two sons.

Douglas was her first child. She said that when he was born she read everything and worried about everything, and followed all the rules. They used to say you mustn't take babies out of the crib every time they cried, or you would

spoil them. So Douglas used to lie in the other room screaming, and her heart would break but she felt that she was doing
the right thing. By the time my father came along, she didn't
bother with all that. She'd feed him any time he was hungry,
and if he cried in his crib at night she'd pick him up and pop
him in the bed between them. "So now look at them!" she'd
say. My Uncle Douglas was an introvert who liked his own
company, so despite all her hard work, she was sure he'd
never forgiven her, while my father kept falling in love and
into bed, and was a bit too in need of immediate gratification.
"You can't win," she said. Douglas had married a Free Spirit,
my aunt Carmen, whom I hadn't met yet.

Free Spirits, like horses, always had to have their own
space. The woman with horses in her hair had her studio, a
single wooden room that stood in the centre of the grass-piece.
Pardi and I only went there by invitation. The room had a very
high ceiling, and a deep, slatted chair that Pardi had built. He
had also made her a long, thin table with planks like a bench,
which had a lot of teethmarks where Mardi's carving tools had
tried out their bite, and where we'd find bits of cheese on a
saucer, which Mardi sometimes left behind from her last visit.
She liked cheese and green olives with gin and tonics.

Opening onto the grass-piece on the south wall of the
studio was a double window too high for me to reach. I would
climb on a brick so I could gaze over the sill at what Mardi
called a thousand years of trees, which turned their heads
this way and that, and bowed and dipped their long necks
above the roof like her horses. In a tall cupboard there were
deep shelves and large, thick pieces of paper, tools, paints
and brushes, cans and old newspapers, and always bottles of
linseed oil and turpentine.

When she let me come with her to the studio, I considered it a great privilege. She'd push one side of the scraping

wooden double door inwards and we'd hear the whole room slowly rise, like an old sleepy dog we'd interrupted who was stretching and shaking himself awake. I'd shuffle through dry pink and brown wood chips and the darker, rougher shells of bark scattered over the floor, stuck between floorboards and collected in drifts around the legs of the table and chair. Everything seemed planted there. She used to give me paper and charcoal and encourage me to draw.

"You know, your daddy wanted to be an architect when he was a little boy. He would use huge sheets of paper like these to design buildings and castles and bridges, overpasses, secret corridors for arrival or escape." These were his practical solutions to intricate problems of space and movement that he solved in his head. They were visible, tangible flags by which he staked his claim on imagined territory.

But I hated the chalky dry feel of the charcoal, which reminded me of a lot of white medicines. She said I was being a Fenky-Fenky girl, and handed me a bar of soap and some sculpting tools instead. When that experiment failed, she put an exercise book on my knees and gave me a pencil and declared, in that decisive way she had when she had had enough and it was time to get on with something, "My dear, *you* are a poet. You get it from your Uncle Roy who died in the war."

And that was really the only thing I ever heard I would be, so that was what I was.

Whenever I wrote a poem, she'd say I should write it for Daddy. She'd send it to him, but she would also suggest what he should think about it: it's really so this, or it's really so that. So subtle, so imaginative, so unique, so . . . .

It got on my father's nerves. He told me later that he used to feel herded.

My grandmother never left my father out of any conversation for long. He was like her crown prince. "Spoiled rotten as a child," my great-aunts used to say, and they would look at me as though I knew very well what they meant.

When my father moved back to Jamaica I was five, and he was this big unattainable thereness with cigaretty breath living downstairs, too long for his bed, too sudden somehow for safety, too restless to pin down. He loved to talk sport. He'd spin a ball with his wrist like Valentine, or crack a shot like Weekes, run through the victorious seconds of Wint and McKenley running at the 1952 Helsinki Olympics. I loved to hear about Jesse Owens infuriating Hitler, and George Headley bringing us West Indian glory at Lord's in England. He'd tell me over and over about Joe Louis fights, and a blow by blow of that famous rematch with Max Schmeling. He'd play with me one day, and then be very serious and not play the next. I used to try to peep at him before entering his room, to judge his mood. Sometimes I'd think he was sleeping; then I'd catch him with one eye open, peeping back at me. I'd know by his clenched jaw when to leave him alone. Sometimes, to make friends, he'd unexpectedly stick his finger in my cheek and when I looked round he'd laugh and say, "Caught you!"

He loved telling slapstick stories, which he could never finish for laughing so hard.

He used to sing a jazzy little song with *de-dums* and *da-das* between "pence pence and tups tups." He said a peanut vendor with a limp used to sing it as he pushed his whistling peanut cart into the school, announcing the price of peanuts as penny or tuppence. Then I'd know he was in a good mood. He only had to look at me and I felt special. He only had to mention a thing and I became inspired. His stories became my legends, his giants my heroes.

He would get annoyed when anyone spilled food, though how he didn't spill his own mountain of rice remains a mystery to me. But more than anything, he hated my cat Percy's frequent coughing fits under the dining table (he had a condition Mardi called tizic, from getting lizard bones caught in his throat), though to me it sounded very like his own hacking smoker's cough in the morning. When he got cross I used to feel scared.

He smoked eighty cigarettes a day, and typed fast, hunting and pecking on his black Olivetti, making his weekly deadlines for a small local paper where he worked as associate editor. He was always swinging into his shirt the way Mardi swung into a stole, and off he'd go in a bigger hurry than anyone else, for his legs were so long and his size-twelve feet were a whole size bigger than Pardi's. "Earning his dues," Mardi would say proudly, as we watched him go hurtling out of the house with his cigarette packet making a square in his pocket, his quick smile thrown like a fastball over his shoulder. And if he was designated sick and put to bed, Mardi would say, "Now Ra dear, it's your job to take care of your father."

In my life my father was always the band's drummer; its heart. He determined my life's rhythm from the very start. In the early stories our lives were tuned to his movements: Daddy walking me in his arms; carrying me up and down the wave-blasted beaches in Cornwall, where I was born, wearing his only tweed coat, pipe in hand. (He was studying Latin to qualify him for entry into university, and the villagers thought him a spy.) Or in London, where I would spend the next two years with him and my mother — Daddy throwing me back and forth between himself and the waiting hands of friends, me laughing and my mother screaming at him to stop.

There is a photograph of him pushing me in a pram in Hyde Park. I am sitting up, and Daddy is tall and his face, even in this small photograph, shows the gaunt ferocity typical of young Manley men. Beside him, turned from view and tantalizingly unseeable, is the comparatively small figure of my mother. I always wished I could see her face, know what she looked like at that moment. I have other photographs of her smiling by herself — she's beautiful — or with my father, their heads together in the small square of paper, but it's here in the picture of us as a family that I want to know her.

I learned to listen for news of my father through Mardi's stories, and to watch for letters, and this cycle of waiting expectation sustained my consciousness of him, as the familiar chorus of a hymn pulls you to the next verse. Our relationship would become no less binding for its intermittence throughout my youth. Maybe I always thought of this as our unique theme, the times away from him threading me to him like the troughs between those Cornwall waves, a hope of continuity, an intuition or a dread, sensing that we would often be separated. But in recognizing this cycle to our alliance, I knew that I could never totally lose him.

By the time my father joined me in Jamaica in 1952, I had become my grandparents' child. They were now my anchor. But the tide held the promise of my father. He would emerge and recede to the cadence of the swells, between one giant wave and another. I knew that somewhere in the need of the crest for the trough, of the trough for the crest, lay my future with him.

THREE

THE OLD YEAR PULLED relentlessly round its last corner, delivering a new one that none of us wanted. There was no way out of that junction in time, no way to avoid the last milestone, not to know that what lay ahead was ominous. We dreaded it, each of us clutching the sides of whatever psychological craft could withstand the oncoming turbulence.

My father always resisted Christmas. He resisted anything that placed expectations on his feelings. I think he regarded the season as a damned bully. Each year he instituted various embargoes on gift-giving: No presents for adults this year . . . . Presents for children only . . . . Only children under the age of ten . . . . No presents whatsoever . . . . But his resolve was invariably weakened by exceptional circumstances. So-and-so has had a really bad year — or, you know it doesn't matter what we say, So-and-so will turn up with a gift.

And every year everyone would get the full quota of presents.

Over the course of his life my father had married five times. If I considered my grandfather's eras marked by elections, my father's I thought of as marked by his marriages. Each year it became more difficult for him to coordinate his family and get everyone together at once. Every few years the dynamics shifted, as the family grew and his partnerships changed. Each year he was faced with the problem of his children feeling torn between separated parents and separate agendas. He felt that for us his holiday dinner was either an accommodation or an afterthought, just one more dreaded ham and turkey for the children to fit in. As hard as he pulled things together, he dragged them askew.

"If you have a short sheet, you have to decide whether you tuck it in at the top or the bottom. Nip and tuck, nip and tuck. You can't do both," he'd say. He had learned that as a schoolboy in boarding school. Life was, after all, a little bit of give and a little bit of take, and where it took, it always gave back compensations. He said this philosophy had helped him negotiate in his union days.

He dreaded hosting the family Christmas dinner, a responsibility that had shifted to him over time. Christmas reminded him that his personal life had become a perpetual untidiness. Every year he vowed that this "production" would be the last.

But the subject of the 1996 Christmas dinner, his last, didn't arise once. The omission, he explained, was an example of life's compensations. He was by now on an almost totally liquid diet of soups, food supplements and fruit juices and, despite the banishment of the scale, he continued to lose weight. Dr. Jinxy's serum, administered each day, gave no adverse side effects. Although his health continued to deteriorate, and he often had a low fever (the nurse pointed out that this had been there before the serum), he was still alive, and we felt we'd landed on a gentler slope. Joseph's graph of the weekly PSA tests, which had moved steadily upwards until November, had now started to decline, a reprieve that we gratefully placed at the feet of the absent Dr. Jinxy.

But Christmas managed to bully us anyway. The more we tried to ignore it, the closer it came. It surrounded us in the sudden cool of December air. When we turned the air conditioner off and opened the windows of his room, it wandered in on the bars of familiar tunes, as though the slanted glass louvres were an invitation: fragments of reggaed Christmas carols that only a culture as defiant as ours would dare to debunk. (Jamaicans reggae music the way they jerk pork — as though, by seasoning something to our taste, we are able to capture it and by redefinition make it ours.) It ascended on the *glunk glunk* of spoons stirring the rich jugs of our seasonal red sorrel sweating downstairs; it arrived in gifts of poinsettias, in the cards with their temperate snow and their mangers and wise men and Santas, on each small anniversary of memory. It faced us in a progression of worrisome hurdles: nursing shifts to be replaced, doctors on leave, the possibility that pharmacies would be closed. The challenge was to keep our course steady.

Glynne had brought up the bridge table and placed it in the centre of my father's room, for meals together and for whenever we wanted to play. It was often strewn with pieces of a puzzle. My father liked this, for when we were quietly scrutinizing the pieces he didn't feel he had to entertain us; he could fall asleep without the fear of losing us. When we completed it, we would lift the table over to him and, securing its edges, tilt it so he could admire some gaudy still life with its joins like a network of varicose veins, or perhaps a dock at the edge of a harbour, with a variety of ships and masts and sails that had taken days to decipher.

He was surrounded by gifts of flowers, which were put outside the room at night. They patiently lined the passage in their pots or baskets or vases, as though waiting for visiting hours. Glynne, who had a knack for window-dressing the illusion of happiness for any given occasion, decorated the room: a small tree on the desk with flashing lights, streamers and balloons, greeting cards over strings looped between the pictures on the walls. These things she offered to take the place of my father's three cupressus trees, which he strategically planted at the top of the hill, and kept pruned as starkly perfect cones, strung with lights at Christmas. They had always stood like visitors arriving from the east over the brow of his mountain. He had called them the three wise men.

Early Christmas morning, Glynne, my father and I opened our presents together. They gave me a silver marquise ring whose sculpted surface of tiny points looked like diamonds in certain lights, and in others like a bumpy road. He had got someone to choose clothes for Glynne from her favourite shop. I gave him pyjamas, and I gave her a set of miniature pottery liqueur cups. I remember that she gave him a pair of garden shears to prune his roses in the hills, and wrote on a tiny card, "For the love of my life." He told me to put the shears with some things that "I have to take up the hill," and the card he carefully placed in the drawer beside his bed with his life-saving air puffers. Family, friends and well-wishers flowed through the home all day.

By New Year's Eve we were all relieved the season would soon be over. Although I had rented a small flat nearby, I was spending most nights at my father's house, in the room across from his. I kissed him good night at nine o'clock and went to bed. I couldn't face bringing in what I had to suspect was his final year.

By now we had installed a hospital bed, and my father seemed almost more bed than man. One morning early in the new year, he was being helped to his feet when, as in an eclipse, something that should logically have happened next — something that should have been — some light expected of day, some universal and predictable truth — was not. He was so committed to his assisted rising that his shoulders and chest, neck and head were still moving towards the perpendicular as he fell. What should be happening was stranded in his head. Below his torso he felt nothing but a waist of pressure where the weight of his dead lower limbs met what was still alive in him, like a desert on a map, a vague beigeness of space. His torso made sense of his intention, but beneath that lurked lumpen disobedience.

The deft scramble that intercepted his fall was irrelevant to him.

"Like a marionette," he explained, choosing the noun judiciously, needing to fix things somewhere, to gain the muscle of control through which he was learning to secure himself against helplessness; and now against this grim truth, this innate dunce in his cerebellum.

"Now, how is Mohammed to get to his promised mountain?"

I tried to think of something to say, to reassure him that things would turn out okay, that this was only a glitch, some small loose wire or a flat battery; that there had been a power cut and we'd have to check with the electric company.

I was conscious of my eyes trying to leave the room, but they only got as far as the window's view of lush green leaves. Today even they turned away, each corona reaching up openmouthed towards the sky.

"Ra . . . ," he said, but I didn't answer and I didn't look round. I didn't want to burden him with my distress. His symptoms kept popping up so fast that I was running out of both excuses and credibility. I knew that my despair had overflowed onto my face, and I feared that my worry might betray the premise that we had constructed together out of odd pieces of hope, alternate suppositions, rumours of miracles.

So he started this foolish singing of his, a thing he did when a situation got tricky. "The thigh bone's connected to the knee bone . . . ," his voice mocking its way, but lovingly, through the old refrain . . . "the knee bone's connected to . . . ," more whisper than song, the hoarse words pattering out of his mouth, small feet on rough, loose gravel, and peripherally I saw his hands ridiculously conducting the tune.

A specialist came the next day. He was a spotless, alert, cylindrical man whose spirit of intellectual curiosity seemed to concentrate itself in the magnification of his spectacles, making him appear inaccessible. He examined the patient with the fastidious certainty of one whose expertise precludes wasted motion. It wasn't till then, as he leaned over my father, that I saw kindness in the vulnerability of his obvious myopia.

The family sat around his bed in a dress circle of outward support and inward dread. We had become my father's new cabinet in a curious democracy of disparate souls, each helpless in the face of fate, whose common interest was my father.

When the specialist had completed his methodical checklist, he sat next to the bed and looked over at his patient, trying to ascertain with similar thoroughness how much information was needed to escort him to truth. My father was exuding pragmatism, so the specialist apparently decided he could unconditionally relate what he knew to a man who, like himself, was looking for answers.

"Yes, yes indeed, it is clearly paralysis caused by pressure on the spinal nerves as the tumour enlarges."

I cannot pretend that I remember much of what they both said, only that the family were stranded at a grim crossroads. The folded wheelchair lying against the wall in my father's cupboard had, up till now, been merely a convenient object that we had borrowed once to take him for radiotherapy, and had not yet returned to the hospital. Up to this point, I had no appreciation of the accommodations made for the wheelchair-bound. I paid no attention to sloping sidewalks or ramps as I passed them, and even felt annoyed when, on a rainy day, prime parking spaces stood empty, reserved for the handicapped by the familiar blue and white sign.

And now here we were, gathered around my father — the common link between us, the single hold on this commonwealth of hearts — realizing that, in the time it took to head for the bathroom, he had become dependent on those very same blue and white signs. What had once seemed merely politically correct suddenly took on flesh-and-bone meaning.

There was a steroid injection that was sometimes used to shrink brain tissue, that could also shrink the tissue in the spine, explained the specialist, but without conviction. My father should try this, for there was a small chance that if the nerves were not actually severed, but were merely being squeezed, it might reduce the pressure and make a temporary difference. He emphasized the word *temporary*, and my father was in immediate head-nodding, word-repeating agreement, as though not to seem to be asking too much of life — as though afraid to lose goodwill in this intricate negotiation, or the off-chance of good luck.

"There would be room enough for the cancer and you without squashing each other . . . for a little time." The specialist smiled apologetically, at either the uncertainty of his usefulness or the oddity of the image, which was at that moment strangely touching. "I'm afraid that's my best shot."

By the following morning my father, a man who to my knowledge had never gone to bed without the full regalia of his long-sleeved pyjama shirts, no matter the heat, had dispensed with pyjama tops, period. It was too difficult for the nurse to manoeuvre another layer of garment. He lay in his white undershirt, which would become the norm. When I walked in, his eyes were bright and he informed me that his fever was down for the second day.

"I hope you have noticed the change in attire." He spread his hands to indicate this new rationalization. He looked a lot calmer than the day before.

"You seem so serene," I said. I was aware of his carrying us all through this; of the incongruity of him buoying us up through rough seas.

He considered this for a bit, and the explanation he gave me, when it came, seemed to answer a question he had been posing to himself. "I am seventy-two, and my personal life is happy. If I felt unresolved . . . or felt I should be taking one of my kids for a walk, you know . . . ." And then he took a deep breath that entered him in spasms: "One has to learn to design life around reality."

As though he were rearranging yesterday's vase of flowers.

I noticed that he was not stroking the edge of the sheet, so I knew he was not in intense pain. Instead he lightly strummed his fingers on the bed rail, which for the first time was lifted into place on both sides, and was propping up some extra pillows to support one of his shoulders.

As he had said, life is always give and take. There are always compensations. With the loss of sensation came the loss of his lower body pain. Now, for the first time that I was aware of, he was noticing twinges of pain in one shoulder.

Later that day he received the steroid injection. It did not help. He hadn't expected that it would. The doctor delivered the news quietly and methodically, explaining each detail with infinite care and analysis, and almost affection, for he was obviously very taken with this alert and uncomplaining patient.

"Bottom line: you will never walk again."

My father nodded and continued watching him alertly. Perhaps the doctor wondered if he had misunderstood, because he repeated himself. "I wish I had better news," he added. He shrugged a little shrug that was slow and even sad.

My father shut his eyes for a moment and lifted his chin in a gesture of impatience. "So tell me what I *can* do . . . ." There was not a trace of bitterness or self-pity, just an urgency to get to any useful point, as he twisted the word *can* till it was tight, with jaws as firm as a pair of pliers.

"You need to get perpendicular above the waist again. Then you will be able to get about in a wheelchair."

"How will we get it downstairs?" asked my father. He was already adjusting parameters, regrouping his troops.

"Wait a minute, slow down," said the doctor, who had placed his hand in a firm stop sign facing my father and then turned it round to face the rest of us in the room. "You will be tired at first, as being upright will place a strain on your heart, which is now unused to beating against gravity."

We all looked at my father. None of us had thought of that. As we fought the odds, as we fought for time, we had unwittingly conceded something so basic.

The doctor described the gradual process, by degrees each day, of becoming perpendicular above the waist. It felt as though he was trying to slow us all down, to keep the room and his patient from galloping away on an unfounded dream.

In the meantime it was easier to tackle the structural problems posed by the house. Could it support an elevator? Someone suggested that a platform could be erected, to lower him through an open shaft that was a feature of the house design.

"I don't want to be heaved up and down in a bucket!"

Joseph and I looked at each other and smiled at the thought of Michael entubbed.

We talked about ramps and electric wheelchairs. It was all part of the great bravado with which we had accepted our father's cancer into the family, paralysis and all — like a foster child we had decided to adopt, or some medieval bastard granted late and grudging acknowledgment.

My father discussed cricket with him; before the doctor left, the patient's mind had already realigned itself to the possibilities of his new condition, and had moved to the more immediate prospect of the one-day cricket match between Australia and the West Indies that was to be played in Australia that night.

His mind refused to be stranded in the parameters of his illness. On a scrap of paper he listed the names of the players he thought should make up the team for the upcoming five-day test match. The names, like tired, broken-legged spiders, followed each other in single file down the slip of paper — Lara, Chanderpaul, Hooper, Samuels, Simmonds, Murray, Ambrose, Walsh, Bishop, Campbell, Adams.

He watched the match from his hospital bed, which was gently tilted to the prescribed first gradation to accustom his heart to being upright. Daytime in Australia is nighttime in Jamaica. His night nurse had been with him the longest; she had come weeks before the other nurses, when we needed help with the overnight shift. She was soft and round and smiling, her views an agreeable selvage to her patient's, and her comfort glowed in the dark. From time to time we turned him, wheeling the bed to where he could still see the television set.

He planned each over of the game, placed the fielders, agreed or disagreed with the batting order, chose the bowlers and strategized beyond the one-day game to the five-day test match ahead. His being had moved away from the dead world of his nether self, which he had condemned to insignificance. He had no time for it, or for nostalgia, as he watched the players in the curious, prideful marriage of physiognomy, personal talent and nationalism that compelled his imagination. He had rescued his soul and salvaged the living from the dead in himself.

He was learning to preside serenely over the indignities of his condition, presuming nothing, as one by one the reassurances were taken from him. "As long as you can all put up with the old, broken-down soldier," he'd say. "As long as you're not tired of me this way." As he had done all his life with defeat and disappointment, with heartbreak, he simply abandoned as irrelevant whatever was hopeless, as a lizard would its tail. He still had life and, however narrow its scope, it provided the chance to endure, to refocus and regroup.

Three mornings later, I arrived and was startled when I didn't see my father in bed. Vita was changing the sheets. He was at the other end of the room, sitting up in his wheelchair, his eyes shining intensely, like wet stones placed too deep in their setting. His face was a small cage. Two large ears clung to the sides, like loyal friends visiting a prisoner. The unavoidable legs were stored under a blanket, his long, thin feet visible beneath, reposing on the footrests with the tips of his toes displaying uncharacteristic patience.

"Life's little triumphs!" he said.

I tried to camouflage the worry I felt in a show of enthusiasm. I was angry at myself for seeing, in this moment of reprieve, more reason for dismay than for optimism. But he gave a little shrug and a resigned sigh, and I knew he saw through me.

I placed myself in front of the long wall mirror, so that he wouldn't see his reflection there. He was just courage and bone. Every now and then he had asked me for a mirror, and I had told him how strange it was that there were no portable mirrors in the house, and had lent him the sliver of one that was on the cover of my La-De-Da lipstick case.

He called my attention to a vase of flowers that his wife had picked and brought down from the hills for him. It was on the puzzle table, amidst the loose cardboard pieces. I could see from the way he gazed at them that he was touched not only by the flowers, but by Glynne's gesture and the memory of the garden they had created together.

"Oh, the mountains have come to say hello," I said.

"Sometimes Mohammed and the mountain must be content to meet each other halfway." He gave a decisive nod of his head.

"Maybe the mountain also misses Mohammed," I suggested.

"Ha, but you'll never hear the peaks complain!"

Mileposts to which we clung, as the waters of destruction swirled around us.

Life's little triumphs.

~

No one knows Jamaica who does not know her mountains. They are the temporal frame worn down to expression by each of the island's passages: its seasons, pauses and hibernations, desertions and reunions, betrayals and redemptions. From history's quixotic lap our imperfections rise as character; scars form our features. Trapped in its evolution, Jamaica has become its own predictable uncertainties. The unfamiliar call this magic.

To live in Jamaica's hills is to be related to this land with the effortless knowing of a sibling — wider than opinion, deeper than certainty, surer than truth. Those who live only in the cities and suburbs, or along the coast, have no connection to this interior landscape. They see the island distantly, as a garment lifted over awakening knees, the land pulled away from them, like an artist's eye, towards perspective. They will remain in the softness of the country's flesh as perpetual tourists.

I associate holidays with my grandparents' small wooden cabin in Jamaica's Blue Mountains. Mardi described it as a "two-by-four," and to tell the truth I thought this was because they had gin and tonics before both lunch and dinner. Two-by-four was really an exaggerated reference to the retreat's tiny square footage. It was a two-storey cottage with walls of diagonal hardwood planks, whose lack of cooperation with each other allowed light and bats and mice to wander in and out. It leaked and it creaked.

Mardi, who loved and understood horses more than she did houses, had discovered the land in 1940 while riding her mare, Firefly, up a bridle track. The first time she took Pardi along to introduce him to the hilltop, she said she expected to have to persuade him to accept this landscape, but Pardi and the hillside ignored each other like comfortable old friends, spirits at ease in their own aloneness. She said he put his hands in the pockets of his trousers and, rocking back and forth on his heels as though settling his arrival, he declared, "I am a mountain man."

This place was that edge of island wilderness that strangers see like the back of a dinosaur when they look up: the place where government censors lose people, the place to which, with the word "interior," trespassing language concedes defeat.

Like everything in our family's personal life, events at the top of the hill stumbled along like backstage prop-swaps and quick costume changes. It was as though the family's commitment to public life was the real thing, and the rest of their time — the hours spent at home, the experience of family — was makeshift, like an outing or a hobby, always interruptable, a state and process that one practised only in the in-betweens. This place was loved because it was never more than a little bit of this and a little bit of that. It was a place between purposes, a point where the inside was almost the outside and the outside wasn't sure where it stopped. Just another pause in one of Mardi's phases, and a dimension of Pardi's favourite hobby, carpentry. And yet it was here, as long as each visit lasted, that I saw the family happiest.

Under Pardi's supervision, a local carpenter built a house of two rooms, one stacked on top of the other, with the upstairs eye of a dormer window inexplicably facing away from the best view. The house rested on a hip of mountain that remarkably escaped my grandmother's compulsion to give things a name. Maybe she thought that, if it didn't have a name, the rest of the world wouldn't find it.

But the house did get a name. It derived from a mistake. There was a natural trench at the entrance to the property, and when it rained, as it often does, this would flood and create muddy "putta putta." One summer, faced with both this problem and the frequent trespass of animals, Mardi commissioned Pardi, my father and Mike — a visiting friend of both generations from childhood, who was now one of what Mardi called our "pioneer poets" — to build a bridge out of logs and display "a forbidding sign." Together the men constructed a low gangway, and erected two gateposts to keep out cattle and goats, on one of which they began vertically painting "No Admittance."

"You'll need to get a gate," my father had told his mother. "A sign won't be enough."

Mardi insisted that some rural people might not be literate, but they could recognize a gatepost with a forbidding sign.

"Mother, that's not the point! It's the cows and goats that won't," my father said.

The familiar discussion of poetry, politics and philosophy occupied the part of their minds not involved in the project, so nobody noticed a mistake in the sign till it was half finished, when Mardi wandered down the path and pointed out that an M had been painted instead of an A. Always looking for the positive in everything, she resolved the problem, deciding that "No Mdmi" was a beautiful name, its origins a higher sign, a cosmic bestowal of title.

"That's that," said Pardi, who had long since resigned himself to the apocalyptic manner in which his wife addressed even the most everyday issue.

"Makes no sense," my father said every time the story came up, with a shake of his head and a fraction of eyebrow raised. (Even though I found my father and Mardi similar in some ways, such as their romantic capacity for sudden, all-consuming enthusiasms, they often appeared to confound each other.) But as far as she was concerned, fate had prompted from the wings. So the gatepost, with neither gate nor sign, forever bore the name Nomdmi.

It was a leaky, creaky, one-eyed house, with an accidental name on the side of a no-name ridge that didn't have a real lawn or a view. I guess it had a lot going against it, but that made everyone loyal and made the house stubborn. So stubborn, in fact, that my first memory of the place was surviving Hurricane Charlie in 1951, a four-year-old huddled with my grandparents in the upstairs bedroom.

Whenever the family gathered up there, life appeared to me to make perfect sense, as if we had entered the country of our natural language. It seemed as though my elders lived their working lives intensely for a world that, instinctively, they kept at arm's length. A landscape they were part of, but separate from. A little like peaks. Like a feature on a face.

As a child I spent weekends and most of my holidays at Nomdmi. Each journey to the hills felt more like a coming than a going, as though the family didn't visit mountains, they returned to them. They would seem to retrieve what they had loaned of themselves to anywhere else. That was where I heard all the old stories of our family history. They have since become one story, and it is our story.

Time shrinks time. Old time becomes simply a number of things that we know, a set of images that are one horizon, like the entire world reduced to a map and the years to one day; a small wooden house fixed between junipers and pines, a white dog (maybe the ghost of all dogs), the sloping roof of the kitchen over a Dover stove baking a runny macaroni cheese pie with six blobs of ketchup, a dank, shivery outhouse where I sat over a hole in the ground with the uncomfortable fear of things in the dark pit beneath. Mountain happiness is the woodpecker knocking all day at doors that he alone discovers along our path, as he searches for some address in startled sunshine; and the isolated solitaire, calling balefully through everlasting mist, is always its sadness. Nights are points of light that one finds between nothingness, a nothingness stoned by stars, the Tilley lamps' sighing circles making something of us. The smell of a mountain's body is citrus and sour begonias, musky mildew and outhouse, wood chips, rotting guavas and the vague sweetness of lilies, woodsmoke and leaves that are mossy, already mulch on the bough, the intimate closeness with trees when the wind lifts their arms, people who still smell like people and life that smells like life. The sound of its voice is my grandfather's axe and the tap-tapping of my grandmother's mallet, and in the distance the drone of an engine that always comes from another world, bringing that misplaced rock, my elusive father, back to me.

In 1955 Pardi became the island's chief minister, the top political post before the country achieved full internal self-government. He became even busier than before. My father had left his job at the paper called *Public Opinion* — a small but outspoken voice of the People's National Party (PNP), the progressive party which my grandfather had founded and led — to become a sugar supervisor at the National Workers' Union. Mardi said everyone was working too hard, and it became increasingly difficult to coordinate family comings and goings.

Mardi and I used to sit behind Nomdmi, on the low retainer wall overlooking our valley, waiting for the men of the family. The hills loomed all around us, like very big people. We felt like a bunched waist from our perch, gathering a skirt of Easter lilies that flowed away beneath us.

Mountain light is always true; its distance is never discreet. Far away we would see the tiny crèche of the forest ranger's house as a moment of the universe. That was where these hills met anyone coming from Kingston; where you parked your car and opened up your soul to the profound proportions above you. I was poised between my world and what I sensed that my family saw as eternity: unending valleys draped between the land's knees.

At the forest ranger's house were stationed the mules that would transport travellers up the hill in their own sweet time. My daddy may not have liked the fact that a mule took its own sweet time, but he knew that was mountain time. Mountain time *was* sweet time. Mardi used to say that the high altitude calmed us all down, brought each of us back to our rhythms. She felt we each had a rhythm of our own, one that we could lose — especially in Kingston. We knew when she had recovered hers, for we would hear her *tap tap tap* her mallet in the little shingle-shack studio that she called Minimus, or Mini for short — with, for her, an unusually terse rationale; well, what else could one call it?

Mardi sat sideways, her arms hugging her bent knees, looking a bit like a small hill herself.

"Sometimes I think I can *feel* the mountain's heart," she said, as she lifted her head and took a deep breath. She always knew things from the inside out; she could see beneath skin, even if it was the skin of a mountain.

"Does a mountain have a heart?" I asked, hoping to lure her towards specifics. I had learned not to challenge the obvious inaccuracies of some of Mardi's statements. She was better at communicating in images. The men in the family sometimes got weary of this, but I found that, if I picked my way through our conversations, hidden meanings would emerge.

"Of course it has a heart. But you have to listen."

"But I won't actually hear it beating?" Sometimes even I needed more evidence.

"You will feel it. It will be like your own heart."

I thought about how to handle this. I could only think of my ears pounding as they did when I tried to run with Little Norman. My cousin Norman, Douglas's son, ran like the wind, according to Pardi, an old sprinter himself. Uncle Douglas had returned from England by then, with my Aunt Carmen and their son, Norman. My uncle had completed his thesis on race relations in Liverpool. My Aunt Carmen was a fascination to me. She was a beautiful, small but fierce-spirited woman whose mocking laughter or sudden flashes of inner light would quicken or frighten me. I never took her for granted.

She always told us mythical Jamaican Anansi stories of a magical spider, some of which she'd made up herself.

Now Mardi was in her stride. "Think of a river when it joins the sea. It can't hear the roar of the waves over its own babble. Not till it's actually there, more sea than river. I suppose it feels lost for a bit, trying to get its bearings. Then, right in there," and she spread her long, veiny fingers with their friendly freckles towards the brightly striped Guatemalan poncho, to indicate a range of possibilities in her chest, "it feels the tug and the pull. You see, it inherits the sea's heart." Mardi had that rapturous, submissive, closed-eyed, listening look on her face. She looked like a tourist suntanning.

I wasn't really listening out for a heart, but for the sound of my father's car. He was that missing piece of myself, the elusive word without which some crucial sentence is incomplete. For me, at nine years old, the other members of the family were givens, but my father had married Thelma and moved out of Drumblair. Although he would come to see me, or I would go to see him, I always worried that he wouldn't turn up, though he almost always did.

My heart had three cities: Pardi, Mardi and Daddy. Pardi and Mardi were interchangeable neighbours, cities in the same province, the secure heartland of grandparents. But Daddy was a lone city, a single culture with its own province; it was like a place one visited, with plans and a ticket and a travel bag and a toothbrush in a plastic case so dust and hairs wouldn't touch it. One went to the city of Daddy like a tourist on a trip — at one's own peril — and saw the sights, or got stomach upset, or enjoyed the visit, or didn't and complained, and came back. Always a journey, always an experience.

My father's new job, though it paid only a small salary, provided a car, as he was required to travel to the sugar estates across the island. The union replaced his old Standard 8 with a long black Studebaker that had a grille at the front like the cone of a single propeller. He chose the car, and Mardi used to say, "Michael takes this business of a car too far," for she thought anything American was outrageous. I thought the car looked like an airplane, but Mardi said it looked like a unicorn. But then, Mardi also said that about the dormer window in Nomdmi's attic bedroom. "I guess I always see horses," she said.

The drone of the Studebaker's engine came up over the lap of lilies. I could hear the automatic gears adjusting to the heaves of the corners. Mardi thought automatic gears were sissy, but then, she still thought of a car as a horse that needed to be able to change its mind quickly.

"I hear the car!" I was always the first to hear cars coming up the hill, and Mardi said I had young ears. She made it sound more like a virtue than a blessing. A small black movement floated along the distant beige river of road, seeming quite detached from the ribbon of engine-sound.

"There they are!" Mardi had spotted the waiting mules in the distance, dark points scattering like disturbed duck-ants as the travellers transferred from the cars. She had ordered three mules for the grown-ups, and a donkey called Dickens, with hampers, to bring up the food. Little Norman would travel on the saddle horn in front of his father, she said. On that, she was wrong.

We watched them as they emerged, no bigger than beads, round the treeless clearings, threading their way like predictable turns in a familiar story. It took fifteen minutes to reach the halfway mark, a now deserted plateau with a weathered, grey wooden house called Hermitage, owned by a Scottish family who had once lived there to escape Kingston's heat. It used to be the only place that could pick up radio signals, so Pardi and Daddy would walk down the hill with the transistor radio to listen to test cricket from there. We looked through Pardi's binoculars. We could see them one behind the other on the narrow path, Pardi first on the dark, temperamental Queenie, and my uncle next on a brown no-name from nearby Content Gap, which we later heard had kept lifting its head up and down. (Douglas said he thought the animal had a canker in its ear, but Mardi said it was because no one had told them its name, so it was still waiting to get acquainted.) My father was third on Doris, the big "so-so" redhead with a sauntering Jamaican bottom, the only one who could bear his weight, and as always he was instinctively holding himself and the more powerful animal back, to keep his place in the family's pecking order. Little Norman brought up the rear, dressed in a Christmas gift of a cowboy suit, with holsters and a Wild West hat many sizes too large for him, brandishing toy guns from his perch between the donkey's hampers.

"Coo-ee," called Mardi across the valley, and the answers came bounding back: "Coo-ee" from the mountains, "Coo-ee" from Pardi, and what Mardi called my father's "Coo-ee Bravissimo," which alarmed the hills. The alternating bang-bangs and Indian calls came from Little Norman.

"Manleys are from a distinguished line of mountain people," Mardi announced grandly. I think sometimes she enjoyed it when her sons visited her alone. "Our family story comes from these hills. We are, in a way, a range of peaks." And I imagined in all of us an orphaned longing, a hope of return to our native archipelago.

In the late nineteenth century, Pardi's father, Thomas Albert Manley, bought a property in Manchester, in the centre of the island, where the earth is bauxite red. It was called Roxburough. I never heard Pardi call it property. He always called it by its name. And because he was conscious of the fact that he had problems pronouncing R's, and offered a tentative W for R that made a child of him, the name came out a little bit as though it were a big boulder he was lifting out of his mouth, with a lot of care and effort. My father seemed to have a similar problem, and was challenged by the words *secretary* and *February*.

"*He* was a character," Mardi would say of Pardi's father, giving the word a separate shake of her head to denote things about which there was nothing to be done. "They were a relatively sober family till he came along. He was a wild card!" She said that Pardi and my father got a rebellious, unconventional, sometimes even reckless streak from him.

Thomas, a produce dealer like his Yorkshire father, was a marketing maverick who landed the family in one financial crisis after another. He was also a great amateur litigant, and he was always suing people, then losing the cases.

By now we had moved to the front of the house to get a better view of the second half of the trip. We could see the distant safari of men ambling its way around the first visible bend after Hermitage. I knew they were approaching the coolest path, a peaceful pass through an isolated colony of bamboo. It was like riding through a neighbourhood. For that short stretch the clay would echo the animals' steps as though signalling a warning, and the bamboo would whisper its objections to the intrusion.

"Thomas loved America. He couldn't be bothered with the British Empire."

Stories heard before, stories heard again, one story.

Great-great-grandfather Samuel Manley was a travelling tradesman from a respectable Yorkshire family. He would no doubt have made a fortune from the island and then returned to England, had he not developed an ungovernable taste for the local ladies he met during his travels. He was said to have fathered three sons out of wedlock, and Great-grandfather Thomas was one of them.

So Great-great-grandmother Who-knows-Who — considered more a valley than a peak by society — was tenderly described by Pardi as "a woman of the people." Through Thomas she became a noble part of our family legend and, in the world of Caribbean politics, the family's legitimizing genetic credential.

On the maternal side, my Great-great-grandfather Shearer had come to Jamaica from Ireland during the potato famine. The Shearer family maintained its middle-class cream colour for generations, reflecting British rather than African sensibility. They craved the indulgence of the former as much as they indulged what they perceived as the follies of the latter. They were part of a small, mildly monied professional and business class whose work ensured that colonial life ran smoothly. This family would have continued its inoffensive social climb quite predictably if my Great-grandmother Margaret had not been mesmerized by Thomas, this handsome half-black maverick.

Mardi told me that Pardi adored his mother, Margaret. Pardi said that I had her jaw and cheekbones, and her eyebrows, which reminded him of the wings of a swallow. She had great energy and drive, and in 1899, when Pardi's father died and she was left to educate her four children, she managed to keep the family afloat, despite having lost many friends when she married a black man. Pardi was only six by then but, living near to the land, he already had a strong sense of who he was.

The sound of voices beyond the putta putta was the sign for us to hurry down the path towards the convoy, which approached on the mules' tidy clops without clips, the animals like fat ladies with delicate ankles and surprisingly small feet.

Little Norman jumped off the donkey and flew past me, aiming his toy guns at us and at the pine trees. The men sat there smiling on the waddling backs of the mules as they glop-glopped through the last muted feet of the journey, a ten-yard welcome mat of mud at the gate.

"I am here despite the rudeness of your husband and my elder brother," announced my father, who was the next to dismount. The splayed animal returned to its original compressed shape without my father's 220-pound weight; it snorted ungraciously and stood there, waiting to be directed.

Mardi always looked at my father as though she was surprised to see him; as if he had recently grown taller. He did rather look as though he had suddenly sprouted from any spot where he was standing. That was how he emerged on any horizon — as if a sleeping giant had suddenly sat up. Things around him tended to get displaced. Like a bright light, he always attracted attention.

Everywhere except here. Mardi used to say that only mountains ignored my father. And maybe that was why he was always in awe of them.

"Oh, Michael!"

Mardi and Daddy always flirted.

"Mother! Dad and Doug were very rude about my car and told me it couldn't possibly make this hill without standard shift," he said.

"So you proved them wrong over the car, did you? Oh, Dougie, what is all this rudeness over your brother's car?"

"Michael is merely relieved that the car got up the hill at all," said Douglas.

"She behaved like a thoroughbred and took us straight to Morgan's without a hitch. She purred her way up the hill like some great cat. I am extremely proud of her." My father always personified cars. He smiled and reached out for me.

"Hello, Michael," I said deliberately.

I always felt shy when I first saw him, so I usually said the wrong thing. I think I wanted to sound grown-up, or to sound like Mardi. Also, there was the temptation to feel that, since his parents were parenting me, we were like brother and sister. I may have been testing this theory. Or maybe I was trying to get his attention.

"Don't ev-er call me that a-gain." He snapped the words out one syllable at a time. Like thunder without the flash of lightning, his monosyllables hit me without warning, before I even had a chance to understand them. He withdrew the offered hug that I had not yet enjoyed. His eyes had suddenly lost their generosity.

He turned to Mardi for support. "I am her father," he explained indignantly.

"Oh dear." She looked imploringly back at him, while her hands instinctively reached out for me.

"I won't have her calling me that. I mean it," he said. His jaw locked like a nutcracker.

"Sorry, Daddy," I said, and immediately relocated myself near Pardi, who appeared not to have heard any of this.

"No, *I'm* sorry, so sorry," he relented. "My fault." He explained that it was all the pressure everyone was under with the politics, and Mardi quickly agreed. My father never stayed mad for very long; it was I who had difficulty recovering. I was coming to the conclusion that politics was responsible for most of the things I didn't like.

Since Pardi's party, the PNP, had won the national general election in 1955, it seemed to me that our family life had become like stolen moments snatched from more important things. I was used to the party's "executive" meetings, but now there was the legislative council; there was what I thought was "the constitchancy," and there was "the ministry," which wasn't a church but my grandfather's new office. Although Jamaica still had only limited internal self-government, Pardi's team was running the country, planning noble schemes like free education and the abolition of bicycle taxes, and dreaming of independence and Caribbean federation. Mardi continued to carve in her studio, but in addition she seemed to meet all the island's "constitchants" in her office on her side of the verandah. Meanwhile, my father was always disappearing to negotiations, arbitration or picket lines.

It seemed that the people I loved always needed to excuse themselves from some more profound cause in order to see me. Everything was "for the country." I began to realize that my greatest competitor, more than politics or unions or art studios or even a stepmother, was the island of Jamaica itself.

Now Pardi held my hand as we moved along the narrow path silky with pine needles, all of us trying to fit into the same place at the same time, but finally resorting to a similar order to the mule climb: Pardi with me in the lead, Daddy with Mardi taking up the rear, and Douglas laconic in his place in between, his eyes browsing the side of the path to check for interesting tubers he could pinch to transplant. Every time Douglas stopped short, Mardi and my father bumped into him like the multiple-car collisions one heard about on a recently built bypass highway, which Daddy repeatedly said was the only road that would truly test this giant cat-car of his.

We reached the house without Douglas, who had ambled off. Pardi, in his red shirt, too-long trousers and cracked leather Nomdmi shoes, climbed the stone steps, crossed through the house and went straight out the back door towards his tool shed. My father, too big for any house but unable yet to conquer mountains, sat down on the verandah, which suddenly appeared even narrower. He looked out at the

Hermitage plateau. He would always acknowledge the hills before he did anything else, as though making sure they were still there, as though clocking in with a master.

My father loved mountains in a visceral way. Not in the way that a man might want to climb a summit or measure a peak; mountains were not a hobby to him. They were not somewhere he regarded simply as a holiday place. Their eminence was real. Mountains he took seriously. Mardi was right, I thought, he must be one of the peaks. I think he saw them as witnesses of time, as history looking down: a fundamental permanence, the still small voice, the ultimate centre, the humorous reproach. A place where nature endures beyond poverty. The nearest he could come to faith. "They abide," he'd say.

As Mardi said, the mountains calmed him down. Whatever restlessness pulled at him, caused him to drive so fast, to look at his watch — always to seek somewhere or someone else — would settle as he gazed across the valley. I never saw him look over the shoulder of any mountain standing before him.

Over the years I must have heard a hundred farms dreamed up by the Manley men on that verandah. Pardi and Douglas had modest plans for corners of the land. Douglas planned to grow lychees on the far brow of the hill, and my grandfather had coffee and ortanique trees planted down the valley. But my father's plans were far more grandiose, and seemed to be influenced by the sweep of "as far as the eye could see." He was always plotting to acquire neighbouring hills.

Manleys have a powerful instinct for privacy. I have no idea whether this instinct was always there, a natural reserve, or if it started as a defensive response to the social isolation endured by Margaret when she wed. It may have developed as a later shyness caused by the constant public gaze. The family preferred not to have neighbours. They all disliked the Caribbean custom of "dropping in." If anyone dropped in at Nomdmi, they had a good half hour to prepare themselves after hearing the drone of a car at the bottom of the hill. Nomdmi had always been "secured" between the rambling wooden house, Bellevue, above, and Hermitage, below. The university used Bellevue as a retreat. The cost to Nomdmi's privacy was only an occasional visit by curious graduates or students, who were usually satisfied with stealing sour ortaniques and souvenir pine cones.

"With Hermitage now unoccupied, we have to make sure we secure the surrounding hills." My father had a way of looking around after he made a point, as though not he but someone else had said this, and was now waiting for an agreeing audience.

"I'll have to try to find out where the owners are," said Mardi, as she poured twelve o'clock gin and tonics, and that was not the only reason I knew the time; days in the hills would stretch like a fully arched bow by lunchtime, with the bluebottle flies sawing the air, green-eyed and irritable, and the brief pate of intermittent grass in front of the house looking like a head just deprived of its hat.

My father was planning more acres of his father's coffee and ortanique trees. He wore his farm-as-far-as-the-eye-can-see look, as he sat there pondering the hills and the future. Mardi said he inherited these ambitions from his grandfather.

"Thomas Albert," acknowledged my father, and seemed proud of this. He always referred to his grandfather by both his Christian names. "Do you know he once launched a campaign to get the parish of Manchester eating fruit and vegetables? And I think he may have been the first Jamaican to ship citrus to the States."

"Well, not quite, dear. You mean he *almost* was!"

But that, he explained to his mother, was not the point. In those days his idea was revolutionary. Jamaica's trade took place almost exclusively within the British Empire, and the market was obviously skewed in Britain's favour. Thomas Albert was aware of growing interest in Jamaican fruit among visiting American importers, whom he would invite home and entertain. He hired a ship and filled it with oranges destined for New York. And *that* was the point. The rest was just "Babluck." (That was the word my father used when fate intercepted intent.) He had not insured the cargo, and either there was a storm at sea or the ship was becalmed; one way or the other, the oranges spoiled and he lost everything. Later that year Babluck gave its parting shot. Thomas Albert got sick and died.

"And, actually, his idea made a lot of economic sense. America was much closer, and a much bigger potential market," my father said.

Mardi, enjoying anything that seemed to put England in its place, reminded us that he was what she called an "Americaphile." She told us how, overjoyed by Pardi's birth on the Fourth of July, he announced it in the papers and gave Pardi the middle name of Washington.

"Come to think of it, even his tendency to resort to litigation was very American!" My father held up his gin and tonic in a toast towards the landscape, where I imagined he was either placating Babluck or seeing the ghost of his late grandfather.

"Ra," my father said, and I turned round to get caught by his finger in my cheek. He was making friends again. "Go and find Little Norman and we'll play broken bottle before lunch." A moment before I had felt like telling him that Pardi was my real father, but a second of his attention was all it took to win me back.

I went in the direction of the cowboy sounds, knowing Little Norman couldn't be far. I found Pardi in the tool room under the vivid mahoes, whose large, glossy leaves and thick-mouthed, moist red flowers made the world within their arms feel as if one were living in a tree. Pardi was already busy, planing a piece of wood at his carpenter's bench. His promi-nent, dignified nose seemed as involved as his arms in pulling each stroke of the tool in his hands.

"Pi." He called me Pi because he said that in mathematics, his favourite subject, pi was times r squared, and that pi was a number that could never be finalized. And r was me. Pi went on for ever, as did his love for me. But it was probably also because of his difficulty pronouncing Rs.

"Par, have you seen Little Norman?"

"I *hear* him. He's shooting his Indians in the apple grove."

Many years earlier, a governor's wife named Lady Swettenham had planted English apples in a natural basin of land nearby. We referred to it grandly as the apple grove, though the trees were almost dead and covered in lichen we called old man's beard. Little Norman could catch a ball. Little Norman could run, he could ride, he could aim a bracken arrow from a bamboo bow and shoot the distant thread of the trunk of a faraway pine tree. He could shoot imaginary Indians in an apple grove. He was athletic like Pardi and his own father, Douglas, who, as schoolboys, had both been ten-second-flat, record-holding, hundred-yard sprinters and amateur boxers. My father admired his nephew's reflexes. He admired all ath-letes, in the way that only a man who could have, should have, would have, but didn't, admired those who did.

"What are they doing back at the house?"

"Discussing the fall of Roxburough," I said.

He laughed. "The fall of Roxburough? Are they indeed? I must take you there one day. It's no more than a shell now, the house, but oh, what a view! You stand on the top of the world looking out over an ocean of hills, with the smell of pimento all around. That is how one learns perspective." He gave a sharp nod of his head on the word *perspective*, as though it was very necessary and that was the only way one could achieve it.

From our own ocean of lilies and juniper trees, mahoes and pines, I tried to imagine another hillside and another time. I tried to picture Pardi climbing the shoulders of old headstones, as he said he often had, all neatly lined up in a row in the valley beneath the house. So close to the island's ancestors, he must have learned that the land was what linked the living to the dead, the past to the present.

"Pardi, do you remember when your father died?" I asked him.

"Yes and no," he said. "I vividly remember a storm of weeping and sobbing in the house on realizing that he was dead. I don't remember the funeral, I only remember that."

I imagined him like Little Norman, sweeping through the time of his youth as swiftly as the second hand on a clock, quickly passing over the decisions and happenings of the family's more considered minutes, and the even slower truths of the land's hour hand.

"You know, it's a great compliment that your father wants you to call him Daddy," he explained, as he cleaned off his plane with his long brown fingers, pulling at the thin fragments of wood wedged like bits of food in a small corner of the blade's lip. "He's very proud of you. And that's a good thing. You only ever have one father."

"No," I said, "I have you too." I had two fathers and Pardi had none.

"You know better than that. I am your grandfather. I am Pardi." He got up and put down his plane and escorted me down the two steps. "Come. Weren't you on your way to find Norman?"

"Do you miss the past?" I asked.

"Never! The past is just that . . . past. You must leave it. The present is much better."

By the time we returned to the house, Little Norman, my father and Uncle Douglas were standing like shrubs between the trees on the lawn, throwing the ball. In broken bottle, if you dropped the ball when it was thrown to you, there was a penalty. One drop, you caught with one hand. Two drops, you caught whilst kneeling on the ground. Three drops, you caught lying down, and if you still didn't catch, you were out. I ran into the middle. Little Norman, three years younger, could already catch a fastball. The brothers side-threw and overarmed the ball to each other and to Little Norman, but everyone underarmed it softly to me. I hated that; I found it insulting.

"Throw me a proper ball," I demanded.

They did, as gently as they could. I kept missing the ball. My temper was making the day too hot, and people I loved were becoming people I found reasons not to love. They threw and I dropped, and a sense of injustice overcame me. I was a bad sport, and now I was required to lie down. I refused. My father repeated the rules of the game. I refused again.

"You are laughing at me." I threw the words at the ugly garden, with the knobbly twisted junipers all tangled up with cobwebby weeds of old man's beard, and the bilberry bushes with their green berries, pretending to be flowering plants and having no right to be there.

"We're not laughing at you," said my father, trying hard not to laugh.

"Your father stepped in a big pat of cow dung," said my uncle.

That couldn't be true, I thought, or fastidious old Daddy wouldn't be laughing.

Little Norman was circling the house, circumventing this tiresome business, slaughtering another innocent village of guava trees on his way back to us.

"If you lie down I bet you'll catch the ball," cajoled my father, who I think was planning to put the ball straight into my hand by this stage. But I would not. So he sent me to my room upstairs, to lie down, as my punishment.

I felt like I climbed those stairs to the end of the world. I was humiliated. It reminded me of the only time my grandfather had ever slapped me, for refusing to share my crayons with a friend. I knew that for Pardi selfishness, and for my father bad sportsmanship, were the darker sins of the world. Everything had gone very quiet outside. I suppose they were giving me time to think. I lay on my bed muttering, "I hope big rocks fall off the cliffs onto your stupid car."

After what felt like forever my father came to the room.

"Come on, pet, we all have to learn that a game is only a game."

"Then why do you care what I do?"

"Because when we commit to a game, we commit to a set of rules. And when we do, we have to see it through. It's a very important lesson to learn in life, and playing a game is a nice way to learn life's lessons, don't you think?"

"I'm sorry," I said.

We resumed play. They threw the ball wisely, and I caught enough throws to regain the perpendicular, my pride and my humour.

And then, shortly before we went in for lunch, with Pardi and Mardi now watching from the verandah and everyone sweating and hungry and hot, my father threw a really fast ball that was low and meant for Little Norman. I saw it as if it came in slow motion towards my right hand, and I felt the breeze in my ears and the tiny accumulation of every lesson of my muscles, as though everything before had been dress rehearsal and somehow the moment had come and I knew it — knew distance and timing and all of my lines, my exits and entrances, knew something exquisite because everything was coming together at the right time — and I ran for the ball.

Just at the moment of interception, my foot hit a stone. I went tumbling down.

"Babluck," shouted my father.

"Babluck," screamed the echoes at first, then, "Babluck, b'luck, luckluckluck."

"I could have . . . ," I wailed. "I could have caught it."

My father was staring at the place where I would have snared the ball.

"I'll be damned," he said with his mouth open in half-awe, half-smile. "Indeed you would have."

He helped me up and walked me back to the house. "It would have been a great catch," he said.

"I tripped . . . ," I started to explain. But I was okay now. I felt like a heroine. I had his undivided attention.

"That's Babluck."

"Why is it Babluck?" I asked.

"It's a trick of fate. It's nothing to do with you. What you will always know is that you *could* have caught that ball. The moment was there for you and you were ready. Like Thomas Albert and his cargo of oranges. The rest is just for reasons of another place."

"What other place?" We reached the verandah, where he sat down on one of Pardi's homemade wooden chairs and put me on his knee — which was very unusual for him, particularly if Pardi was around.

"A place we don't have any business in; a place that is no measure of who we are," he said firmly.

I thought of Pardi losing his father at six. He must have withstood that injury as a broken bone waits in a body. Healing would come. However cruel the toss of fate, Babluck was no more than mood or climate; its rage might intercept a ball or end your days, but it could never dispossess a deeper umbilical truth. Was Babluck a drastic and daring gene that could somehow graft itself onto the land, fusing its ill fortune onto the family history?

My father kept his arm around me for a little while before we went in for lunch. I felt vindicated. I knew he understood. With him around, time never managed to simply pass by, but always presented some useful lesson.

I leaned back with my head against his chest. I could hear the mighty subterranean rumble of his voice as he told everyone it would have been a great catch. I listened to a huge, pulsing diphthong that sounded like a big finger falling slowly off a tight bass string inside whatever cave lay at the centre of him. Like Mardi, I had found a mountain's heart.

FOUR

"SYLVIA SAYS THAT UNTIL 1972, when she walked down the street in her own country, she always felt she was somehow walking in borrowed shoes. Since 1972, every step she takes, she knows her shoes belong to her."

My father smiled. 1972 was the year he first became prime minister.

I was helping my father with a special file that he kept in his bedroom, labelled "personal correspondence." This was our latest project. He had moved his office from a commercial building in New Kingston to his townhouse many months before, when both his health and hopes for a thriving consultancy — a business he started with Joseph after he retired — began to falter.

His assistant, Grace, who managed his affairs so seamlessly that for a long time many people did not realize how ill he was, had thoughtfully provided us with this project, knowing that it would give my father something useful and gently absorbing to do. The growing file of personal letters from friends and well-wishers had to be answered, but my father insisted on composing each letter himself, and nowadays he tired easily. Sometimes, as soon as he started, he'd fall asleep;

after a few minutes he'd wake up again. With me there in the mornings, the file and the scribe were always on hand. Opportunities would present themselves.

There were many letters remembering my father for some thoughtful deed, help for a child or a sick friend, or from someone he'd rescued from an injustice thirty years before, none of which I had known about: an artist he had helped to support for years, mothers of children who had benefitted from his sweeping educational reforms — each now writing to offer thoughts and prayers in letters that sometimes appeared laboriously crafted. I felt it was good for him to know that so many people still loved and respected him, remembered his work over fifty years, noticed his quiet kindnesses.

"People are kind," he sighed, his expression woven of many sadnesses. It was as if, behind all this praise, he heard dissenting voices, as if his critics too were announcing themselves. I glimpsed in my father a sense of futility that reminded me of Pardi's despondency in his last years. He looked thoughtfully towards the television set, as though it might have been responsible for the thought that troubled him. But somehow, wherever he was, although most gossip bored him, my father's antenna was always up. He knew what there was to know around him, even protected by what one might assume was the insulation of his sickroom.

I knew his pragmatism would survive any momentary gloom brought on by criticism, as it would outlast the bolstering of praise or the comfort of flattery. But I was glad for tangible proof of his worth from voices that mattered to him. I believed that each kind thought added a small drop of healing from a vial of life's potions.

Grace was one of the small crew who now guided the leaky vessel of my father's day-to-day life. Glynne and Joseph were at work on weekdays. In addition to round-the-clock nursing, there was Mousey, who was police security, and Desi, a quiet spirit of self-effacement who simmered soup for my father as gingerly as if the contents of the pot were the patient's feelings, and steeped his teas: mint for his stomach, and for his nausea, ganga (which would mysteriously arrive in minutes if he needed it), and an enigmatic barky brew recommended to stave off cancer.

I was the alchemist in charge of the *guzu* — those magical potions I discovered along the way, with which I was hopefully plying my willing patient. In addition to these various libations, arrayed on a section of the desk was an assortment of brown bottles ordered from a health centre in one of America's Carolinas. Four times a day I would assemble this weaponry — four capsules of this and that, and three of these and two of those — opening their shells into halves and spilling the odd-smelling powders into a little glass bowl, adding honey or marmalade, then stirring the reluctant consistency into a bitter-tasting, gluey mass that stuck to the spoon and was a problem for my father to swallow. The various drops, ranging from twenty to forty, I'd add to his juice to wash it all down. "Little drops of blessing," he'd say as he swallowed it, covering all the bases in case. "Wearing braces, belts and overalls," he said. The production made us both feel virtuous, even if it had no physical effect.

And then there was Rennie.

Nowadays, in my father's world, matters tended to get handed over to Rennie. He had first come to work with my father when there was enough space for a real garden. He was a large man whose strength seemed to have accumulated so steadily over the course of his life that his limbs displayed no demarcation of surprise at the muscles. He had a quietly determined face that expressed a truce with defiance. Rennie could arrange a cactus with a rose, a bachelor's button with a fern and a stone, and compose his own harmony. He moved through his routines methodically each day, understanding that wherever he planted his charges, there they remained; only he could provide a fresh start each morning. He turned the earth around them as if they were beloved invalids who needed their sheets straightened and their positions changed; who had their own times of day, their own need for shade to feed, or sun to grow.

He moved with my father to the townhouse. Large as he was, Rennie helped scale down every green thing to a smaller life. He helped to soften the new walls of this corner unit, giving it a unique face that distinguished it from its uniform row.

"Wha' happen now, Mass' Mike," Rennie would say as he entered the room, as though it were not a question but a statement of rallying intent.

"Rennie, my prince, they say I mash up Jamaica." And my father gave such a sad little sigh.

Rennie would laugh. "Only some people say so. It's a question of point of view. The way I see it, sir, the way things used to be *had to* mash up . . . . I say that's good. You see, now it's '*who* 'fraid fe *who?*'"

My father's weary smile through the fabric of lurking shadows made his face seem slightly torn.

Rennie would come to vacuum the room, water the plants, hang a picture, discuss the cricket team, appraise the state of the nation, move the furniture, chase out a lizard.

"Don't kill it," I'd plead.

"She's having a crisis of conscience," my father explained once. "She thinks that if we spare it, God will spare me."

"He will spare you till He's ready." Rennie's philosophy: the good don't need justification.

"Truth is, I worry I've got so small the good Lord may accidentally trample me underfoot!"

"Not Michael Enormous!" I'd say.

Or Rennie would come to lift my father, because he was the only person strong enough to do it by himself.

It was Rennie's trusted arms that turned Michael Enormous now.

~

In 1959, when I was eleven, I went to boarding school. It was my own decision, inspired by a description of the school by my grandfather's eldest sister, my stern Aunt Vera, whom I loved and was always anxious to please. Knox College was a coeducational Presbyterian school in the centre of the island, near where my grandfather had lived as a child. Spaldings, the school's town, was in bauxite country. Run by an innovative Scots minister, Knox placed as much attention on agriculture, carpentry and business, on self-reliance and creativity, as it did on academics and exams.

Pardi had just begun a second term and was now the island's premier, his title having changed when the island achieved full internal self-government in 1959. In his first term he had worked to secure greater autonomy, placing Jamaica on a path to national independence. He had also begun approaching other leaders of the English-speaking Caribbean with the concept of forming a federation of our island nations, including mainland British Guiana. In his second term he became increasingly focused on this goal, which would result in a short-lived political union between 1958 and 1962. This meant that my grandparents were almost continually travelling, either visiting the other islands or negotiating with the Foreign Office in England, as Pardi thrashed out the terms of our Caribbean future.

Before my enrolment at Knox College, one of my aunts often came to keep me company at Drumblair when my grandparents were away. Sometimes my father and Thelma came to stay, with my new brother, Joseph. My father took pains to explain that he was named not for the biblical carpenter but for Joseph with the coat of many colours, whom my father considered the first person in the world to use collective bargaining, hence the father of trade unionism. Though not a religious man, like the rest of my family my father regarded the Bible as grand literature, with riveting stories. He often plundered it for its symbolism, and borrowed its characters' names to give his children.

Joseph was born in January 1958. It was soon obvious that he was a highly intelligent child, which did not endear him to me. It only increased my resentment about sharing my father with anyone. I had just got used to having a stepmother around. There were times when I loved Thelma and times when I was jealous of her. My father was very proud of her. He marvelled at her physical bravery, relating the occasions when union clashes had got ugly, and she was often the only person left standing beside him, as grown men fled or hid under their chairs. Thelma tried to be mindful of my feelings. She never bought a piece of fabric without including an extra yard and a half for me. She entered me in a costume contest, which I won with her design of an exotic plant, my face at the centre of the blossom. She was a professional dancer who had studied ballet in London, and modern dance in New York with Martha Graham. She tried to teach me in her children's dance class, but I only managed to disrupt everyone — probably because I felt entitled to special attention.

It was thought my life would be more settled at boarding school. My father and Mardi took me to Knox College the day before classes started, when boarders were due. It didn't look like a school to me as I came over the brow of the hill. I was expecting a formal façade, a da-da-da-dum portico leading into some hallowed hall that would echo mightily. Instead there was a lot of red clay and nature, the kind that gets bright green in rainy weather, and dotted here and there were small, unimposing buildings whose cream walls had surrendered to mud.

We followed the hill curving halfway round, circling a deep green basin of playground neatly scarred by a circular running track. The road looped from the gate and back in a wide circle, like the perfect throw of a boomerang. Oh God, I thought, as my dream took on structure and shape, what have I done?

After depositing me with the house mistress in my dormitory, they kissed me goodbye and left, having decided "not to drag things out." I felt utterly alone. What did it matter to me that I was there in the legendary hills of my grandfather's birth? My homesickness was fierce, its immediacy perhaps connecting me to an older sense of loss. Each strange new thing I saw, every unfamiliar person, compounded my feeling of desolation.

And yet distance forged a new bond between my father and me. A personal conversation started between us through letters, in which we found our way around a mutual shyness that had developed during those early years apart. The first letter I received was from my father. The letters of my name sloped along the envelope in his familiar leaning-over-the-cliff handwriting, proof he had not forgotten me.

My darling Ra,

I could never begin to tell you how proud I was of you last night. I so well understood how you felt because I can remember very clearly how I felt twenty-two years ago, when I went to boarding school for the first time. But you rallied like a true Manley, my dear, and we were all so proud of you.

Strictly between us, I could have cried myself because I am going to miss you terribly. Anyhow, that is how life is and what is important is that you should be happy with your new friends and with the wonderful, busy life of a boarding school.

I personally feel you made a most intelligent decision to go to Knox. I have a strong feeling that you are going to like it. We will all, between us, come and see you regularly and there will always be the holidays.

You know, darling, I have great faith in you and believe you are going to grow into a grand person. You are my first child and there is a place in my heart for you which no one else will ever take. I know I am grumpy and preoccupied sometimes but don't mind that. You, my pet, are never far from my thoughts. So good luck and God bless in your great new adventure.

Write me when you can and remember to let me know if you decide you need a tennis racquet.

I'm coming to see you soon and will let you know when.

Lots of love, darling — and a big kiss, Daddy.

Every two weeks Pardi, Mardi, my father or Thelma took me to lunch. For the first few months I lived for the sound of the Humber or the Studebaker growling up the hill, the clatter of small stones flying in all directions. One of my father's later visits I remember clearly, because I sensed that somehow his life was changing. He had come back from a holiday in Cayman. I didn't find it strange that he had gone there alone, but now I realize that it must have been when his marriage had started to break up, and another era was ending.

As we climbed into the car, he hugged me, patted my back (I was a small child, very thin and bony, described by the boys in my class as the daughter of a pirate who had buried my chest) and said I obviously needed to eat. Was I ready for a good lunch? He was starving. He was always starving. He seemed in a great hurry. I dreaded him looking at his watch, but he only glanced at it now and then, maybe just to reassure himself of eventual departure. He drove full speed to a gracious guest house on a knoll of green hill.

We could smell lunch as we climbed the steep stone steps to an elevated verandah criss-crossed in white latticework. (The sight of steps leading up to verandahs and latticework still makes me hungry.) Beyond lay the dining room, which felt like a church when we entered, leaving the sunlight behind. The surrounding nature had bled the room of its colour and light. Even the furniture was no more than a hardening of shadows. Two sisters, who appeared to own the place, welcomed us and asked after my grandparents. We sat at a large square table already laid with crisp linen placemats and napkins and highly polished, mismatched silver plate.

There was a young, thin, nervy man sitting at the next table, restlessly strumming his fingers. From the verandah came the sound of a woman chatting on a phone. After a while she came in, wearing tight pants on tippy-toe mules, and joined the stranger at the table. She was very pretty, with playful eyes, and she kept looking over at my father. I could feel his renewed commitment to our outing from the moment the lady was present. He stopped looking at his watch. I think he felt an audience had arrived. One of the elderly sisters brought us a menu, and whispered the name of the man, who she seemed to think was quite famous.

"And who is the lady?" asked my father with surprising urgency.

His companion, she explained, was a former Miss Jamaica. She emphasized the capital letters, obviously sure that such company made her place swanky. Despite my father's indifference to beauty pageants, I knew we were going to have a good visit. I only worried he might run away with the former beauty queen.

Sunday lunch arrived on dainty plates, none of which matched either the side plates or each other. Roast chicken with rice and peas. The thought of the school's pork fat with imbedded spikes like rhinoceros hairs, and the endless days of "stew peas and rice," in which I sometimes found tiny stones, made this homely Sunday lunch the best food I had ever tasted. Boarding school fosters a special hunger that it seldom satisfies. At school, I liked only the still-warm bread from the bakery, its doughy body needing thumbs to pull it apart.

My father was throwing himself into both the visit and the meal, but I was acutely aware of the lady at the next table. He would glance over at her when he felt he had related an amusing point. I am sure, in retrospect, that they were flirting. "Have you noticed that my waistline is distinctly *down*!" he announced, after wiping his mouth and pushing the edge of his napkin under his belt again. "But I expect that after this lunch it may creep back up," he added, and looked apologetically at her. She batted her eyelids. The other man glanced over and, meeting my father's gaze, looked genuinely pleased. He nodded, muttering, "Mr. Manley."

"Fishing calls for very tall stories," my father now advised me, and he described a Sunday on a boat with some friends. They had taken lunch with them, as they wouldn't get back till late, and were hopeful at the news that, the day before, some fellows had caught a blue marlin weighing 267 pounds in the same area. It was not an altogether successful day, he explained. They caught eight barracudas in seven hours, or maybe it was seven barracudas in eight hours, but for the longest time he himself caught nothing. The man at the neighbouring table laughed so we turned round to include him, but he was telling his companion some story of his own, and the beauty queen looked mildly contemptuous as she picked her teeth with a toothpick.

"I made up my mind that I was going to catch a fish, if I had to climb overboard to get him! In fact I caught only one for the day — barely two feet long — although I had a line out for the whole seven hours!" As he said this, he turned towards the next table and jiggled his fishing wrist to demonstrate.

The plates were cleared, and my father became thoughtful. Time was slipping by.

"Now tell me all about school!" He wanted to know about classes, about tuck-boxes and if there were tuck-box thefts, if I had joined the choir and how much I got paid for my hours of duty in the bookshop. He heard about bus rides to Olivier Shield soccer matches in Mandeville, rehearsals for *The Mikado*, and my creative writing classes. He heard about our visits to church on Sunday mornings, where the local epileptic once fell into fits, interrupting the sermon and frightening us. I showed off about my cross-country training, leaving out the mornings when I waited behind a tree undetected, joining the others on their way back. I wanted him to think me an athlete.

But then the young couple rose, and smiled at us as they collected their things and left. My father looked sadly at the door after them, and immediately started glancing at his watch. I wished I were a beauty queen. I knew that this signalled my journey back to school.

I fought back tears during the drive, and when we arrived at the dormitory steps he stopped the car very gently, as though making sure he wasn't the one to spill them. He handed me some tuck Mardi or Thelma had sent.

"Nip and tuck," he joked, "nip and tuck." Nip and tuck, for he was in a hurry; nip and tuck, as with me on the verge he needed to be deft.

"Be a trooper!" he said. A time always comes to say goodbye. That's life. "It's been a great day." And he hugged me.

Once again I was waiting for letters.

Time became a trail of red clay on the bottom of my shoes, on the sleeves of my shirts, even sometimes on the ends of my hair, which through habit I'd stick in my mouth then spit out in disgust. On my skin it looked like scratched mosquito bites. Each building had a hem of ruddy splashes spat out by the rain. And it rained a lot in that part of the island, which is probably why old Great-grandfather Manley had such juicy oranges to offer America in the first place.

There were consolations to my year. I didn't draw or paint very well, but I discovered the art of caricature. I could take a weakness or a strength in a feature and exaggerate it so that I had the feel of the person, even though I couldn't get a likeness. I used to draw my family over and over: my grandmother with a face like a lantern, with a sharp, inquisitive nose, and hair like a horse's mane; Pardi with a nose that could face all consequence, and hair streaming behind his thoughts; and Daddy with his big bat ears and small mischievous eyes, and a nose that turned up *whoops* at the end. In creative writing class I learned to reach into my memory and pull out things that I loved and missed. I learned the art of patience and the second-thoughtedness of distance. I learned that from far away I could beam a long light. I could retrieve lost things and place them on the pages in front of me.

The year turned by its country seasons, and the freezing cold early-morning showers became warmer in the spring. I discovered the comfort of the "san," a small sick bay in the school's clinic, and got sick on days when I had games, which I hated because the boys would see the outline of my vest under my T-shirt (the other girls wore bras), and my knock knees in shorts.

Eighteen months later, when I was leaving for the last time, I bound my poems in a small book and embroidered the cover, which I had made of orange linen, dedicating its contents to my grandmother. I showed my creative writing teacher. He carefully lifted the cover and flipped through the poems, most of which I had written during his class over the year. He smiled enigmatically. "A writer once said that the soul of another person is like a dark forest," he said. And he closed the book and knocked its edges gently against his desk, as though further straightening the pages. Then he handed it purposefully to me and said, "I hope you'll keep up your writing."

The last letter I received before I left was from my father.

Darling Ra,

I don't know when I've enjoyed a day as much as my last visit. I really look forward to my trips to Knox — sometimes I think that when I'm with my kids are the only times I ever really feel relaxed and at peace with the world. More and more I find that the only enduring reality in life is one's family — and particularly you and Jo-Jo.

You know that wonderful note you wrote me? It is very strange. I don't know when anything has touched or moved me so deeply. And yet it made me very shy. I didn't know how to answer it. So I kept putting it off and finally wrote a meaningless letter, which I didn't send because it didn't say a damned thing of what I really felt and wanted to say. I think it is partly because we haven't been really close for so long.

When you were a baby, up until you came to Jamaica, we were tremendously close. I used to push you in your pram every afternoon in Hyde Park, and later take you for walks. I was ridiculously proud of you. And whenever I came home in the evenings from the university, you used to dash down the steps of the house where we lived to meet me. But somehow, when you came out and we had to separate, and later when I got married, I became hopelessly shy of you. Isn't it extraordinary — and silly really! But that's what happened. It was as if I had failed you and so feared I might fail you again. I don't know really.

Do you know what I did when I was in London last week? One whole afternoon I went back to Hyde Park, to the places where I used to push you in your pram! I walked and walked and thought of those days and of the years between and of today. One's sense of time is a strange thing. In a certain mood time can telescope until the past is today, and today the past. In Hyde Park today and the past were with me together, and I thought of how surprised the you of today would be to meet the you of then — and vice versa! At this point I laughed and a passerby looked at me strangely — as if I might have escaped from an institution. Then I came back and read that little note you gave me again and I was so moved — and reassured. But at the time I couldn't find the words to say what it had meant to me.

Forgive me, dear — and understand. I love you and am proud of you more than you will ever know. I think it will be like it was in the beginning again. I am sure of that now. God bless, Daddy.

Memories leaning on him, unremembered by me but leaning on me, numb and undefined. Perhaps a good weight. In a wall one brick doesn't touch every other brick. In that dark forest one tree may not touch every other tree.

FIVE

ONE PARTICULAR EVENING stays with me, not because of any unique happening among the sad pleats of that time, but for the way an odd fragment can attach itself to the mind and narrow the gap between generations, making us aware of ourselves as cut paper-dolls holding hands in a cycle that is eternal.

Before an additional practical nurse became necessary in the evenings, I'd assist in turning my father. Every two hours the night nurse would wake me gently where I slept in the room across the passage, vacant since David, Beverley's son, the youngest of my four paternal siblings, had gone abroad to school. It was a little like waking up to feed a baby again, like the nights a quarter of a century before when I had to feed my infant sons, Drum and Luke. A small part of the heart is always on guard for one's charge. Love keeps forgiving even before a thought can stray to consider this an imposition. Though tired, somehow the body knows when it's needed, before the quiet touch of a hand. One gets out of bed while trying to keep sleep intact, the same sleep in which one hopes soon to enfold oneself again.

From where I lay, although I could hear no sound, I

always knew when my father was awake. If I lifted my head to look over the foot of my bed, I could see the softly flickering light of his television under the crack of my door. I used to get urges to peep at him. They came like premonitions, but were probably inspired by no more than my awareness of the peril in which life had placed him.

"We had a good day," my father had said after his midnight turn, settling into one more motionless, lonely, two-hour spell of nothing but his thoughts, his imagination's struggle against pain — or his dreams, if the night was merciful. But as I was leaving the room he seemed comfortably tired, and the nurse had given him all his medicines, including something to make him sleep.

He had been reluctant for the afternoon to end. He had enjoyed his talk with a student who was to be his assistant on a new project. The University of the West Indies campus at Mona had established a chair in political science in my father's name, and had offered him the first professorship. It meant a lot to him as, despite the recent conferral of an honorary doctorate, he regretted having had little opportunity over the years to share his experience directly with Caribbean students at home. Though bedridden and frail, he embarked on the project with his usual enthusiasm. Rex Nettleford, a friend and then a university pro-vice-chancellor, discussed ways this scheme could be made workable.

Mardi used to call Rex a Renaissance man. Involved in many disparate fields, his thought and work examined and embodied so much of what being Jamaican had come to mean. Rex and my father often talked to each other in parables, the meanings of which both were quick to decipher. Their lives had crossed each others' for years, through dance, unionism and academia, and most of all through friendship.

"The mountain can send its messengers to the prophet," he advised my father.

"I hear you," my father said, understanding his meaning: an assistant could come to the house for sessions.

"There are modern ways to communicate with young Turks."

"I hear you," he said again; students could be communicated with through e-mail. All this till he became strong enough to go to his office on campus, he said with certainty.

"I hear you," Rex said back to him.

When the assistant arrived for her first meeting with him, her youth in that room struck me as incongruous, her freshness an awkward innocence. I left them there and went to have supper with a friend. I returned around eleven. When my father saw me at the door, his eyes lit up. "I'm hungry," he said.

The nurse and I looked at each other as though our patient had sat up after weeks in a coma.

"Scrambled eggs?" I asked him.

"With bread and lots and lots of butter."

I fixed the eggs the way he liked them — beaten without milk to a frazzle and then scrambled, but still so soft they spread like jam — and cut heavily buttered bread into cubes, as I would for a small child. The nurse placed a napkin under his chin, and spooned the eggs and bread steadily into his mouth while she gave little *mmm* noises. My father's eyes went no farther than the next mouthful.

"Not too fast," admonished the nurse. "We don't want you to be sick, now."

"My dear," he said as she wiped his mouth, "I'm so damn sick already it hardly makes any difference."

He settled back on his pillows, appearing totally satisfied, made sleepy by the comfort of the warm food going down. Life was as good and as simple as that. I waited till midnight to help turn him, shut off the television and went to bed feeling peaceful, grateful to life.

·But about an hour later I woke, automatically raising my head, and there was the dreaded sliver of light, the telltale witness of sleepless pain. I got up and crossed the corridor. The nurse whispered an explanation, picked up a bundle of linen and went downstairs. He had been sick and was now in great pain.

"Ah, my Ra," he said.

I felt his head. He was eerily cool.

"Maybe a bit too much food too soon," I suggested.

"He giveth and He taketh away," he muttered. "Stay a little bit?"

I got a blanket from the other room, and curled up in the chair beside him. I lowered the nearest rail and held his hand, resting my head next to his shoulder on the bed. And as if the mind finds songs for comfort in the night, whether the young are old, or the old are become the young, I found a song. One my father used to sing for me, with three verses about a cherry. It was his rendition of an old English folk song, and in the past, whenever he sang the first line, he would have to sing the whole song.

"I gave my love a cherry that has no stone." And there would follow a chicken with no bone, a story with no end, a baby with no crying.

"I used to sing this to you when I put you to sleep in your crib," he'd say. It was a simple song and the notes moved one at a time, unevenly, like someone all alone picking his way through an overgrown path. My father's voice, which though urging was not melodic, would seem to tumble inside him like the cement in a big mixer when they throw in gravel — stones in lugubrious mud. As I grew older, it amused me to listen to it wander ponderously, word over word, in his chest.

The final verse provided the explanation for cherries without stones, chickens without bones, babies without tears and everlasting stories. It reminded me of his world. It reminded me of him.

Now I sang the song for him, in my thin, high, equally unmelodic voice, with the world a small, frightened place no more steady than the flickering television. But I knew that this love had flowed down the river of years, and I was meant to return it to him.

~

"That's how you build Jerusalem. From scratch!"

My father would take a sentence and make from it two sentences or four. He would take a qualifying phrase and make it stronger by giving it its own breath. The truth is, he could do anything he wanted with language, once he learned to master the stammer that ran like one of those ropy lines through the length of otherwise perfect silk.

"Why is your father building Jerusalem?" my Uncle Douglas asked me, for it always appeared that he and my father had an arrangement not to speak to each other directly.

"Something to do with Oscar Niemeyer," I said casually, as if I knew all about him. I had only discovered the existence of the famous Brazilian architect the night before.

"Oh, that," said Douglas, and lifted his head as though what had been said either made perfect sense now, or wasn't worth bothering about. It seemed to me that, if my father was fire, my uncle was water, each instinctively avoiding proximity to the other. I loved the yin-and-yang tension between them.

It was late 1963. My father was now chief negotiator at the union, and had been appointed to the Senate at independence a year earlier. He had helped found, and became president of, the Caribbean Mine and Metalworkers' Federation. They worked to get a better deal for the region's natural resources and set up joint ventures for processing raw materials. He had returned from Trinidad and Brazil, and had brought me a scarf whose softness reminded me of the subtle taste of furry roseapples, and a pair of white leather high-heeled shoes. "Size eight," I had lied, and they were too small; like so many other manifestations of my small-footed dreams, they would remain unworn in my cupboard.

I have always been unable to come to terms with the size of my long Manley feet. Two years before, in 1961, I had asked for tennis shoes in size 8 for school. My grandmother, who knew I longed for tiny feet like my stepmother's, like the descriptions of my mother's, said there were no half sizes, and bought me size 9. They fitted perfectly but I looked like a small bird with big feet, and I got so cross with her, and behaved so badly, that she said she couldn't take the strain any more. And for that serendipitous reason, at age fourteen, I went to live with my father.

I did not know, then, that everything in my life was going to change. The year when I diverged from my childhood was also a watershed for my family, with closings and openings, endings and beginnings. All the sad things seemed to belong to my grandparents. Pardi lost a referendum that he had hoped would secure a Jamaican mandate to remain in the West Indies Federation; success would have given its members greater power to face a neo-colonial future. But the federation's brief four-year existence had been plagued by inter-island disputes and conflicting interests. Then he narrowly lost the general election to the more conservative Jamaica Labour Party (JLP), led by Pardi's older cousin, Alexander Bustamante. The man whose vision had inspired and designed our independence would not be our first prime minister.

By independence in 1962, not only had my grandfather suffered these two political defeats, but he was totally broke — a detail my grandmother cited as consolation, pointing out that it was proof of integrity in public life. The land on which Drumblair stood was sold for development, and with it the house. Pardi and Mardi moved to a small bungalow they had built on land next to my father's.

"Find me a name," she charged me.

With all the sadness that lay on their shoulders, I suggested she call their new home "Regardless."

The island had come of age with independence, and was supposed to be starting anew, yet it stays in my memory like a sky with only its clouds in transition — as though life was the same, only its expression was different. Things were changing and yet not changing: Drumblair turning into Regardless and my father's house, Ebony Hill; my father changing into my grandfather.

And yet, in the reshaping of those times, two violent images spring to mind, both involving bulldozers. The first was the developers tearing Drumblair down; the second, the demolition of a ghetto in Kingston called Back O'Wall. Pardi witnessed the mangled boards torn from our treasured family home of over forty years with sadness and resignation, as though they represented the years of his life. The destruction of Back O'Wall he received like most of Jamaica, with horror.

Although Back O'Wall was a collection of flimsy shacks, it was also a neighbourhood, a community of homes. The JLP demolished it, and replaced it with Tivoli Gardens — a set of concrete high-rises for constituents of the right political flavour. This was politics under a different guise. It was the prelude to an island divided against itself, an island of bloody ghetto wars between two well-armed tribes.

To Pardi it must have been like watching the dismantling of the world he had helped shape. He especially despised the presence of guns. He felt that this scourge of armed violence was the most evil thing to enter our society since slavery, and that its effects might destroy Jamaica as we knew it. We all lived with a sense of regret over the breakup of my grandfather's dream of federation, of what Jamaica might have become with Pardi at the helm. As for me, I began to understand the force of Babluck that surrounded my family, with its constant reminders of what should have been and wasn't.

Before Drumblair was sold and razed, my father had been given an acre of land beside another that Pardi kept for himself. This was where Ebony Hill, and later Regardless, were built. Designing his first home reawakened my father's early architectural aspirations. He hired a maverick builder whose experience was limited to roads, and enlisted him to build a small cement house, with a shingled roof, on a knoll that leaned over the street. The house looked as though a child had drawn it, with its predictable windows and single door between yellow pouie and ebony blossoms that Thelma had insisted must not be uprooted, and a steep path like a ladder straight up the hill. The house remained an uncomfortable migrant caught between the perpetually irritable nods of the ebony trees that gave it its name.

Inside, too, the design followed a child's presumption of an adult world: one big L-shaped room, for living on one side and dining on the other, and a corridor like a simplified concept of time, with bedrooms branching off like consequences. Every year my father knocked out a wall, added a window or turned one into a door, added a cupboard, widened the patio, enlarged the kitchen, redesigned the perpendicular driveway, or elongated his corridor, which stretched farther and farther — an avenue of unfolding projects, summer by summer,

child by child, room by room, each pausing with the reassurance of a door, a manifestation of something hopeful in his
nature.

I entered the challenging, shape-shifting world of cherries
with or without stones when I went to live at Ebony Hill. I
think my father was glad I came, for he must have been lonely. Despite our public profile, we remained a shy family and
my father was a very shy man. Like Pardi, he did not become
a different man in his job, but coped with the need to be
extroverted by donning an extra layer of skin. For both men,
work was as natural as breathing. It was my father's emotional life that seemed to perplex him. At home, among ourselves,
the extra layer of skin came off.

My new home was the waking remnant of one of my
father's lost dreams: his second marriage, to Thelma. Thelma
was gone, with her pretty clothes and perfumes, taking five-
year-old Joseph, with his dinosaurs and toy trucks and trains.
She and my father had quarrelled so much that the agitation
gradually but inexorably severed their bond.

Although I believe my father often felt lonely, it was not
company he craved, but the certainty of one other person in
his life with whom he could design a reality. Living with me
at Ebony Hill provided his life with a predictable scaffolding.
To me it was anything but predictable; it was like living near
a bright light. I seldom felt secure, but life was exciting. In
my youthful intuition there always lurked the sense that my
father was not fully present, that although he might be looking at me, even if I didn't see his eyes wander, he was really
searching somewhere over my shoulder.

Times like this, when he was single and alone, were
troughs, valleys between peaks, the loose-bellied wandering
of a wire between two posts. And the places where he was
and yet wasn't were places in which he searched for a new

companion, as though searching for another version of himself. In the meantime I was just glad to have a chance to have him, as Mardi described it, "all to myself." His trough became my pinnacle.

My Uncle Douglas, whose marriage to my exotic Aunt Carmen had disintegrated over time, now lived in what had been my brother's room. He was surrounded by Thelma's books and Joseph's few remaining toys, and kept Joseph's cricket bat under the bed as protection, along with a tin of aerosol insecticide for anything that moved, and mosquito coils that scorched the tiles when their ribbons of still-burning ash fell to the floor. At times, bewildered by the marital problems of her sons, my grandmother was uncertain as to whether Douglas was still married or whether he had forgotten to go home.

Kik, a school friend of mine, came to stay with us when her family moved to Barbados. We were four separate souls in a house that, though full, rarely stopped echoing. It only ceased to sound hollow when Mardi came to visit, as though she awakened the voices of each inanimate thing.

Each morning was the same but different. I'd venture down the corridor, summers past marked by a different pattern of tiles for each extension, to the plywood door at the end. I would knock as though to check the existence of this long-awaited room (whose far wall had a further door waiting for the future), and the reassuring presence of my father there. When I heard his reluctant mumble I'd go in and he'd say, "Be an angel, pass me my cigarettes." I'd pass him the Albany box and the silver Ronson lighter given to him years before by a group of sugar workers, which got lost almost every week in one place or another. I'd wait for the snap of the cover and then leave him to get up.

Soon Astrud Gilberto was introducing us to a girl from Ipanema, who I was certain was somehow responsible for my father's present enthusiasm for Latin music and South American self-assertion. He had recently mastered the cha-cha, with the guidance of a brief romantic liaison, and he applied this step, when he could, to whatever music was playing — even to half a bar of John Coltrane. Those little Latin American syllables became indispensable to him.

Today there was a boxer sitting in the living room. This was not unusual; I can hardly remember a time, in those years before my father entered politics, when he was not training some boxer to conquer the world. My family loved the sport. My grandmother, who was the first woman to sit on the Jamaican Boxing Board of Control, told me that she felt this welterweight would really prefer to be a cabinetmaker, but that he didn't want to disappoint my father. He was waiting for either his breakfast or his lunch. My father, who co-managed him along with three other men (they grandly referred to themselves as a syndicate), had decided he must eat steak and drink eggnogs every day, as he was in training for a bout that weekend. I resented these boxers eating steak when we only got macaroni cheese. Despite this, I offered him a *Ring* magazine, which now lay open across his lap. It had apparently put him to sleep.

In the mornings it was father's rising that seemed to rally the world, rally the house. Ebony Hill, like a man's dog, wakened with him.

"Brasilia is a *birth*."

My father was in the small hallway that housed the telephone, the long cord trailing after his passionate conversation. His large presence was pacing but at the same time hunkered down, as he carried the phone in the crook of his arm like a small person with whom he shared this conversation. It felt to me as if the attention of the world received this news. Each of his preoccupations was a huge furnace eating up energy and oxygen, a magnetic field that attracted every shard in its reach, a gust that could enter any opening, suck things in, blow things apart — to me he was infinite possibility.

"I need my socks," he mouthed away from the receiver, and I happily brought him one of the folded clumps I found in his sock drawer. It never dawned on me to consider myself anything but honoured when he asked me for something. I felt not only that my assistance would free his time for more sublime activity but that I was endearing myself to him. The truth is that he was terribly spoiled by everybody, and that we all loved doing it. He nodded appreciation, stuffed a quick three syllables of cha-cha into a line of Gilberto's bossa nova, took the neat arrangement I offered him and fiddled with his left hand till he got it unfolded.

"I am not sure you can build nationhood on the back of colonialism. Tell me when it has worked. That damn place got me thinking. In Brazil they have built from scratch a totally new capital, in a brand-new location, far from the old ideas, the old corruptions and bad habits. Far from people's custom-ary *perceptions*. This is a *symbolic* break, a profound commit-ment to that break and the construct, *physical* construct," (he could speak in italics) "of a new beginning." And he looked crossly at the sock and shook it to encourage its mate to come loose, but it didn't, so he cupped his hand over the speaker. The daily conspiracy routine of "Who has stolen my sock, and why?" was enacted above the covered receiver.

The boxer woke up, startled by the shouting, and looked at the magazine again, bending his elbows with difficulty, as his shirt sleeves strained to span his muscles. Hawthorne, the cook, disapproving behind her severe black spectacles, handed him an eggnog in which I thought I could detect the golden orb of a yolk.

"He will die of protein shock," said my uncle, who was another of the placid boxer's managers. "Only your father could find us a boxer with a good heart and a glass jaw, and think steak and eggnogs will help." Douglas had squashed my father's newspaper into a splayed fold under one elbow on the dining table, and was working steadily on the crossword puzzle with the arduous diligence of a left-hander writing with his right hand. I had no idea what he meant, but I was used to his droll comments, like a layer of condensation on the surface of all circumstance.

"Spence say the cow dem eat down you hibiscus."

The tall, skinny, ropy-veined Hawthorne always brought bad news.

"Oh Lord, why you always bring me trouble, Hawthorne?" asked my father, who was at last off the telephone.

"A Spence weh mek bad ting 'appen, sah!"

Spence was the gardener. Spence and Hawthorne. Dog and cat.

"Spence!"

"Spence gone to tie up de cow."

"Tie up the cow? How you mean tie up the cow? You mean a cow eat down my hibiscus and Spence is the gentleman going to escort cow with rope and offer him pastureland? Whose pastureland, I ask you, Hawthorne? Whose cow?"

My father had the liberal middle-class instinct to concede certain corner-cutting features of dialect, without actually mispronouncing anything himself. He did it with enough flair and enthusiasm to suggest only a minimum of condescension.

"A Spence cow, sah."

"Spence's cow? *Spence's* cow? Tell Spence he's fired!"

Spence was fired every now and then.

My father looked down at the table to the further annoyance of the crumpled newspaper. He sighed. His brother was as foreign to him as a country one has never thought of visiting.

Days with my father were always epic. His was a cluttered, moving world like the edge of a beach, compulsive and yet unpredictable, leaving everything behind him beneaped.

My life fell apart whenever my father was away. While he visited Brazil, I decided that my heart was broken, when a footballer who had promised to take me out had forgot even to call me. My father returned from Brazil in the middle of this humiliation. A new Buick Electra, ordered by the union for his island-wide travelling on their behalf, waited for him at the airport. The workers had christened him "Young Boy," in inevitable comparison to his father. As Young Boy drove proudly up the road towards our gate, he discovered me running in the opposite direction, with the household trailing after me. I was escaping barefoot, dressed in shortie pyjamas, with the family doctor trying to keep up, a hypodermic in his hand. I was drunk on several rums and had faked suicide with a bottle of Aspirin, flushing the contents down the toilet and leaving the bottle ominously open beside my bed. My uncle, a sociologist, had arrived home in the middle of the uproar, characteristically smug as he described a friend's lover being pulled out from under a bed by the friend's wife.

"She's only drunk," he had remarked after a cursory look at me. "Probably flushed the pills." He had gone to his room, chuckling at everything going horribly wrong, with me screaming after him, "Oh no, they would stay in the loop! Pills don't go down when you flush them." I knew this, for they had taken ages to dissolve. And that was when the doctor had arrived and I had made my escape.

My father stopped the new car carefully. The window slid down smoothly and he stared out at the procession in the road, which had regrouped at the side of his car. He looked questioningly at my grandmother and opened the front door for her. She got in gracefully, as though a limousine had been sent to fetch her up our steep hill, and the rest of the exodus climbed into the back. As we were swept up the brief slope by the Buick's eight cylinders, we breathed in the expensive smell of a new car and were introduced to the sloping dashboard and all its features: air-conditioning, radio speakers, automatic windows and a cigarette lighter. Even the doctor appeared to be enjoying himself before he left.

We all sat around my father's seven-by-seven-foot bed. (He said he had designed it so there would be room for his feet, but Douglas claimed that husbands made beds big enough for themselves and their wives to cohabit without having to speak to each other when they quarrelled.) This was where we usually ended up, listening to each others' problems. And that was when Daddy heard about my lapsed footballer, and we heard about the planes with not a single pretty stewardess, and the second-rate hotel, and the crack-of-dawn flight to São Paolo with three hours' driving from the airport, and the kitchen closed at the awful hotel, and the long walk to the café where they finally got eggs bathed in grease. And we knew that, like all my father's tales of adventure, even the stories of his dates, this would end up in sunlight, with some redemptive reason, however small, for everything to be considered worthwhile.

Oscar Niemeyer had saved this trip, with the dream city of Brasília.

"They have built a brand-new capital. They have created their own structural *engine* to drive the country's government."

"Ah, an engine, but surely not a beating heart," said Mardi, who Douglas said was invariably sentimental.

"Of course not! That's the point. Brazil already has a heart, a culture, an identity. The point is that all colonizing countries — the Spanish, the English here, the Portuguese in

Brazil — they leave behind the structures and machinery of their dominance. We inherit these with our independence. We whose sweat built their dreams, we are taking the reminders, the symbols of their dominance, and trying to translate them into what is new for us."

"Oh heavens, Michael, I see what you mean! That is *brilliant*. Trust you to see that." Mardi always jumped in to fill any breach left by the family. I glanced at Douglas, who looked impassive. I found Mardi's habitual fascination with my father's words somewhat embarrassing in front of my uncle. "Isn't that something!" she added.

She looked at each of us in turn, last of all at Kik. We usually appealed to Kik, only mildly interested in anything going on around her, as witness or audience. Now we all stared at her.

"It is, it is," she said, and smiled co-operatively.

The idea of Brasilia must have attracted my father in those dry days that followed our own independence a year before. The JLP was in power, but I still considered it the opposition, even though it was now the government; to me, opposition was anything that opposed my grandfather.

"Years ago," my father continued, "I had an old tailor in Kingston who would refurbish my suits for me. Sometimes he'd only let out the waist or a hem, because I'd got too fat or I'd grown or something. But sometimes he'd change the width of the collar or take off some pocket to make my clothing more contemporary. He would always charge me according to a system that distinguished between "changes" and "alterations." Changes meant you had to remodel. Alterations were just that: alterations. They were minor. They were tinkering. They cost much less. 'It don't have to *refigure*,' he'd say.

"Independence is a little like those alterations. We had a whole lot of hoopla down at the National Stadium. We pulled down the old red, white and blue flag and hoisted our own —

gold, green and black — sang our own national anthem, appointed ambassadors and set up fancy missions, named our national wood and national flower, a drink and a dress, a this and a that, even our own heroes. And so what? Most of it's only cosmetic. It don't have to *refigure!*"

The brothers managed to discuss this subject for a bit, looking at their mother while addressing each other. Douglas shrugged off neo-colonialism as unavoidable, but my father would not be silenced.

"Whether we design it brilliantly, as Niemeyer has, or we don't have the money or expertise, but only the 'facetyness' to say to hell with the past — let Spanish Town be a dinosaur of Spanish history, let Kingston be a fossil of British history, we are going to build our own Jerusalem *here*." He stabbed the air with a stiff forefinger. "You name it! It's our damn capital. And wherever that is, that is where we build Jerusalem."

The phone rang; Pardi had come home next door and was looking for Mardi. She told us she must go and check on him, because he was attempting to heat up a can of soup. I saw her to the front door, which she insisted on using because one must respectfully say hello and goodbye to a house, even though our kitchen door was no more than twenty steps of Mardi's long legs from her own place.

Kik and I sat with my father for a while, after Douglas had gone to read in his room.

"So what was all this about heartbreak?" he asked.

I told him.

"When I was a boy . . . ," he said.

My father had fallen in love. He had fallen in love with a girl who had a beautiful face and a withered leg. She had suffered from polio. To Michael her face was the face of a wounded angel. She became his cause, a Holy Grail he set out to discover, to reach, to defend. Only he knew the bravery of her heart, the brilliance of her mind, the creativity of her spirit. Only he knew how to rectify the wrongs that had been done to her. He would march round the house, scowling and furious, speaking to no one. It became a madness in his head, and he would see her face before him, wise and beautiful, his bright bride. He thought he'd found his fellow guango tree. She was whatever Mardi was to Pardi. He plucked up the courage to ask her out, or was it the courage to say hello? For some reason she declined, or didn't answer; whatever it was, it didn't go well. He hit his parents' liquor cabinet and drank so much he nearly died.

I felt only partially consoled.

Then he asked how my exams had gone. English was easy for me, but I hated learning the dates of history. I liked the stories of the Tudors, the personalities of the kings and queens, but got confused by the machinations of the various European wars; I was too lazy to learn the names of acts and treaties. All this we discussed as he came and went, unpacking his clothes, dumping laundry in a basket and arranging what was unworn, fold to fold, in the deep, gloomy shelves of his plywood cupboard — painfully attempting to be neat, but knowing he would be rescued, so that Kik and I took over the job and released him to go to the bathroom. He reappeared in fresh grey pyjamas. "History," he said, and settled himself on the far side of the bed, with his head on a stack of pillows against the wall. He lit a cigarette. "To study history, a certain amount of work cannot be escaped. But I think one has to get a sense of pattern, of ebb and flow, where basic motivations are similar. Spain and England were fighting for the New World because it meant trade, land, gold — all the elements of wealth. And each had to rationalize and disguise this raw impulse under the trappings of a religious crusade. Later England and France fought it out for Canada."

"But it's so much to remember by heart."

"One has to feel for the connections that make sense of great conflicts in terms of man, whose character, impulses, needs, are much the same everywhere and at all times. And if you relate history to your own time, you'll be surprised how many echoes and parallels you'll find. But don't be overawed. It is Pardi and Bustamante . . . or Castro and Kennedy . . . only in different costumes. See what I mean?"

"I guess," I said, but I was tired and didn't feel inclined to talk of history.

He was hungry and wondered, who was the angel who was going to make him must-be-soft scrambled eggs? He always asked so nicely for favours. Kik looked at me. She knew I basked in any chance to win my father's approval. We both would, I volunteered. I was following Kik out of the room, but he called me back.

"Ra, you know what you do? Always get at the story of people . . . who need food and need to be comforted, and will put their faith in false prophets and submit to despots rather than have no faith and no order. The struggle to have freedom and an end to despots, without losing comfort and order, is the most fascinating issue of all. So go for the characters — look for hunger and poverty — and you will have the two great factors whose interplay makes history tick."

I'd try, I promised.

"Despite your insistence to the contrary, you have a fine mind. All you need to do is use it. In the meantime, be a pet . . . make haste with my scrambled eggs."

"So where was your sock?"

"Someone apparently decided, quite rightly, to give it back!"

My father with his make-believe shame-face, dropping us to school. The thin top lip formed a neat hem to the sensitive area under his nose, which had its own pulse and a single left-of-centre tiny mole, and I always thought it the most loyal part of my father, for it kept back his secrets and would tighten over his teeth in defence of him, or concentrate itself into thought, flicker at his amusement or play coy, its pucker only a small slip of innocence, asking forgiveness, as it did now.

"What would anyone want with one sock, anyway?"

He is in a good mood, and fiddles with the car radio. He adjusts the rearview mirror to see if Kik in the back seat is really there. We pick up Marie and Audrey, starched uniforms waiting, annoyed and late, farther down the road. These will be the days when the Buick Electra reigns as his "true dream of a car," sleek black with electric-blue upholstery. Its lines are what I think American hotels and houses and presidents and tourists' luggage and tourists themselves are: spacious, wide, fast, blatant — or, as my father put it, un-British.

The car and my father are eager to inch the speedometer beyond yesterday, but we are held up in rush-hour traffic. The smoke from his cigarette curls around us, and this, with the new-car smell, makes us all feel modern and grown-up.

Today I have a headache from my antics the night before. I carry an excuse to present to my physical education teacher: "My daughter was not well yesterday, and in fact the doctor had to be called. She is still not feeling one hundred percent but is anxious not to miss school. Please therefore excuse her from P.T. class and afternoon games this week."

When my grandparents drive me to school, I ask them to drop me outside. Truth is, they are old and embarrass me. But I am proud when my father swoops in and stops in the middle of the one-way circle. This is my second-hand moment, my place in reflected limelight. I know that, facing the driveway, the upstairs verandah rail will be lined with the elbows of older girls, each faithfully leaning over to await her daily glimpse of my father with catcalls and hand-blown kisses. Heather, a large senior whose rounded shoulders yield to an enormous-breasted torso, calls out a lisped "Sexy." Her braces are so darkly alarming that she seems to have spilled ink in her mouth, the pewter-grey obscuring any charm in her rapture.

That's how I remember the mornings after the nights before — getting him to drop us to school, Kik always the last to the car, usually without breakfast, which is dispensable to the late riser. His musings, socks missing, phone ringing, jazz or something mellow and ungrandparently playing, monosyllables from my rumpled uncle, Hawthorne complaining, cows versus my father, Spence under threat, cigarette smoke like our daily breath, cities rising into the sky, poverty as the story of people, history as passion. This was a world where cherries were blooming, chickens were pipping, love stories could be never-ending, and babies were peacefully sleeping in some other life.

"Let me catch a glimpse of m' boy," shouts Heather, a latter-day Juliet dreaming from her balcony, between snorts of her own laughter. "Michael — Young Boy, Kennedy gone! It's only you left now. The last hero!"

SIX

THE MORNING ROUTINE BEGAN with Vita's shift at eight. By then my father had completed breakfast with Glynne, who read him the morning papers before going to dress for work. Books and even newspapers were too heavy for him to hold. Vita would give my father his bed-bath, then I would shave his face. At first I was nervous holding the whizzing shaver. I had never been so near to my father's face, never stroked his cheek. To me it felt almost blasphemous. But things had been turned on their head, and once I was sure that I wouldn't cut him, and I learned to push the tiny flat saws against the grain of his face, I looked forward to the ritual. "Harder," he'd say, from the direction of the far cheek, where his mouth had been pushed out of the way to stretch the skin. Then he'd run his fingers over his cheeks. I'd see by his expression how well I'd done. His face, behind whose walls most of his being was forced to retreat, was still a safe place, one of the few that one couldn't hurt.

For a large man, he had a small face: a face that cartoon-ists had found easy to caricature, with its strong, square jaw, protruding ears and optimistically upturned nose. A boyish expression always gave an impression of hope. Although the skin on the front of his neck had slackened with age, "wobbling," he said regretfully, "like a turkey gobbler's," it was clear that, no matter the years, his face would never succumb to its age, never fall into its frowns.

My father had not always used an electric razor. I associated the compulsive drone with my grandfather, whom I would watch when I was a child as he sat on his swivel stool at the Drumblair bedroom window, conferring with a small silver shaving mirror, pausing to stroke his face and lengthen his gaze towards the world of the quiet road beyond the house. Curiously, the older man had trusted his grooming to the impersonal efficiency of modern technology, whereas my father, a generation later, had only recently abandoned his hand razor and the insertable metal blades which often cut him.

While I was sawing away at his sharp bony jaw, he lifted his hand like a patient in a dentist's chair, and squeezed my wrist to stop me. I moved my hands away and straightened, worried I might have hurt him. But his eyes were bright with a thought. "You know, when I look back, I feel such pride about my work in the union. I never feel quite that joy, that satisfaction, about politics."

"I suppose the issues are more straightforward," I suggested.

"We were all men who led factions that *hated* each other," he continued, as if he had not heard me. "But the unions have grown up. They have mellowed, really, in a way that the political parties never did. Maybe the friendship between Hugh and myself had something to do with it." Hugh Shearer, a man as tall as my father, was thought to be our distant cousin. Each week he came to visit, bringing coconuts, oatie-eatie apples and pawpaws. He had been my father's counterpart as island supervisor of the rival workers' union founded by Bustamante, and later became our third prime minister. Once adversaries, they were now old lions who had cut their political teeth in similar fashion, and seemed prepared to lose them, eventually, in a spirit of camaraderie.

My father let go of my wrist and his eyes scanned the room, as though, with his range of movements limited to his torso, they had undertaken the job of pacing. Then they settled on a speck in his miniature universe that made him frown. "Truth is, in some ways I hated politics."

Vita, who was waiting to give him Coumadin by injection straight to the stomach, looked sharply at him with a bemused expression, as though a child had announced its refusal to go to school.

"Not the big picture of politics, but the constituency work, the endless invasion of one's privacy, people's sense that you were to be accessible at every turn . . . turning up at one's home, oh how I hated that . . . and the constant need to compromise over issues."

"The nip and tuck?" I suggested.

"Yes, right, the nip and tuck." But his expression changed, for when it was put that way, he remembered he liked the nipping and tucking. He relaxed, and I went back to shaving his face.

Despite my father's protestations — "I'm out of it now," he'd say — he kept abreast of current events. Nearly every day he'd talk to one of his friends from the party now in government. They would call to check on him. When he had something to say on some issue, he'd call a cabinet member — "Can you get here by nine?" — and the frazzled minister would have to rearrange his schedule. After one such visit, his close friend, the minister of finance, took me aside and whispered affectionately, "Your father thinks he's still in charge, you know."

In the middle of February my father invited the trade union presidents to see him. He was concerned about a dispute with the bauxite industry that might result in American and Canadian companies pulling out of Jamaica. Vita and I busied ourselves with logistics, circling the hospital bed with chairs. My father expected the meeting to last an hour, from ten o'clock. Vita and I would wait beyond the small connecting bridge outside. He would signal if he needed us. Although we couldn't see him through the window, if he raised his hands we could see his long, thin upper limbs, like branches, as they wafted for attention.

I tried to remember what was familiar about this exercise, and then it came back to me, how once, thirty years before, we had created a tabernacle for my father's dying third wife so she could take communion from her sickbed.

During her illness, a lot of the rituals were the same: the timetables of pills, the waiting for results, the visits of friends or doctors, the moments of reprieve and the inexorable sinking, the shrine of the hospital bed at whose edge we came daily to worship. After her death, my father seldom spoke of that time. Although we never spoke of it now, I was reminded by the similarities, which prompted ominous comparisons in the silence of my mind.

"Dad," I said, "suppose I ever have to face a situation like this? By then I probably wouldn't have you around. How do you deal with it?"

"It is dealt." The words came perched on a brief, resigned shrug.

I felt suddenly helpless, out of my depth — like learning to swim at Cable Hut Beach, but no longer sure he'd be there.

"The generations, Ra. You have your two strong sons . . . Drum and Luke . . . They'll be there, just as all of you are here for me now."

"I don't have your courage," I said.

His eyes wandered to a big sheet of paper propped up against the books under the window. "I LOVE YOU," it said in large capitals, and it was signed by a friend who couldn't face sickrooms. He bit slowly on his dry bottom lip, pulling the minimal skin upwards from his chin, which seemed to tighten more every day of this siege.

"It's not courage one needs, but knowledge. Get all the knowledge you can."

"Did Barbara?" The question slipped out.

"No. Not at all. Knowledge was kept *from* her. That's how things were handled then. That was a mistake."

I was surprised how quickly he answered, how unsurprised he was by my question; either her sickroom or her memory had not been so far away after all.

"But she had faith." He offered a tender, self-knowing smile. "I'm not blessed with faith," and a strobe of mischief crossed his eyes, "so I need knowledge!"

"For we walk by faith, not by sight," came a whisper from Vita, who was entering notes on the chart. She kept her back turned so the Book of Corinthians spoke for itself.

"Do you think about her illness?" I asked.

"I try not to. I think of her life instead."

~

In my father's life there was always the thing that was and the thing that could have been. Every now and then these two pictures would become the same, but then they would diverge, and one would feel torn between the reality and the haunting possibilities.

From 1964 began a time that pulled my father into the national spotlight and towards the heart of our country's politics. It must have been inevitable. He was a unionist in an island whose two political parties were firmly aligned, each with one of two major unions. His father was a political leader and, of course, he was his father's son. But most of all it had to do with the person he was.

He was so much a mixture of the philosophic father and creative mother, and his personality reflected the combined extremes that make Jamaica what it is: African and English, passionate yet skeptical, intuitive yet logical, robust yet too sensitive. He was intelligent and shy, articulate yet reticent, visionary yet activist — curious contradictions that are part of what we call magic in an island, and charisma in a person.

At the centre of the glory and troubles and heartbreak of that time, in the rubble of memory — severed and merely emblematic now — I can still see our bright flower, Barbara.

I don't think my father could have known that it was one of those defining moments, designated apocalyptic by Mardi, when two union delegates at the Jamaica Broadcasting Corporation (JBC) were fired. One of the men had committed only a minor technical violation of news reporting, and the union considered the other to have done nothing wrong at all. It brought to a head a series of incidents seen as government interference since independence. The dispute was not only about the station's news reportage, but involved a growing concern that the government was becoming oppressive, limiting freedom of speech in the press, in the university, in popular songs and even in sermons aired on the radio. On February 1, 1964, the union went on strike.

Kik and I were preparing for exams in May. After exams Kik was returning to Barbados. I would join her for the summer, and my Uncle Douglas was going to a job with UNESCO in Africa, taking Little Norman with him. My father planned to rent out the house and get a smaller place, for in September I was leaving for England to finish my last two years of school.

Before going to work that first morning of the strike, my father had stormed up and down the hall, twisting knots into the length of the telephone cord as he talked. How dare they? Did they realize the course of history can change because of some small nettle of injustice? They had better reinstate these men or face one hell of a strike. He sucked up all the energy of the house and, dropping us off at school, roared on to battle. I knew the scenario by heart. There was always some crisis in the union; there was always some crisis in my father. Sometimes just the intensity he exerted on the simplest thing — a cough or a sneeze, a lost sock — made it seem like a crisis. No one could have predicted, as we left the house that day, that my father's life would never be the same afterwards.

The workers had gathered outside the Jamaica Broadcasting Corporation. My father pointed at the small station, an unlikely building to be a symbol of oppression. "There are the walls of Jericho!" he announced.

"Joshua," shouted someone from the crowd to my father.

"Tear them down," the workers cried, and cried again as the day dragged on and the sun got hotter.

That very same day, Barbara walked uncertainly into my father's life.

Barbara went to the station that morning. She worked in advertising and had planned to record a commercial, but she refused to cross the picket line. My father saw her arrive in her yellow sharkskin suit, which shifted minutely at each of her long-limbed, thoughtful steps; he noticed her make what he considered a principled decision and he noticed her depart, with a graceful yet uncertain gait that my grandmother would later describe as her substance trying to walk in tune with her shadow. When Barbara was gone, my father imagined that she had left a stillness behind. He would remember this years later.

The young broadcasting station had limited means and a small audience, and so to win a strike my father knew he had to arouse public sympathy. He began to see the incident as a metaphor for the times. So much more than a union dispute was at issue here; much that his father had worked for was at stake.

A wide range of Jamaicans boycotted the station and donated to a strike fund. Even the rival union — traditionally sympathetic to the JLP — contributed. By March the workers resorted to civil disobedience. Traffic was blocked. Kingston came to a standstill. My father lay down in the streets side by side with the workers. A police vehicle actually rolled up to his head before it stopped.

He was in the newspapers daily, photographed in moods of defiance, his jaw always leading the way. On the rival radio station, his name dominated the top story of every hour. His familiar voice came over in passionate clips. "He's like the oboe," said Mardi sagely, as though she had expected all of this. "The whole orchestra will have to tune itself to him!"

At school I began to hear "Michael Manley" in a way that riveted people's attention. It was like hearing a name for the first time from the outside in, instead of from the inside out. It was the way I had always heard "Norman Manley" — delivered as though the very sound spoke of nobility and honour and integrity; as a child I thought it had a sort of majesty that made me very proud. Now my father's name was also a thing that belonged to other people.

"Michael Manley" said this, and "Michael Manley" did that, like gully stones rattling down a torrent. And sometimes, under their breath, "Her father is Michael Manley." It made me feel self-conscious to say my father's name. It felt like repeating gossip, or being "stuck-up."

"Michael Manley lie down in the road, and the traffic drive right up to his head and have to stop!" the girls said at school.

"Passive resistance," noted my grandfather with obvious pride.

"A legitimizing moment," explained my grandmother, who had an instinct for symbols. "Busta was seen as a man of the people from the moment he led the striking workers in 1938 and the country heard he went to jail."

Although change had been the outcome of Pardi's political endeavours, he was not widely thought of as a radical in the way that his cousin Bustamante was. But my father did not concur with that view. "The word 'radical' comes from 'radix,'" he told me, "it's Latin for 'root.' Although Bustamante cut a dashing figure as a hell-raiser, when it came down to fundamentals he never wanted to change anything at its *root.*"

The way my father explained it to me, in politics you had three types of governments: the fascists, for whom power was a goal; the idealists, for whom power was a tool; and the political tinkerers, who accepted the status quo for what it was, merely mending and darning as the immediate need arose, without ever "refiguring." He considered independent Jamaica's first government to be needleworkers — tinkerers.

Independence had been granted, yet the years of colonialism had left subservience in the grain of the people we had become. The British had ruled us by dividing us, and they left us with our divisions, nowhere more so than the middle class. The inequalities glared at us in the streets. The rich were still rich and the poor were still abject, and there might as well have been an ocean between these two extremes. Yet each extreme was Jamaica — as though there were two countries. The middle class was growing, but the basic tenets of a just society were still missing, and it was an absence we had lived with for so long that most people shrugged off the weight of conscience with the thought that it was now too late for change.

"Jamaica might have been a different nation if its leadership at birth had been imaginative," my father said to me years later. But whatever we were, he believed we didn't have to stay that way forever. We could change things; we could take anything from here to somewhere else.

After ninety-seven days the strike ended. A board of inquiry found one worker justifiably fired and the other innocent. The latter was offered a pittance in compensation. Many said the early spirit of the station was never to be felt again.

"We could not win because, short of revolution, you cannot make an elected government do what it does not want to do unless you are able to bring tremendous economic pressure to bear," my father explained.

But something irrevocable had taken place. As in 1938, a labour issue had become a national issue, and this time leading the way, indelibly printing his image on the political psyche of the public, was the emerging figure of my father. Though the strike was lost, the controversy began a hankering for an ideal state, a Jamaican quest for Camelot. And those who searched became the constituency of my father.

In a way I could sense but not explain, Jamaica had fallen in love with him. And he had fallen in love with Barbara.

"She can't fry an egg, but she can use an Agfa Rapid."

This slogan beneath her picture in a newspaper advertisement for a camera was all we really knew of Barbara. And that she was the town clerk's daughter, sister to a beauty queen, wife to a local actor. And that her name was spelled out on the Ouija board when Kik and I posed our perennial question, will Michael marry again?

"I think he's found the apple trees . . . ," said Mardi.

She used to call the early days of her love affair with my grandfather "the apple trees, the singing and the gold." I had no idea exactly what that referred to, but it became her code for people falling in love. Pardi had gone to England to study law at Oxford University, and she had been a young art student studying sculpture at St. Martin's in London. She lived in digs over a fish shop and my grandfather would come to visit her on weekends. They were first cousins, and I always considered this kinship a reinforcement in their relationship, like the steel that ran down through the blocks of my father's cement house to strengthen it against earthquakes. It was difficult for me to imagine a time when they hadn't been together. But in fact they were almost total strangers when they fell in love.

Although I hadn't seen these apple trees in my father's life before, it was said that he had fallen in love with my mother that way. When he met her, Jacqueline was beautiful and bright, he said, so utterly irreverent about all the shoulds and should-nots of life, so gay against the grey of her own life that first day, having lunch with her earnest husband at Drumblair. He was a friend of my grandmother, who had met my mother while he was studying in England. While the company discussed plans for a junior centre, my father became fascinated by the gregarious Jacqueline, who had given up on dreams in her husband's land where nothing much happened and everything seemed to her to be a contradiction of one's dreams, who passionately hated empire, and who was now being gently but firmly ignored by her husband.

My father didn't see my mother again for two years, by which time the war and her marriage had ended, and she had returned to England with her daughter, Anita.

At Ebony Hill, my father's romantic life had been no more than an entertaining subplot that I had come to enjoy. If it was a dancer he dated, he became a choreographer, throwing himself into theatre hours and rehearsals. If it was a teacher, then the rescue of education became his crusade.

He'd enter a woman's unsuspecting world and astonish it with the possibilities engendered by his enthusiasm.

During these spells, Kik and I screened his messages, and sometimes made up excuses for him. We would watch him disappear into his bedroom with the phone, the long cord snaking under the closed door. I enjoyed the hours he contrived to spend at home so we could get acquainted with some lady, the music he played to introduce her to his world. He usually began with Nat "King" Cole, and after she left he would play Brubeck's "Take Five," if he felt things were going well. We would laugh at him, and he would laugh a little at himself, then take it seriously all over again. Now, despite the loss of the strike, "Take Five" was playing a lot.

Mardi had noticed him batting make-believe cricket balls with an imaginary bat. She said this was a sure sign he had fallen in love. "He falls in love so *colossally*," she observed. I always had the feeling that my father's excesses came from her.

In the past, I had often taken advantage of the kindnesses my father's various dates bestowed on me in their anxiety to please. I had never felt excluded. This time it was different. There were no shortcuts, no compromises with Barbara; there was no in-so-far-as or just-as-long-as. My father had told me that sometimes in life you had to pick a team. I felt in my gut that he had now changed sides. Before, I had always remained at the geographic centre of his world, his home, the place he planned around or excused himself from, the place he kept safe, the place of his return. But now his heart had found a home elsewhere. The realization made me insecure and jealous, but I was sufficiently mature to know that the rules had changed.

At the time she met my father, Barbara's soured marriage was unravelling. Under a barrage of disapproval from her family, and friends of her family, Barbara became a defiant quest for my father, a wounded life he must save, a compelling victim who inspired rescue. It was an alliance of two against a seemingly hostile world.

"High drama," said my uncle wearily.

Mardi concluded, "I think we've entered the reign of Barbara."

Barbara came like a beam of light dispelling a dark time in our family. We had been exhausted by Pardi's successive defeats; they had left us emotionally and financially thread-bare. For all the displays of democratic sportsmanship, we felt like victims of a calculated murder. We had seen Pardi stand there as witness to the new national flag rising yellow, black and green on Independence Day, but on someone else's watch. There was no grave to give a shape to grief, yet it was like a death in the family. Life had become a formless business of keeping up spirits. A left-overness, an emotional shabbiness like furniture soiled, or walls needing painting, a worn, depleted overexposure had made its way into our spirits.

It was into this bleakness that Barbara came. She was a happiness I noticed in my father, an ebullience, as though his life had got a fresh layer of paint. He hovered near the phone wherever he was, and answered it immediately. His other personal calls dwindled away. At the end of any conversation he would start to say something else, and his eyes would be asking some question, beseeching support. It was unsettling, yet his fullness was uplifting us all, making us feel hopeful, even happy again.

From the first day I met Barbara, I liked her. I was packing for England, though my departure was still weeks away, and she was sitting on Kik's old bed, giving me advice about what to take and not take, thinking of things she could lend me. She was respectful of each small piece of my life she encountered as she addressed Brumus, my ancient stuffed bear, and even my baby pillow, which she patted lovingly before leaning back on the wall and placing it behind her head. Despite my reluctance towards the fact of her, I liked her. I liked the way she called me "Kiddo."

Her face was all planes and square bones, like a carving, but one that she had meticulously painted. Her makeup seemed more part of her nature than her face. Its volume and care suggested that she had made a concession to the world: "Here you are . . . take my face!" She had separated it from herself, and wore it like a mask, a perfect picture from behind which her black eyes, which she further blackened in outline, peered out with detached curiosity. She always seemed to be listening, even when she spoke, and then she cautiously dropped her words, as though apologetic about offering a contribution she thought inconsiderable.

I knew I could never win a war over her, even if I wanted to. But my jealousy over what she meant to my father made me antagonistic towards him.

I left Jamaica in September, with my father, who would spend a month in London to settle me in school. We arrived on an overnight transatlantic flight and picked up the keys of a house we had rented through an agency, at 23 Clanricarde Gardens. When we got there, my father climbed the steps of the cream-white building and stared at the number on the door.

"My God," he said, "would you believe it! I have been here before." I thought he was having that shivering feeling one gets when someone walks over one's future grave. "Come to think of it, so have you," he added, letting us in. "We lived here!" I had left England before I was three so I had no recollection of this.

He entered the place as one follows memory, stopped at the ground-floor apartment now temporarily ours, and looked up the stairs towards a flat whose entrance opened off the hallway above. "That was where your mother and I lived with you and Anita when you were little."

The quiet hall and whatever ghosts looked back at us meant nothing at all to me. I could only think of Brumus. I wondered what Mardi would see as the cosmic significance of all this, and suddenly I missed her.

My father put down our bags, reached out for me and hugged me.

"We're back," he said softly, patting me. "My baby, we're back."

I stood before the small figure of the mother I had not seen for fourteen years. I hugged her, and noticed how much shorter she was than I. From the moment she looked at me, I felt that indefinable authority that nature gives a mother. I can't say that I expected anyone different, for there was no surprise when I saw her. But in all the stories I had been told that she was a tiny French lady, so when I heard her speaking like my English teachers at school she became very real to me, and sobered my fantasies in a second.

My mother had a small converted mews flat in Denbigh Close, off the Portobello Road, which had originally been an old stable. It was a scaled-down world in which everything was reachable and neat, and my father kept bumping his head. "I paid for it myself," she explained proudly to him. She addressed everything to my father first, and looked at him fondly, almost proprietorially, when she spoke, glancing at me repeatedly, as though I was part of what it meant to talk to him. I found myself trying to look at both of them at the same time, but not knowing what expression to use. Nothing came naturally. I smiled at each thing they said till my face ached, and I caught myself trying to imitate my mother's English accent, impressed by her quick repartee when she jousted with my father.

She was a petite woman, but her presence compelled everything around her. Her face reminded me of my grandmother's. Her eyes were always teasing, debunking. I found myself gazing around her flat, searching for lost pieces of my own puzzle. Could this be my homeland? The only photograph I saw was a large picture of a dog, a German shepherd called Beau Beau. There were several delicate ornaments, most of them animals. Even her books looked small, with many treasures of poetry no bigger than my schoolgirl's missal.

Each thing I saw, each thing we did, was a minute tile I placed in my new mosaic. Even watching my father eating my mother's breakfast.

"I see you haven't lost your touch," he said, as he gulped down her fried eggs. The yolks seemed larger than in Jamaica, yet less intense.

"And I see you haven't lost your appetite," she answered. I tried to imagine the three of us when we had been together before. I conjured up a belonging I hadn't known, an intimacy of towels and old shoes side by side, of shared cupboards, of laundry democratically soaking all our spills and soils together, of rumpled sheets in a smoky bed with me between their younger selves like a seed in a pod, proof of a love no longer evident.

But I saw my father glance at his watch, and I knew this wasn't going to be a new world of Daddy, Mummy and me. This wasn't just my special trip any longer. He asked if he could use the phone. I was not surprised; I had felt his restlessness coming over with him on the plane. I knew what he was like when his emotions were stretched out of shape and he wanted them back in place.

I kept buttering more bread and heaping on the very red jam.

"You like bread and jam?" She looked amused.

"It's my favourite food," I said sheepishly.

"You get that from me," she said, and seemed pleased to find a connection.

My father returned with a look I recognized — tight round the lips. It was a bit of guilt, and a lot of defiance waiting to take its place if he got any flak. He didn't sit down, but stood behind the back of his chair, poised to push it under the table.

"I've heard . . . quite by chance, of course, a friend of mine . . . well, it's Barbara . . . ," and he looked pointedly at me. "I think she may be in town."

I was irritated. Why did "high drama" have to follow us to London? Because she was still married, everything to do with Barbara became some form of conspiracy. The secrecy irritated me. She might as well have come over on the flight with us.

But my mother just said, "I see," as though she saw straight through him, and changed the subject to my clothes. She frowned at the bright yellow and black plaid sweater I had been lent by a friend, over a tight hobble skirt. "She will have to go to Marks and Sparks. They won't let her into school dressed in *that* dreadful gaudy thing." I was taken aback by her bluntness. I was used to my grandmother, who quilted each word with her tact.

My father made an excuse to leave, and there we were, my mother and I, alone for the first time in fourteen years. And with everything in the world that I wanted to ask, I couldn't think of a thing to say. She asked me about school and how I felt about being back, and I explained that I had no sense of ever being here.

"How far back *do* you remember?" she asked me.

"An April Fool's morning. I wanted to take a box of April Violets talcum powder to Edith, the laundress at Drumblair — it was her birthday — and Mardi told me she had died during the night. I must have been about four."

She looked wistful, and I wished I could have said something that included her. I wanted to know about my father and mother.

"He just turned up on the doorstep in London one day as your father would do," she explained.

"How did he find you?" I asked.

"You know I never asked him. Good Lord! When I met him in Jamaica, I was married. I told him there was no way there could be anything between us."

"Was it love at first sight when you saw him again?"

"There was love at first sight long before that," she said. Watching her expression relax — even her sharp little nose softened — I felt the pleasure of finding the piece in my father's romantic experience that related to me. "I turned him away. But the cheeky monkey got another chap to invite me out to a New Year's party. Oh lovely, I thought — stuck at home with my kid and my sister's kid, my life wasn't very bright then. So I'm at the station waiting to go to this party and Mr. Michael Manley turns up, so tall and handsome in his air force uniform. 'Oh, I'm so sorry, Jacqueline, but Jimmy is ill and he couldn't come so he asked me to take you to the party.' So I said, 'And if I could believe that, I'd believe anything!' And we went to the party, and we didn't stop seeing each other after that.

"He lived in a grotty little flat in a bombed-out road — one or two houses were still standing — with a cold kitchen and a cold sitting room and a cold bathroom. He'd furnished it beautifully and had electric fires, but the electricity was unpredictable — you'd never know when it was going to be on or off. He had odd bits of furniture from his various aunts — your grandmother's sisters — all very tasteful, and lots of books.

"Anyway, I got divorced, and we got married."

"Did you plan to go back to Jamaica with Daddy?"

"I was never happy in Jamaica; I never thought we'd go back. Not that anyone ever said so, or made any promises. The subject never came up. Your father liked England. He found it interesting. He wanted to be a political economist, a political journalist." She looked up, frowning uncertainly, as though searching an attic for memory. "I never saw things in terms of politics, I saw things in terms of our life here together. You could have knocked me dead with a feather when he returned to Jamaica and became a trade unionist. He always wanted to find his own separate path. I had just never seen Michael in that role. Though he was a natural-born political thinker. All his friends were. They were all going to change the Caribbean — change the world."

She folded her napkin and stroked stray breadcrumbs into the palm of her hand, then dusted them thoughtfully onto the empty plate.

"I think I never saw your father as a politician because of his gentleness. It sounds a silly thing to say, but he was very gentle. Despite a privileged youth, and even though he'd been very spoiled, I never saw him as a pampered man. He had a tendency to spoil his own. He spoiled me and he spoiled you children."

"What happened?"

"To us? Oh, I don't know. It got all pear-shaped in the end. I wasn't well. I wasn't coping. Two kids, a constant *stream* of guests, people to feed. Your father was absolutely marvellous. I think he was too young to take on all the domesticity he did, but he threw himself into it heart and soul — washing, ironing . . . all your nappies — he'd do anything, even cook Sunday dinner."

"He'd wash *nappies*?"

"Good God, yes! He'd do anything for you. Oh, he adored you! Sometimes I think the thing was just so good it couldn't last. I got terribly ill — went to hospital with a breakdown — and we sent you kids off to Jamaica to give me a break. I think once you'd gone he had a sense of freedom, he was able to go to his classes and he didn't have to rush home to everything . . . ." Her voice trailed off as though diminishing with the fated marriage.

"Was he faithful?" I asked.

"In his way," she said, and smiled slowly, like a let-go paper package unfolding itself. "But it was a lovely time."

That night I met a brand new family at Clanricarde Gardens. A grown-up Anita was there with her husband, Brian. My half-brother, Jeremy, came early with his wife, Brenda, who roasted a duck for our dinner. After the family left, as I was about to go to bed, my father explained that he had to go out for a little while. I knew he was meeting Barbara. I felt betrayed. I was overtired and probably suffering the effects of jet lag, but I couldn't go to sleep in the creaky old flat, with the night and the glass of the extra-tall windows imprisoning me like panes in a frightening lantern, so I decided to wait up for him. By three o'clock I had worked myself into a fury, and decided I hated them both. I started rifling through his briefcase, and there I discovered several letters from Barbara. I did the unthinkable. I read them. I raged at their intimacy. And then I took one of his lighters and set them on fire, one by one.

The coming together of the past and present was not bringing any harmony. My father and I quarrelled for most of the trip, mainly because he shared what I considered to be *my* time with Barbara. I tried to make him feel guilty, and he probably did, but he resented me for it. One day I joined him and Barbara for lunch after school. It was cool so I wore my new grey duffel coat with the toggle buttons. Barbara arrived looking like a movie star in a smart black wool coat with a tire of shiny black fur at the collar. When I saw her, I felt suddenly despairing. I was so plain and unequal to this sophisticated city; unequal, I suppose, to my father. I became sulky, but she was sensitive to me and tried to find out what was the matter. I wanted to resent her but I couldn't, so I kept sniping at my father. He looked bewildered.

As we were leaving, I admired her coat, and she hugged me close and whispered to me, telling me to be brave. I think she was shaking. She thanked me for being understanding, and said it was a difficult time — something about pressure and snatched moments, and needing courage too.

The night before my father left, after I had unpacked my things in a narrow room at a students' hostel, he took me to dinner. I was disappointed that there had not been space for me to live with my mother. I found the day school, without uniforms and with few rules, disorganized and perplexing. Everything was strange to me, and everyone but me seemed to know where to go and what to do. My father and I talked about the future; I tried to reassure him that I liked Barbara, and he tried to assure me that nothing in our lives had changed. I told him I was sorry about the letters. As always, he found it easy to forgive.

I spent the last night at the flat with him. He sat on my bed before I went to sleep.

"I am very proud of you," he said.

"But I haven't *done* anything."

"Maybe I am proud because you are growing into a nice person."

I winced. I knew I had behaved very badly.

"No one values ability and talent more than I do. But when you boil it all down, I believe that to be a real person you must have the capacity for generosity, for kindness, for tolerance, for affection. All these things I think you have. We all make mistakes, and this is a difficult patch. You wouldn't apologize to me unless you were a big person."

He told me to let these qualities grow in me, for they would bring me happiness in a way that achievement alone never could. Achievement would bring me satisfaction, but that was not to be confused with happiness. "Most men tend to achieve in their work, but they are not happy because they have nothing else to give life except their efficiency. Most women tend to achieve husbands. Then neither they nor their husbands are happy, because they have nothing else to give except good meals. You will not be like that because you have this other side — the side of the heart. Like Mardi. Never deny it."

As we were leaving the flat the following morning, he presented me with the beautiful black coat, which Barbara had left for me. And he had placed a note of his own in the pocket: "Make a calm promise to yourself to try a year of steady work as an experiment in a new experience. You have great intelligence but have to learn like all of us that intelligence is not a substitute for work, but rather a guarantee that you can put work to good use."

England was a hiatus, a waiting period with which I had learned to cope through my earlier experience at boarding school. I rocked my emotions in the hammock of a predictable cycle of days that I marked off on the calendar each morning before committing myself to their "good use." I think that was when I realized how much my father had come to mean to the day-to-dayness of my life. In the midst of Beatles songs and my fascination with Mick Jagger, the electric youth of sixties London, unaffordable Mary Quant clothes and Vidal Sassoon hairdos, the clumpy shoes, the op art and the Cockney muddled up with Liverpudlian, I anticipated his letters as much as those of my grandparents. I awaited word from a world that had little to do with any of what I was experiencing.

My first year went badly. I failed my exams, and my grandparents came over and moved me into a boarding school in Chorleywood. I felt safe there. I liked the stodgy British food, which reminded me of childhood meals at Drumblair. The headmaster was my history teacher, and I learned to share my father's passion for the subject as, step by step, he taught me to hike through centuries of European treaties and détentes and rapprochements, tracking the steps of power from which extended the stories of people and poverty that my father had told me to follow. But I longed to go home.

Barbara wrote me sometimes. Towards the end of my two-year stay, she and my father started planning their wedding. At first it was to be on my birthday, at Regardless, and then, for reasons I never discovered — probably because her parents relented — the date and the venue were changed; it would be held later that month at her family home, instead. We planned my dress and Barbara drew stick-figure designs with explanations in her always cheerful handwriting, her words seeming to kick up at the end like little jetés.

I returned to Jamaica in the summer of 1966, moved in with my father and Barbara at Ebony Hill, and enrolled in the University of the West Indies at Mona. I had the required distinctions for Sussex, but an English university would have been too expensive for the family, and even after my two years there, although I was getting to know my English tribe and had planted a genuine kernel of friendship with my mother, the ties were not sufficiently binding. I still wanted to come home.

I think of aqua when I remember the wedding. There were aqua flowers all over the bride's family home. Barbara wore aqua chiffon trimmed with aqua feathers, and had aqua buds in her hair and in her bouquet. The room was decorated with aqua balloons and ribbons. My dress was aqua. Even the cake was iced in aqua, which Pardi thought unfortunate for a cake. In fact, I think of aqua when I think of Barbara.

I was both happy and sad at the wedding. I was glad to see someone who had become my friend and my ally join our family, but I had lost a special space that I had shared with my father.

Everything seemed to have changed. Barbara chose smart aqua-upholstered furniture (Mardi said it made *her* furniture look like logs of wood she hadn't got round to carving). Though I never saw Barbara cook, the menu included more traditional Jamaican dishes than Mardi's unspiced fare, or even Thelma's chicken pies and undiluted tinned mushroom soup on toast, both enhanced by much garlic. Thick, quilted covers replaced the old Drumblair chenille spreads on the beds, carpets replaced the straw mats on the floors and fresh flowers replaced the sore-throated rasps of dried arrangements. For the first time the two adjacent homes were separated by a fence. Mardi was not very pleased about that.

"All he cares about is *her*," I griped.

"That's not true," Mardi gently contradicted. Although she must sometimes have found the closeness of her son's relationship disconcerting, she always tried to be fair. She quoted one of her favourite Jamaican poets, George Campbell: "'A cloud that was the faintest breath, / Within a time of gentian blue, / And telling more about the sky, / Than any dreamer ever knew . . .' For Michael she is that breath of cloud."

I tried for a while to live with my father and Barbara again, but my father and I couldn't get along. I had too many friends visiting, or my music was too loud, or there were too many phone calls and my conversations were too long. I was rude to him, I was unpleasant to her, sometimes even unpleasant to her family, who always seemed to be around.

My jealousy over my father tormented me. They would emerge one by one from their room at the end of the corridor, looking crumpled and smudged, with an intimate brilliance, making a visible effort to connect to me in the world outside themselves. I felt uncomfortable and excluded but knew that I shouldn't, and therefore found other things to gripe about. One day, after a terrible argument in which Barbara had to intervene, my father asked me to leave the house. I went to live with some friends in a flat.

Pardi and Mardi were no longer at Regardless. Pardi was still broke. So he rented out the house in 1966, and they moved up to Nomdmi. But the hills no longer enchanted my grandmother. She had used up every passion of mountain spirit creating her earlier cosmos, and now the faraway place was like a spiritual carcass; it made her feel irrelevant, stranded, almost exiled. Every morning my grandfather drove down the hill to attend Parliament, to be personally abused as has been no other national leader in Jamaica's history, and then he'd drive back up again late in the evening.

Later that year, Barbara — who had been told by doctors that she could never have children — discovered that she was pregnant. The baby was due the following April.

My father and Barbara turned their downstairs study into a one-room flat for Mardi and Pardi. Barbara was often resting in her room, feeling unwell, and Pardi's favourite place became the chair at the foot of his daughter-in-law's bed. All the men in the family loved her. Douglas, who periodically returned with Little Norman from his various UNESCO postings in Africa for his holidays, took an uncharacteristic shine to her. They shared a wry sense of humour. "It's disgraceful how they gossip," my grandmother would scold, though secretly pleased with the new harmony in the family. Although Mardi's nose was slightly out of joint, she respected Barbara. Barbara gazed at us all from her vantage point on the pillow as she often lay there, flat on her back, through the months of her pregnancy. We became homing pigeons to her roost.

I would visit and borrow Barbara's clothes, which she didn't need for a while, and borrow the books she had kept since her own days studying English at the university. I was still in love with the footballer. I would sit by the bed telling Barbara my secrets. Once she said to me, "I gave up university for love, and look what happened! Don't you dare do the same thing, Kiddo! Live it for both of us!"

My three years at university coincided with the family maelstrom, one that would prove far more compelling than life as an undergraduate. At first it added a glow to those in its circle. The family came alive again as we watched my father breaking through like a new butterfly, transcending us, as though we had been only a chrysalis in which he prepared for his true role.

The scandal over his marriage soon subsided, and most people reacted favourably to the union, for my father and Barbara made a handsome couple. They were both tall people, wide-jawed and definite, articulate and bright — not just intelligent, but shining with energy and humour. They reminded me of two phosphorous surfaces that quickened each other, sharpened and exposed, probed and debunked, dared and encouraged. Barbara used to say, "The nubs fit." Despite my own selfish reservations, I believed that there could have been no better match for either.

In March 1967, three weeks before the next general election, my father was persuaded to run for a constituency seat. He had a long talk with Barbara the night before. I don't think her influence alone convinced him, for I believe that decision always lurked in him, but with Barbara he found new confidence at a personal level. He had begun to trust life. She had provided him with an emotional base. He felt capable of anything now. He agreed to run in Central Kingston, a constituency disillusioned with the People's National Party — an almost impossible seat to win.

In Half Way Tree Square, where over the years so many national decisions had been announced, a crowd of thousands gathered under the clock tower. It was the night before nomination day, and they had come to hear the candidates named. Pardi left my father's introduction to the very last. He stood there in his old grey three-piece suit, swaying back and forth, the trousers over the heels of his shoes slightly trailing on the rough wooden platform.

"And I am the proud father . . . ."

He stretched out his hand towards my father, who rose as though the cheering of the crowd willed him to his feet, and walked over to the party leader, who appeared suddenly shrunken next to the tall, gently reluctant figure of his son.

"And I am the proud father . . . ," he started again, but the voice of the crowd was like a drenching from a pipe that had been waiting for decades to open, " . . . of a son . . . ."

He never had a chance to finish the sentence. Nothing but mindless, long-decided emotion could be heard after that, in wave after wave of "Michael, Michael, we want Michael."

And he ran, and he won a seat that should have been unwinnable, by fewer than thirty votes.

When Sarah was born in April, by Caesarean section, Barbara was diagnosed with cancer. My father was told in the dusty parking lot outside the operating wing, before his wife had emerged from the anaesthetic. We were all passing the time, which had extended beyond the shadows of the dusk into some great undefined space of worry. First came the brief introduction to the baby in its swaddling of green operating-theatre sheets, and then came a surgeon, a friend of my father, who was assisting in the theatre.

"It's cancer," he told him, "and it has spread like wildfire."

Cancer. The months of weakness and tiredness, and the frailty of my stepmother, which I had secretly found a little too precious, suddenly made sense. She had come to my father with death at arm's length, patiently waiting for her — as though she was meant to walk only part of the way with him. Deep inside each of us there now lurked the suspicion that her presence was only borrowed. Soon she was off to New York, for cobalt therapy and whatever hope was offered by modern medicine.

The baby thrived, and for a while Barbara seemed to get better. She even returned to work. Then one day my father took us to a test match between England and the West Indies at Sabina Park. We were there to witness the great Garfield Sobers. There was a disagreement about the umpire's decision, and the crowd started to throw bottles. The police used tear gas to quell the disturbance, and the wind blew the fumes into the members' stand where we were seated. It was then that I realized that Barbara, who had come to mean so much to our family, was going to die. It was something in the way my father whipped out his handkerchief and held it over her face as he hustled us out of the pavilion, with her calling to me, "Kiddo," and pulling me by the hand, and the fear in my father's eyes, his love a trapped, helpless emotion. I knew it then. She was going to die.

She started to fade again, and her skin got yellow and she ached and felt tired. The doctors said she was very anaemic. My father took her back to New York. The doctors there gave her only a few months to live, though she was not to be told, a decision that my activist father found deeply anguishing.

One afternoon after her return, Barbara was resting in her room and had fallen asleep. My father, who in addition to his

political role still worked with the union, had gone to a workers' meeting. Barbara suddenly woke up agitated. She had
dreamed that she was watching her husband speak on television, when he suddenly fell forward out of the screen. When
she told me she was very upset, but we agreed that it was only
a "worry dream," probably reflecting concern over the outcome of his trip.

"What does it mean?" I asked Mardi, who knew these
things. "Does it signify death?"

"Not death . . . not the end of life, more the end of life
within life," Mardi said shrugging sadly. "You see, it's a screen
within a screen. The TV screen within the screen of their life,
and within the screen of her dream."

The minister who had married them escorted Barbara on
her road to death for a while, and then their roles seemed to
switch, and she became to a certain extent a spiritual escort
to us all. She returned to her faith reluctantly, "like a bucking
bronco," she said. She fought to recover, to mother her daughter, to live for her husband. But, near the end, when it became
clear to her that she wasn't going to be a Job — that her suf-
ferings might not end, that no restorations would be made to
her — she began to see herself as the bearer of a lesson.

"Maybe it is Michael who must learn humility," she said
one day to the minister.

If my father had drawn the best straw at birth, he began
to realize that he would have to pay for that. That nothing
would ever be easy. He learned that he would always have to
fight, no way would be made simple for him, that all things
would come to him at a high price. But it wasn't humility he
learned. His life became a rage, as though fate bore the familiar face of the bullies of his youth. The light might be turned
out, but he would make his way if he had to, even in the dark.
Life itself, the very thing whose taste he couldn't live without,

whose brilliance and dark shadows, whose lascivious joys he craved and devoured, whose cruelties he rode bareback — became his adversary.

Barbara died in June 1968. My father had been called out because of a crisis at a bauxite plant. She waited for him to return. Her months of pain, her fevers and the paraphernalia of keeping her alive were already gone when he came round the door. She was no more than a light going out under the lid we had all watched coming down.

"A being that was full of grace, / Right through the blue and mixed with light, / A cloud that would be lost at night . . . ."

"Goodbye, bright flower," was all my father said.

SEVEN

IT IS SAID, IF YOU WANT to get rid of a headache, get a toothache. But if you fix the toothache, will the headache come back?

The body language of pain is subtle. When he lost feeling below his waist, the pain in my father's upper body became our new problem. He said that it had been there before but he hadn't noticed it as much. Now his upper back and right shoulder were constantly hurting. His hands, which had kept his rhythm of calm during the regime of lower back pain, now seemed gingerly paused, each digit set in its own separate clench, avoiding the slightest movement that might disturb the irritable upper limbs to which they were attached.

We were referred to a pain specialist. He arrived to tend my father, a sturdy and dishevelled angel of mercy. No white coat or neat tie, no steady composure or technocratic order, simply a soldier who had left one trench to make his way through the constant reality of battle towards another. There was something comforting about his casual clothes, as though pain was just an everyday circumstance, and relief had a rec-ognizable shape no more imposing than the friend who comes to reprogram one's satellite receiver. He moved swiftly and softly, in tennis shoes, as if speed and silence were necessary weapons for his swoops.

He wasted no time on formalities, but placed his bag on the floor beside the bed, and held my father's feet around the ankles long enough for his patient to see a connection that he couldn't feel. Leaving one hand to span them, he moved round the bed to place the other on his subject's forearm, as though he were unthreading the setting of a bomb. He then released my father's ankles and his hands met halfway, at the pulse in the patient's ticking wrist. All the while he was talking quietly to him: "My name is Doctor So-and-so, the traffic was rather heavy, yes indeed, it is a strong pulse . . . now you say the pain is where? Here? Oh, a little farther to the left . . . we'll get to it in time. When you lean forward, does that hurt? Is it worse now? Here? That's fine, no, the morphine doesn't always work as specifically as this. I have my little bag of tricks . . . here we go, gently. You leave the pain to me." His sturdy figure remained motionless as his hands dipped deftly into his bag.

After assembling his arsenal, he administered several local anaesthetics, all the while addressing the pain as if it were an animal he was taming — "Here you are . . . there, now . . . settle down . . . settle . . . down" — and pricking my father's back with little dives of his needle. He pressed here and there on the still surface and submerged the needle beneath the skin again and again. "Does this hurt?" he asked each time. My father smiled; "So what's new?" he asked straight back.

At last, though, the patient's hands became still, and I imagined the animal whimpering now, beginning to submit.

"This will last for several days, and will relieve the topical pain. It's my magic brew. I'll change it in a couple days. We have to keep the pain guessing." I asked him if he had ever met a pain he couldn't penetrate, and he said that pain and he were long-time adversaries; that you had to get to know each pain, know its personality and anatomy. Like everything in life, it had a cause and a source, so you needed a map.

The exorcism was complete. My father had repossessed his body, and smiled wanly at the departing doctor as if he only half-remembered him. After we'd resettled him, he stared out at the nothing in particular always there in front of him and said quietly, "Now I think I'd like to play a game of bridge."

Before long, I'd assembled Joseph and Ainsley, and we played on a hospital table we'd borrowed from Regardless. It had been for Pardi's use during his final days, and Mardi kept it afterwards, installing the sentimental keepsake beside her own bed for her books and her asthma equipment. Ainsley, a close friend whose passion is bloodlines, had arranged to repaint the table, saying fondly, with the mischievous purse of his lips, "It has a history." It swung over the prone figure of my father like a diving board over water, so that we could play.

But my father soon tired. We decided to finish the game after one rubber. When we dealt the last hand, I passed him his cards, which he sorted, lifting his eyebrows as though they were doing the counting. He flipped through the cards again, as though hoping to find a hidden ace. He appeared not to. He muttered good-naturedly: "Oh, what shall I do to be saved?"

We had not noticed the change of the nursing shift till, from the back of the room, we heard the serene voice of the devout afternoon nurse, a stealthy woman of textured silences, gently suggest, "Only believe."

Card games were the currency of love and interrelation in my family. When we were children, Little Norman and I used to play, he flippantly and I ponderously, with our grandparents up in the hills, and my uncle and father would play when they came up. It was a tradition that had started with the long summer holidays when Douglas and Michael were boys. They were teaching us to be good sports, and teaching us to have fun in our spare time; only a Manley, who considered life to be first and foremost an earnest responsibility, would think fun needed to be taught.

At first Mardi taught us to play donkey and strip-me-naked, simple games to teach the suits, and then we got to play with Pardi as we graduated to rummy and then to whist, and finally to bridge. Pardi and Mardi had played serious bridge before they entered public life, but now it was what they called kitchen bridge, an intuitive version played by the seat of our pants, with a lot of laughing and no post-mortems.

It was really through bridge that my adult friendship with my father began. Two days after Barbara's funeral, he left for England, where he spent time stitching himself back together, knotting loose ends left by two years of emotional tearing. He wrote several letters, which started arriving in Jamaica at almost the same time as he returned. He thanked his parents, he thanked Barbara's parents, he thanked the doctors and the nurses, always paying tribute to what he described as "the glory of what she was" to everyone, "a great lady."

To her minister, who he felt had claimed her towards the end of her illness, for a faith he could not share, he wrote: "For me she was merely the light, and it has been turned off. The world will never be the same again."

To me he wrote a letter dated June 16, 1968.

My darling Ra,

As long as I live I will treasure the letter you handed me at the airport. And equally, I will remember how utterly sweet and thoughtful you were to the end. This is not going to be a long letter because I am tired

— not in the sense of sleep so much as in the sense of inwardly dry — can you understand what that means?

I have my fingers crossed for your exams but feel your sheer ability will pull you through well. You have it, kid. I am *so* proud of how you have grown — so delighted to watch you come through the wars and the devils and the hurts and indulgences and the emptinesses and the too-fullnesses and to know this is my kid, my first-born, who has the guts — to survive despair and work up the slopes and the reaches of excellence. Because when the banalities have gone to sleep, succumbing to the coma of their own flickering fatigue, it is the people who say, "I will climb Everest because it is there" — and it represents that intangible, inexpressible, indefinable thing, excellence — who count and matter and make history and pay a price that is not as great a price as the coma.

Forgive your prickly father who spends a lot of time at and in defence. Don't be hurt if there are a lot of women when I come back — but I will love all my children the same way and I will work hard and I will hold my values and I will not be crude. But she was hard to lose so soon and not all of me is tough — only the surface and the centre — in between is distressingly soft really.

My love to whoever you think deserves a word of greeting.

And for you, baby — much more than you will ever know or than I will ever be able to say out loud — Daddy.

When he returned from his trip, having no anchor, he gravitated to me. He brought a shattered self that could be seen in the pronounced grooves on his forehead and the flat and dispassionate regard in his eyes. It could be heard in the leanness of his words, which dealt only with the matter-of-fact, failed to dwell on anything too long, and in his laugh, which shot out like a short rebuke when it was called upon. When occasionally he smiled, one sensed a tide of deep regret beneath.

The life my father shared with Barbara had been quickly dismantled. At his request, her family had removed her clothes and personal effects, and my father arranged to take from Ebony Hill the furniture he would need. He rented out the house and moved back to a small apartment on Mountain View Avenue that he had lived in years before, once when he was first married to Thelma, then again when they were divorced. Despite its address, the flat had absolutely no view of the low mountain that lay behind it.

Mardi cleared out Ebony Hill for the second time. As she sat waiting for new tenants to arrive, she wondered, "Do houses have a destiny or do people follow a pattern?"

"People follow a pattern. Their pattern becomes their fate," Pardi concluded.

All our fates had shifted around. Pardi and Mardi were back at their home, Regardless. I was living on campus, in the female residence, in a narrow, cheerful room shaped like an anchovy can, which extended over the porter's lodge. Joseph lived with Thelma, and Sarah lived with her maternal grandparents. When I visited my father on Mountain View, the small flat appeared to have shrunk and aged and faded, and it glared at its occupant like a reprimand. The stadium opposite flaunted Jamaica's flag like the glory that, for all their work, had eluded our family.

Not even a photograph of Barbara was evident, not a photograph of anyone. "Don't you miss her?" I asked him one day.

"I don't miss people," he said thoughtfully. He explained that he was always compelled by the present, to which he felt he owed a duty. "It's all we have," he said, "that connection." He never lived in the past, despite his prodigious memory, so when it came up, the past seemed to surprise him. "I did all I could till there was nothing left I *could* do . . . ." I dropped the subject. I would discover years later that a friend of mine he was dating had complained that displaying his late wife's picture beside his bed was morbid, and that it had disappeared permanently after that.

My grandfather shrugged when I told him my father kept no photographs of Barbara. "I expect he doesn't dare," he said.

I had come to realize that this was something they all had in common: they could be ruthless about departures. They could leave a thing behind, or buried inside. Mardi never went back to a piece of her work, my father never went back to a woman, and Pardi, who said that only a dog goes back to its vomit, never went back to anything.

Pardi became more frail after Barbara died. "She was a woman I greatly admired and deeply loved," he confessed. "An irreplaceable loss." Before the funeral, Pardi visited the site of his daughter-in-law's grave, and the newly dug edge slipped under his feet. He slid down with the loose earth to the bottom of the hole and had difficulty scrambling out. The gravediggers nodded knowingly and said he'd be next. This omen worried my grandmother considerably.

He was slower and his irritability was no longer explosive, but more like a dishevelment of spirit. The world had become a place that annoyed him. The soup and the coffee were never hot enough, everyone talked too much on the phone, people kept leaving their radios on, and because he was growing deaf he heard the sound system thumping from the neighbouring town more clearly than his own. Life was wearing him down — the slugs in the garden, the autobiography he didn't feel able to write, his deteriorating health, the problems of the country and in our lives that he couldn't solve, his own poverty, the death of Barbara. His pants trailed sadly behind him as his steps dragged across the tiled floor of Regardless. He hadn't the energy to pace any more, but instead sat in his chair and read Hemingway — "He blew his brains out," he told me — or sat in his chair and refused to remember memories, listening only to Mahler. I didn't spend as much time with him as I might, but I knew he was there, like the presence of laws in a just country.

My father displayed a contradictory mixture of intensely directed focus in his work, and uncharacteristic wafting in his private life, like a lost item being passed from hand to hand in search of ownership. A lot of women pursued him, and he pursued a lot of women. Some of them were my friends. Part of me enjoyed the power I imagined this gave me; another part was secretly uncomfortable.

He kept pushing the shadows behind him. In a personal sense he appeared to be without a compass, and his large and imposing figure was oddly vulnerable as he searched for himself in the recognition and affections of others. He had given up smoking ("just stopped cold turkey," he'd say with pride), and to be sociable he needed several gin and tonics. It was the only time I knew him to drink heavily.

Like his father, he had very few friends, and would rely on his partner or, failing that, his family for company. He seemed more at ease with things he could handle at arm's length. My uncle once remarked that his brother was no good with less than twenty thousand people. In all things personal he tended to be awkward. He was always "trying" at happiness, or love, or marriage, or even at family. I remember a childhood friend of his telling me that her earliest memory of him as a teenager was seeing him at a party one night, standing self-consciously with one leg propped up behind him against the wall, his arms crossed in front of him. He remained in the same place for the time he was there, staring, she said, at a spot on the floor in front of him. And then he disappeared. He hadn't spoken to anyone. Some might have considered him unfriendly, but she sensed that he was painfully shy.

I understood this. Although I am more gregarious than my father, living in Jamaica with a very public name, I always had a sense of being watched. When you're supposed to be on stage you know what to do, but how do you act when you are just a bystander?

Because he was shy, my father used to take me along with him when he went out in the evenings, or on weekends. I liked being part of his world. He had a small group of friends, some of whom he'd met during his marriage to Barbara, others through me. Most of them were between my age and his. They surrounded him with solicitous concern and apparently unconditional support; my father seemed to attract devotees. There was one couple who kept an open house where there was always a well-supplied bar, and easy Latinesque music that could be danced to or simply swayed to by the steady stream of couples or singles (it was difficult to tell which) welcomed by the excessive generosity of their hosts. And day after day, during what seemed like one endless party, there was always a game of bridge.

One day we were playing bridge on the porch, and a lame dog kept limping up to the table and cowering. The dog looked dirty and I could see that it was upsetting my father, who was squeamish, but he didn't say anything — just kept pulling in his elbows, and glancing at the dog to make sure it wasn't going to touch his legs under the table. Every now and then one of the other players would adroitly shoo the dog. Then someone started to pet it.

"Don't encourage that dog," someone else said.

"But he's so loyal," he crooned to the animal, who was now slavering over him.

"He's not loyal, he's needy!" snapped my father, obviously unable to take it any more. Everyone looked at him curiously.

I sympathized, for I was fastidious myself, and the dog was upsetting me too.

"You don't like dogs, Michael?" someone asked without rancour.

"I like the dogs I have got to know," he said, "but that's not the point. It's the neediness I don't like." He found charity in any form humiliating, feeling that it was society's responsibility to ensure that none of its members ever needed to beg.

Another visitor, a rugged-spirited woman with an unadorned, bony beauty, was an ardent Catholic. On another day there was a heated discussion on religion, passing over our heads where we were seated at the bridge table. Suddenly someone at our table asked bluntly, "Michael, do you believe in God?"

"That's like asking me if I believe in the universe," my father said. "The universe exists and I am connected to it . . . so far. If you mean, do I believe in a specific religion, or believe that there is a heaven and a hell, that I don't know. So I must be an agnostic. I suppose I'm an activist, really. I believe in connection."

"So you think that when you die there will be nothing?" asked this visitor, mildly affronted.

"No. Not at all. There will still be everything . . . but me! The universe won't end, but I will! My connection to it will be severed."

One or two mumbled in agreement, and the woman raised her brow knowingly, and dropped the discussion, maybe leaving the unbeliever to the justice of a higher court.

"I like life with its mysteries," he muttered. I knew he felt under attack when he added, "I don't need my imponderables filled in for me." But if nine out of ten people agreed with my father, he would lose interest in the nine and worry about converting the tenth. So I knew he was upset.

Mardi worried about us. She said my father was drinking too much and burning the candle at both ends, knowing that the time he spent with his friends was often a fringe at the edge of the sometimes sixteen hours he shared between the union and his political work. At other times she worried about the distractions, as I had to sit my final exams that year. "Whenever you get too embroiled in your father's life, it's trouble!" she'd say. Mardi had always been our common language, the joint to which my father and I connected. Now we wondered if she was becoming a little jealous that we were close.

It was 1969, and the Black Power movement in the United States caught the imagination of youth in our small, predominantly black country. It was immediately popular at the university, where young ideologues saw it as a route to black pride and self-assertion, and some thought the realization of Garveyism. But all too often it lead to simplistic conclusions and naive demands for easy solutions or an immediate new order. The entire status quo was seen to have emanated from Westminster, and was therefore bad and must go. Despite the fact that he had fought for independence, my grandfather and his politics were included. These students branded Pardi as "the same old story," one that had sold out national interests to imperialists. They produced a thin journal in which they attacked Bustamante and him as stooges of colonialism.

"That rag is a travesty," said Mardi, but Pardi was thoughtful. "They cry down the work of the past and deny its value. They did not live when we were working for self-government. They know nothing of the dangers we faced . . . the fights we fought, and how and when we overcame . . . to win this generation the tool of political power they find in their hands."

"But I am of *this* generation," my father would say to me.

On the campus, anyone who was not black was suspect. The lighter you were, the harder you had to try to prove yourself. As a beige-toned mulatto I found myself constantly trying to prove something that I didn't then realize had nothing to do with the equation I needed to solve. Yes, I could wear dashikis, and tie up my hair (which was "too straight"), and I could even try talking in dialect, but it would never get me accepted. Colour and class had become muddled. For the first time in my life I began to feel like an outsider in my own country. I couldn't bear to hear my grandfather criticized, yet I couldn't defend him without distancing myself even farther from them. *Them.* Not all the students, but the vociferous ones, the cheerleaders, the more blinkered extremists who referred to themselves as "the student body," and set an arbitrary standard for acceptance that was designed to keep out everybody but themselves.

My final year at university began with a crisis. Walter Rodney, a Guyanese history lecturer on the Jamaican campus, had been proclaimed *persona non grata* by the government. Hugh Shearer was now prime minister, as the aging, ailing Bustamante had retired and his successor had died shortly after assuming office. Although Shearer came from a similar union background to my father's, he was a political conservative, and Walter Rodney was a fiery Marxist known for his radical views. When Rodney returned from a lecturing tour, Shearer's government — probably overreacting to the universal upsurgence of youth protest, and possibly mindful of the experience of France in 1968, when students and workers had united to almost topple De Gaulle — refused him entry. The ban galvanized the faculty and students to organize a protest march, which many of us joined, and which the police suppressed with unnecessary force.

A geology student, a friend who would not participate in the march, shrugged when I asked her why.

"The continent of Africa is pushing up the Alps," she said.

All the attention the students received gave them a certain political legitimacy. The most radical ideologues continued to be iconoclastic, but more thoughtful students began to consider their options. They turned to the Member of Parliament for Central Kingston, who was emerging as the new hope for change and the possibility of social progress without violence. My father was touted to be the person most likely to succeed as the next leader of the opposition party. The students approached me to be an intermediary. I was delighted to have any opportunity to win their favour, and my father cooperated, hoping to attract young membership for the PNP.

In all this, my father was steadily building his name in the party. He was not an exemplary Member of Parliament — he disliked the role of constituency caretaker — but he had a gift for persuading other people to get involved. His constituency soon benefitted from the organized help of both university youth and the middle classes, some teaching, others helping to build sports centres or giving medical assistance in clinics. There was a feeling of give and take that infected those involved with patriotic fervour, an energy that brought out the best in those it touched.

Barbara had been elected branch president of the women's movement in my father's constituency before her death. Now I was invited to fill the role for a year. This was the first time

I had been asked to do anything political and, although I felt honoured, the invitation bewildered me. What did the president of such a movement do?

On the day of my first appearance at a group meeting, I almost became ill with nervousness over my speech. My father was not surprised. Although few people knew this, as a shy man who had conquered an early stammer, he had spent his public life fighting that very fear. He had not made his first speech until he was twenty-six. He helped me prepare my brief presentation. We ran through it several times. "Write it down this way," he'd say, showing me how to break a line for effect, or underline a word for emphasis.

He felt I should go by myself. It was, after all, a women's group. He dropped me off at a small schoolhouse, where a dusty yard in front of the building was used for meetings. A large and amiable woman who was the soul of the movement and the constituency met me at the side of the road and nestled me under her arm, squeezing me close, like a chicken she was carrying to the slaughter. She introduced me to the ladies, and gave me a lemonade sweetened with cherry syrup.

The women had placed a table with an elaborately crocheted white cloth in the centre of the yard, under the only tree. My grandfather's picture hung above us, tacked to the trunk, and my father's stood to one side of the table, next to a small picture of Barbara, propped up in the middle. The picture was accompanied by a friend's eulogy on newsprint. "She had the sort of courage that was a palpable thing. A woman like her was why we try to make a decent polity," it read. The table was like an altar.

A more confident chicken kept strutting in and out during the meeting, as if checking the items on the agenda, and there were two dogs sleeping in the dust, with flies on them, and a third dog which, mysteriously, was chased away each time it appeared. "A JLP dawg," someone declared. The ladies sat in a circle on long, low school benches in front of the table, and the meeting was called to order. I was voted in as president, unopposed. I told the lady in charge that I felt undeserving. "Stop that," she commanded, "what you mean! You're Joshua's daughter!"

My credentials were evidently in order.

I rose to my feet, the paper shaking in my hands, "It is my honour to be here this afternoon . . . . " My voice kept breaking and I swallowed often, and my eyes never left the page with my father's slanting instructions, like little bodies leaning to pull me behind them. When my speech was over, despite my poor showing I got a standing ovation from the audience. Then one woman arrived with a cake, and another frail old lady, with a pronounced hunch in her shoulders, brought a box wrapped in orange crepe paper, the party colour, and presented it to me shyly with a small, embarrassing curtsy which I could only accept by returning it. I was charged by my caretaker to open my present.

Inside was a pair of handmade straw sandals embroidered with colourful raffia. I kept my grandmother in mind when I mimed surprise and pleasure.

"Take them out," they demanded. I did.

"Put them on," they ordered. I tried. I couldn't. I looked at them in despair, and started to explain tactfully to my lifeline that both were two entirely different sizes — one at least a size 10, and the other as tiny as a child's slipper — and that both were for the left foot. Why did my life always boil down to the size of shoes, I wondered. I held them side by side, two lopsided kidney beans facing the same way, to illustrate my point.

"Go on," shouted my committee.

"Nu matter," commanded my guardian presence. "In politics all shoe is the same size!"

They all laughed and gesticulated to each other, and forgot about me and the mismatched gift. I was left standing there holding onto them.

My father came to pick me up. Driving home, he said, "You've been a real trooper!"

"I *hate* politics," I said.

"But life *is* politics, Ra." He looked across at me for as long as he could in the traffic. "Politics is the human reflection of life."

"Anyway, what does it matter?" I said. "Do you know that Africa is slowly pushing up the Alps?"

"Now that's a comforting thought," he said, and smiled.

But he was speaking to the fool with two different-sized left feet. I knew my brief political career had just ended. I told him that I felt like a patronizing fraud. All the cynics at the university were right; we were just a middle-class family from another world that didn't begin to understand the Jamaica the anthropologists wrote about.

He argued with me all the way home, insisting that one did not have to be poor to understand the problems of poverty. People we passed on the road recognized him, and I could see their look of surprise. If we had to stop, some would give him the PNP sign of the clenched fist; others would nudge each other; children would laugh and run towards the car. He waved modestly, sometimes returning a fist in solidarity. He had a feathery wave and mischievous smile that he kept for older ladies and children.

"Mother is a great egalitarian. She likes to nurse birds with broken wings," he said. "I am no good at that. That's why you all get vexed with me when people come begging at the door and I get mad. I am not like Mother. I resent the intrusion. But you better believe I will rage on the bird's behalf! That business of people telling me, 'See that little lame mongrel . . . he's so loyal . . . ,' I know he's not loyal at all. He's being denied his living right to dignity. Don't pat him on his back. Damn patronage! I'd rather he not be loyal. I'd rather he not bother with me at all because he's off about his own business. Then he's not needy any more. You don't simply feel sorry for people. Charity is as humiliating as want. I suppose that attracted me to the union. You can make things better. You can have a crack at making things just."

He lectured me about injustice; about frustration leading to anger, and anger leading to violence; about the fact that oppressed people did not have the power to help themselves.

"But I can't make speeches and negotiate wages," I protested. The prospect of a political future loomed dauntingly before me.

"Then you must find another way to contribute. Be a teacher, be a writer . . . enormous influence there, and opportunity to help . . . to guide people and change things." He brooded for a bit. "You see, there is so much cynicism and sometimes plain indifference nowadays. In a sense it's not knowing how to make a difference, and that's understandable. But a lot of the time it's damned laziness or selfishness."

I nodded, hoping he didn't think I was guilty of this.

"What I want to do is open up the doors to politics for everyone — doctors and teachers and lawyers and house-wives and insurance salesmen, like our friends in the bridge group. They have a stake in this. Then you have the angry radicals at the university. Instead of treating them with cruelty or contempt, we should harness their enthusiasm and their energy. They are our youth! The country's blood!" And on and on. He was treating me as if I were an audience of twenty thousand. But this was my father. His enthusiasm became an infectious energy.

Looking back at that time, without realizing it then, these

various strands to which my life was only loosely or accidentally connected, were woven into a plait by my father's deft fingers, a confluence of spirits that helped usher in the seventies.

On Pardi's seventy-fifth birthday, in July 1968, my grandfather had announced his intention not to seek re-election as party leader for the thirtieth time. He told his party that in the following February they must elect a new leader prepared to shoulder the weight of history's judgement. "I pray that he will, as Antaeus of old, draw strength from the earth, from the courage of the people, the feel of their hands and the sound of their feet, the roar in their throats, and the love of their hearts."

In February 1969, my grandmother and I sat by the radio at Regardless to wait for the results of the succession election. It had been a hard-fought two-man race. The election of officers was not open to the public, but even if it had been, we would not have gone. My grandfather insisted that the race be a fair one, so that if my father won there would be no suspicion of nepotism, no suggestion of a dynasty, and our presence might remind the party of the close connection.

We crossed our fingers, and my grandmother touched the wooden radio for luck as the familiar repeating tone announced a news flash. My father had won. The quiet room absorbed the information. It was a profound moment. We could not hear the cheers, or know the excitement as speaker after speaker rose to welcome their new leader, but the news seemed more awesome for its detachment. I suddenly felt I might never see my father again. Mardi smiled briefly, as if to say, ah well, that's settled then, but not happily — more as if someone had asked for her opinion and, just as she was about to reply, it had become unnecessary.

"It's all out of our hands now," she said. But it had never been in our hands in the first place.

EIGHT

"*'CUT, CUT THIS SURGING THROAT / To flood the world with dawn.'*"

My father looked across at the light streaming through the window, which ended in a small puddle he could not see on the floor at the foot of his bed. He drew his index finger across his own throat as these words spilled from his memory like renewed life on the bright morning.

"Oh how glorious," I said. "Now who wrote that?"

"Shame on you!" he replied looking very smug. "M.G. Smith!"

"Mike Smith. I should have known that. A lifetime family friend, and another of Mardi's pioneer poets."

I turned on the small tape recorder and placed it on the table, near my father's voice, where he lay with head propped higher than usual on an extra pillow.

"Tell me about Arthur Wint," I said. Dr. Wint was the Jamaican track athlete who had been a gold medallist at the Helsinki Olympics. His daughter was planning a book to remember her late father.

The room seemed full of grace bathed in this light. My father's hospital bed appeared less ominous, its rails no more than gingerly ornamental.

"Arthur was one of the greatest match performers that athletics ever produced. He represented a kind of 'cultural first' in Jamaican experience. He was also utterly, patriotically selfless," he began. Only the week before, he had had to turn down two writing projects on sports that he hadn't the strength to accomplish — one a history of boxing in Jamaica, which he aptly handed over to his brother, and the other on his friend Herb McKenley, another Jamaican medallist who ran with Wint in the winning relay team in Helsinki.

He was cheerful this morning, and he still felt hungry, even though he'd had porridge. Rennie always said that porridge was a food that never satisfied, it only "opens up the appetite." His observation seemed to have some truth to it. Whenever my father ate Desi's porridge, cornmeal or oatmeal nutmegged with lashings of condensed milk, within the hour he'd be asking for this or for that. Earlier he had asked for "those nice little finger foods . . . devilled eggs and those thingys" — little motions twirling his index finger — "that come with toothpicks." He did have a mischievous smile on his face, but I went into the next room and called a friend who did catering — just in case.

My father needed no prodding to speak about one of his heroes: " . . . He gave us the sense of the Caribbean as a great centre of potential excellence, a tiny part of the world with a very small population who were running world records, Olympic records, who were taking on the best at the highest level and winning. They were burning into our souls the conviction that we were the equal of any group in the world."

After a while his tribute was interrupted by a tight cough, small enough not to unsettle whatever temporary peace reigned within the war zone. I gave him some coconut water. He was starting to flag, and I decided he'd done enough for one morning.

"If you had only a few words to sum him up, what would they be?"

"Who, Arthur?" He frowned. "I'm sorry. Nothing comes," he said. His face furrowed into attention, and his features, his shoulders and elbows, even his fingers clasping their counterparts, all pulled themselves into a posture of considered irritation. "My mind doesn't work that way," he said curtly. "I can think of ten thousand words to say about Arthur Wint, or none at all."

When the gift of a picturesque tray of hors d'oeuvres arrived later that day, his appetite turned out to be no more than a mirage in his relentless desert. Seeing them in front of him made him feel ill. The nurse gave him an anti-emetic and he fell asleep.

Meanwhile, I played my grandmother's demon patience on the puzzle table, dealing two packs of cards slowly and neatly face up, eight across and eight down, the way she used to — except she would chew the side of her tongue — shifting and sorting and grouping and plotting, dealing one card at a time from the remaining deck. She'd decide beforehand what she was playing for — the health of a friend, the sale of a carving, the outcome of an election.

I hadn't been able to get a single game out, not one, in the five months that I'd tried at that table. And though I never dared tempt fortune by saying, "this is for Dad," in truth they were all for him.

~

To read a book is to begin to know the end. A page at a time, like a landscape that, layer by layer, adds a shadow of green, maybe the density of a single leaf, to the forest of what we understand. Written into the book we hold is everything we will discover, one line at a time. The fate already written into the grain of my father, he would uncover step by step, chapter by chapter. In a way it was like that with Mardi's carvings, whose full meanings would emerge only gradually, over time.

In 1943, the year that my grandmother awoke the "Horse of the Morning" from its log of Guatemalan redwood, she also discovered "The Generations" sleeping in a piece of mahogany, and she pondered the perennial question, do all men seek renaissance through their sons? It was part of her "cosmic" period in the mountains, and the piece was part of the series she called Dying Gods.

In "The Generations," at the centre of the dense, oblong mass, a porthole opens like a space for an eye, and two human faces flank its hollow circle on either side. The face on the left is the young God of Day, a sun in the morning rearing back to look at us from the vantage point of dawn. He is rising from a lean shoulder, like Neptune bursting free, a fierce bow arching out of the sea, paused for the moment to cup his hands, one above and one below, to receive the light from the dying God of Yesterday. Lower down, on the right, the old god's heavy head sets, and his eyes appraise the aging westerly light, his chin resting on the carving's horizon. His eyes are scorched, bulging globes burned away by day. He seeks the sea in which to extinguish himself. His light is darkly old and inner, and we know, as he passes the rays behind him, that he is leaving the genes of the universe to his son.

As with most things in our family, Mardi's metaphor would come to life. The old god's hands seemed to stretch across three decades from before my grandfather first ran for a constituency seat (and lost) in 1944, till my father won the PNP leadership in 1969. "So do the generations pass, and the days repeat themselves in time's everlasting cycle," said Mardi.

In February 1969, a small photograph was taken at the PNP party conference that would remind me of that carving. The picture shows only the back view of Pardi, the curly grey hair at the nape of his neck, and beside him his son's face leaning onto the father's shoulder. There is an awkward male tenderness. My father's smile is only tentative, and his eyes have a concentrated expression; he is counting life's rhythm, like a dancer whose pause must anticipate the timing of his next movement. He is holding the older man, his right arm embracing Pardi around his back, as he cradles a spirit trapped in its diminished humanity; but with his left hand he squeezes his father's elbow fiercely, as a child might, clutching onto the certainty of a parent.

Somewhere in that faded photograph, in the mix of two men's shoulders and their arms and their hands, in the clichés of torches and batons passing, the changing of guard, in the mysterious passage of time as it ages and renews, darkens and withdraws, I find my own way back to the beginning of another journey.

At the beginning of September 1969, after a short and self-willed battle with himself, my grandfather died. Eerily, it was on the day of the by-election to fill the constituency seat made vacant by his resignation. In his farewell speech to the party conference that previous February, Pardi's concern over the future had been apparent. He reflected on what he saw as a missed opportunity at independence to rededicate the national spirit to a sense of purpose and a deeper unity. He charged the JLP with destroying that very spirit by fighting bitterly divisive campaigns between 1961 and 1962, in which it seemed that victory justified any means. But he declared that his generation's mission to achieve self-government for Jamaica had been accomplished. The mission of the following generation would be economic. He charged the party to "struggle unceasingly to change those things in our economic and in our social life which deny to the masses of our people their proper place in the brotherhood of man."

I had spent the summer before he died with friends in the Bahamas. My exams were over and, when a three-year relationship with my first love ended, I did what was instinctive for me; I escaped. Shortly before I left Regardless for the airport, I handed Pardi a slip of paper with my examination results. I had received only a lower second, a modest degree, but he stirred from his thoughts over lunch and looked at the brief notation long enough for me to notice the clock ticking. "Well?" I urged him.

"Pi got her BA," he said, as though I were already gone and he was registering my small achievement on the consciousness of the family.

My grandmother was left by his side for the duration of that summer. She tried to keep him awake and focused through the months, as though the reasons to live were there to be seen if he would only keep his eyes on the horizon. She brought in friends to entertain him, some with whom he listened to his beloved music. He remained weak but sufficiently alert throughout July to see man walk on the moon, on a nineteen-inch black-and-white television screen. In August he kept playing a small piece from Mahler on his stereo, and it sounded so sad to Mardi that she told him it was breaking her heart.

Towards the end of August, when the house was unbearably hot and the fans were irritating her, for she hated breeze in her hair, Pardi suddenly asked to go up to the hills. She drove him to Nomdmi and he walked slowly to his study overlooking the valley behind the house. He sat for a while gazing at his country, the same heartland he had known as a child, as though from the other side of a long journey. He didn't speak of what he saw. When he was ready to leave, he walked to the desk and patted it, and looked at each thing he had chosen to surround him there: the old rocking blotter; a silver letter opener he had used through law and politics and retirement, which amazed him because it was always sharp; an aluminum reclining chair with a green plastic seat; a high bookshelf with his wife's maquettes perched on top; his blood-red cardigan that hung over the back of his swivel chair; the straw mat where his dog would sit and scratch at fleas.

When he came down from Nomdmi, he went directly to bed. Over the remaining days Mardi encouraged him to speak, gave him pieces of paper on which to write. He compiled meaningless lists with amounts of ortaniques or gallons of gas. She gave him cheques to sign, but he merely wrote half a date, in the wrong place, or signed the name of his dog, Uhuru. Meanwhile, my father was helping the PNP campaign for the upcoming by-election to fill his father's seat. He would drop in each day and update Pardi on the party's progress.

On the last day of August, between sleep and the steep, slow, arduous steps of his breath, Pardi said, "I have a train to catch." Mardi begged him not to leave; we all needed him, she said. Then she berated him for being damn bloody-minded, but he insisted that, though he didn't know its destination, he must catch the train. His bag was already packed. He even knew the clothes he wished to wear.

Later that afternoon he asked my father how the voting was going.

"Not until Tuesday, Dad. Today is only Sunday."

After my father left, Pardi said to my grandmother. "So it's Tuesday, then. That day the book will be closed."

"Why don't you stay with us?" she fretted. "We all want you. Don't bother with the train — stay with us."

But his reply was final. "Life here costs too much."

Two days later, on Tuesday, September 2, 1969, he left us. I came back to Jamaica by chance the night before, but didn't see him till the morning. In his pale blue, long-sleeved pyjamas he was smooth and still, except for the vivid concentration behind his face, and the occasional mutinous heave from his chest. His mind seemed locked in a struggle to take a body that was not yet ready to go. I brushed his hair for a little while, and thought of how much he meant to me and regretted that it was now too late to tell him so. I left him there, alone with Mardi, afraid of the unalterable certainty of seeing his death.

My father was also absent for his father's departure, because he was busy on the day of the election. The show must go on. We would not be able to make an announcement till the polls closed, for this might be misconstrued as seeking a sympathy vote. Even in mourning, the lines blurred between the private and the public.

We waited for my father in the perilous calm after death, as though it were up to him how we coped, which face we must wear for our grief; who we would be after this. He came to the house shortly after Pardi's death. He walked out to the small patio and faced the gully; in the distance beyond had stood Drumblair, where he had spent his whole childhood with his parents. The small, flat-roofed bungalows of a housing scheme looked back at him now.

He paced in a short, tight weave like he was darning a single tear in the fabric of his life, back and forth, back and forth. His face was a child's face, each feature separating into its own expression, each of a thousand sorrows, like the ears of an animal questioning. He turned and lifted his chin towards the hills. "We must look after Mother now," he said. Then he started the long process of contacting Douglas in Africa.

In the next few days he worked around the clock to help with the arrangements for the state funeral. Pardi was given what many remember as a full hero's burial, complete with a display of affectionate respect, a twenty-one-gun salute, a distraught wife and the heartbreak of his family and nation. I remember it for its un-Jamaican quietness, which felt like a great weight, and for my grandmother's grief — her stilted stillness, her unbreakable reserve, like a wordless reproach to the mourners gathered.

But my father had felt his death from that afternoon at the National Arena, as Pardi's mantle descended on him like the settling of a shroud, and someone took the snapshot that would appear in the news for one fleeting day, as though one day or one date or one hundred columns were enough to absorb anything so utterly complex as a life.

Someone should tell us that when a grandfather dies, every branch on the family tree will start growing in a new direction. It is as though a huge tree has been removed from a forest, or a tall building from a skyline. There are so many things you see for the first time. Everything is now different, exposed in a way it never was before, and profiles bear an altered significance in their landscape. Or so it was with us.

Pardi's death profoundly changed the family. Whenever I think of that day, I remember Mardi standing in the doorway, looking out from their room in a quandary, poised to announce his passing to Little Norman and me but transfixed by uncertainty. She had no idea how to proceed.

A few days before, she had been in the studio facing a large new canvas, with a piece of charcoal in her hand. In her frustration she had begun to cry, and the tears were burning so she put down the charcoal and squeezed her eyes with her thumb and forefinger. She then swiped the top of the canvas with her dampened digits. The result was two lines that converged like a fork in a branch. This morning she recognized those lines as the frown on the face of the angel who had come to fetch Pardi. Over the following days she would draw the remainder of the face — an indomitable one, with flat surfaces for cheeks and forehead, graven and unchangeable. In the lids almost completely lowered over the eyes, one sensed an indifference, a universe blind to our desires.

I moved back into Regardless to keep her company. With the help of my friends I painted the blue walls white, like a fresh page, and brightened its moments with buttercup yellow on curtains and lampshades. I encouraged Mardi to rearrange the pictures, which in our family symbolized recommitment to life.

A few mornings after Pardi's funeral, Mardi returned to her work. She said she thought Michael wise to go to the damp of England after Barbara died; weather would feel more sympathetic if it mirrored one's mood. As for her, she agonized. She would disappear half-heartedly into her studio, as though she feared what she might find under the shadows there. She made a small clay maquette, a sheltering figure of an angel carrying a man cradled in its folded wing. A few days later, as though the bare concrete floor echoed footsteps from memory, she scattered it with curling chips like fallen forest leaves; she returned to wood.

The week that Pardi died, I did two useful things. I sat my driver's licence exam, and got a job teaching English and history at Kingston College, a boys' school in the heart of the city. It was the most rewarding job I ever had, and the best work I ever did. My life had become meaningful. It was as much as I could do to show Pardi, if he was hovering as Mardi said, that his influence had not been totally in vain.

Without the philosophical centre of Pardi, the family seemed to have separated into its different souls. At times I thought Mardi must have lost the logical lobe of her brain. She became like an infinite glitch, a stutter that wouldn't come unstuck. She appeared to return to a state of inner chaos that I suspect was actually her true being, one that Pardi had helped her disguise and channel into a source of creative energy. Although her inspiration to work survived his death, my father and I now realized how much he had contained her excesses, as we became sponges absorbing a spill. She trailed a nervousness around her like a wake that threatened to overturn the rest of us. At times she appeared affronted, as though her husband's departure were an indictment of her. At other times she stared out at life like a perplexed faun from the edge of its forest. Always independent of spirit, she was curiously dependent in other ways. Although she rode her life with bareback intuitiveness, her independence was selective. Faced by mundane practicalities, she resorted to a quaint but irritating obstinacy. My father had to teach her to write her first cheque at the age of sixty-nine.

I seldom saw my brother and sister; Joseph would spend weekends with his father in Kingston, and Sarah would receive visits from her father at Barbara's parents' house. Norman, now at our university, remained the closest thing I had to a sibling.

My father's grief did not belong to Pardi, though his death extended what had already been there, like the emergence of a new length of scarf pulled out of a magician's pocket. Grief had become his nemesis. It seemed to be the high price life extracted for its use. Yet he was determined that life must go on. He was most of all a survivor. Life at any cost, he said.

I suspect that Mardi had secretly hoped grief would deliver

her son into our laps like an injured child or a broken-winged bird. Although I became his sidekick, he had initially distanced himself from the family nest soon after Barbara's death. He tended to insulate himself against anything that stirred her memory. With Pardi gone, he did indeed seem to return to his mother. And that was probably when, with adult eyes, I began to see the dance between the two of them. It was like a love affair — without the affair. Maybe I hadn't noticed the intricacies of their connection because Pardi had stood between them. I saw myself for the first time as their child, as the third side of a triangle I hadn't perceived before. Sometimes I felt like a little bead wobbling up and down on a string connecting them.

Mardi was determined to sustain her husband's memory. She helped Rex Nettleford collect and publish a selection of Pardi's speeches, with his fragment of an autobiography; she sanctioned an independent committee to start a foundation in his name and launch a yearly award for excellence; she was already leafing through submissions to a competition to design his tomb, searching for the one that plucked the most familiar chord, knowing that all this could be no more than a full stop dropped at his story's edge.

But my father became perplexed by Mardi's passions and rages. More and more, he left me to cope. One had to know Mardi to understand anything in our chaotic new life. But who knew her? I think at that time my father *dared* not know his mother, for if he looked at her too deeply, he might discover his own reflection looking back. Maybe I came closest to knowing her, for in many ways she created me to be her repository and witness. As though she had placed her genetic makeup in a bottle for me to guard, hoping it would outlast the vicissitudes of her stormy life, turning up, in a million years, on the far shore of a descendant.

"Life never stops," she declared mysteriously when she'd finished carving *The Angel*. And then she returned reluctantly to us.

After a year of living with her, I fled to England. I was briefly married to someone I had known for only ten days — an impulsive act that reflected the emotional clutching at straws to which I was prone. I would pay for this when I found myself alone, pregnant and destitute in London, too proud to ask either my English or my Jamaican family for help. But rescue would come, as though reaching out from an early nest. Estella, the matriarch of our neighbours at Drumblair, took me into her London home, feeding and tending me as though I were one of her own.

In 1971 I had my first child, Drum. I was torn between giving him the middle name of Norman or Michael, so I settled on Manley instead. Mardi came to stay with me for my labour. It lasted thirty-six hours, during which time I held my grandmother's hand and felt the ghosts of my past like ancestral roots knotting in me. At the end, when I had spent every ounce of strength, to my astonishment I recognized the face of my son.

My father waited on the tarmac to greet us when we returned. "My first grandchild," he announced proudly, looking briefly at the baby, who was fussing. Like Mardi two decades before, he charged me to find a name the baby could use for him other than "Grandpa."

My father was deep in an election campaign. At his request, Douglas had returned to Jamaica, at great personal sacrifice, to enter politics and run for a rural seat. I could feel the immediacy of politics around me again. Driving back from the airport, I saw "Time for a Change" and "Better Must Come" on bumper stickers, painted on walls, stretched out over T-shirts with my father's face. The new voice of Jamaica was heard in songs on the radio, and from the PNP bandstand at meetings all over the island, in the ironic shrugs of Bob Marley, and Peter Tosh, and numerous other spirits of reggae, as they toured with candidates night after night, investing in a struggle to which they were all committed.

My father spoke everywhere — to thousands in large squares, to mere handfuls of people at roadside stops and in cane pieces. Jamaica's poor, he explained, were his "true constituency." He communicated well with the crowds, displaying the easy rapport he had always shared with workers through his union days. He made economic nationalism the centrepiece of his platform. It was a program of democratic renewal, of social improvement, of national assertiveness, the revisiting of independence with a social conscience and an acute awareness of our demographic reality, our overwhelming population being of African decent. He spoke almost evangelically about the politics of participation, about a process of social change in which every man and woman would play a role. "Did anyone ever *ask* you what you thought?" he would challenge the crowds. "When you clocked in to work, did anyone ever ask you for an opinion?"

"No, Joshua, no." They replied as one voice.

Everywhere he went, he carried a rod that was a gift from the emperor Haile Selassie, on a recent trip to Ethiopia. It was thought by the Rastafarians to have mystical powers, and it was thought by my grandmother to be a lucky omen. It became Joshua's "rod of correction," and accompanied him through thousands of campaign miles.

"Michael Row the Boat Ashore," the crowds would sing after he had spoken, as though he were landing them on the shores of Jamaica for the first time.

"The word is love," he would tell them as he left.

When the election date was announced, Mardi predicted victory at the polls. Her rationale was purely superstitious, based on the date; February 29 was her birthday.

Joseph and I were beside our father when he became Jamaica's fourth prime minister. He was lying in his bed sleeping after supper, his rod at his side. As we stood there watching him, he seemed so peaceful, not yet aware that he'd won. I felt intensely proud and intensely sad. In saying hello to Joshua, I felt, I was saying goodbye to my father.

I could hear the cars arriving outside, and voices filling the house. I knew that he would wake to a different world.

NINE

"MY THREE EARLIEST MEMORIES are vivid. The first, a mastiff called Biggums. The second, a dream in which I am almost over-whelmed by the vomit of a huge dog. The third," and my father's eyes became fixed on a sharp point of memory as he spun an index finger in steady, compelling rotations, "my moth-er turning in a slow pirouette to display her new dress. And in that precise order," he added, unprompted, "one, two, three."

I worried that, like a drowning man, he was seeing his entire life passing before him.

"Biggums," he repeated softly, as though the memory of the mastiff was a visitor he was surprised to be welcoming.

I wrote them down. Although he thought the order of his memories was significant, why this was so appeared to be unclear to him. I offered him an unprofessional interpretation: that when he was a child, the world around him appeared to be made up of giants that loomed over him, and that he was afraid he might be obliterated by the weight of their prolific outpourings; and that he had discovered early on, through the wiles of his mother, the choreography of seduction in his bid to survive an overpowering world.

"Now how can you get all of this out of it?" he asked me.

I sat with him quietly, talking about this and that — trying not to awaken the pain, yet still governed by it, knowing how easily it was aroused by any cheerfulness in his tone. We discussed the possibility of him writing a book about his father. Although he had written eight books, on subjects ranging from unionism to politics, from economics to sport — my favourite was a history of West Indian cricket — my father had always avoided personal biography. He said it made him shy. I told him I thought a book on his father was an excellent idea. His perspective on both the public figure and the private man would be unique, since he was both a natural and a political son. I could take notes as he lay in bed. Better yet, we could use his customary tape recorder. Like a newly lit candle, the idea seemed to flame brightly in him for a minute.

"I was thinking how best to remember him the other day, when they were preparing to celebrate his centennial," he said, "and the thing that really struck me was the painstaking, tireless way he built concepts into something permanent. Enshrined everything he touched in a construct . . . the party, government, the Bank of Jamaica, the Boxing Board of Control, Banana Producers, Jamaica Welfare . . . you name it . . . he *built* a nation. In his hands, ideas became bricks." His own hands stacked his father's achievements in the empty air in front of him.

I asked him what he thought was his father's ultimate contribution to Jamaica. He lay quietly but his eyes fidgeted, and each small movement seemed to be registering more what he thought than what he saw.

"I'd say it was his ability to transfer a dream of nationhood from his own mind into the collective consciousness of the Jamaican people."

He spoke haltingly, the words waiting in his mouth until his lungs could provide enough breath to deliver them. Sometimes I found myself inhaling deeply, as though trying to breathe for him. I felt thoughtless for having taxed him with another of my questions.

He steepled his fingers above his chest, weighing the evidence as he spoke. "You know, glory is the mirror image of disaster . . . and they are the thickness of a coin apart. He initiated all the fights but enjoyed none of the fruits. When he should have made a comeback in the sixties, when we so needed his leadership, people didn't see him as a figure of renewal. He had suffered too many defeats."

"Did Jamaica break his heart?" I asked.

"Not Jamaica itself, but towards the end its prospects may have. He was already seeing what a sham political independence can be without financial independence. And he recognized political violence as a growing cancer in our society."

"Could Jamaica break your heart?" I asked.

He looked startled. "Jamaica has *already* broken my heart." He owned up to this without apparent bitterness, not dwelling on it, reverting to the subject of his father. But his breathing was laboured, so I picked up a book that I kept in the room to read when I wanted him to rest. I could feel his mind continuing its engagement.

"I would call it *The Long Shadow.*"

The book. I smiled. "I know about long shadows," I said.

"I guess you do. And you should also know that a time comes, at midday, when the shadow shortens till you and the shadow are one." And he shaped his hand into a pistol, with one outstretched index finger pointing at me.

If you ask most Jamaicans what they remember about the seventies, they will tell you, with responses that range from love to hate, that they remember Michael Manley. When I think of the seventies I think of my father too; I think of his absence from my life, and of my sense of exile from him.

Soon after the 1972 election, my father remarried and moved into Jamaica House, the official prime minister's residence. It's an odd house, with no entirety, no coherent body — just a series of obligations connected by halls downstairs and passages upstairs, and two ostentatious circular stairways that lack genuine grandeur, as they seem too big for the small halls from and to which they ascend. It's like a skeleton without flesh, a rib cage without a heart. It encourages no affection, offers no alliance; as though it knows the temporary nature of each tenancy, observes the neutrality expected of its station in the civil service. Because of its distances and separations, there is no ruminating, no sympathetic dawdling; no ghosted memory left, nor the small embroideries adorning the fabric of family.

From Hope Road, Jamaica House appeared pompous and tasteless on the flat, sprawling land that flows down from the governor general's house, formerly the colonial governor's residence.

"And they could have had Vale Royal," my grandmother mused. Vale Royal was a gracious colonial two-storey house with sweeping verandahs. Pardi's government had restored it to become the official residence after independence. When he defeated Pardi, Bustamante had peevishly, though arguably appropriately, opted to build something modern. Vale Royal was demoted and became the comfortable home for the minister of finance. Instead of returning to his father's plan, my father decided to stay in Jamaica House. He felt that a young country needed to develop traditions, and that you couldn't keep chopping and changing; and anyway, moving would seem churlish. After all, that was exactly what the other party had done.

My grandmother, obstinately partisan, said Jamaica House was a Labourite house. She considered it brash, modern, inartistic, ostentatious; architecturally thoughtless and ill-considered, unconcerned with the human frailties and needs to which even figureheads were subject.

It was quite a palaver to visit my father at Jamaica House. First you were stopped at the gate and made to produce a pass to be vetted, and a phone call would announce the imminent arrival. You would then climb the front steps under the pretentious columns of the house, passing the amusing anachronism of a soldier on guard with his bayonet, studiously attempting the fixed, impersonal attention of his role model at Buckingham Palace.

In a way I had never remembered before, the family seemed to have been turned inside out. We were a garment with our seams on display. Everything in our lives had become public.

"Oh, it's all too silly," Mardi would say.

It is impossible to describe the euphoria of that period. There was a feeling of almost universal goodwill. It was as if some huge cosmic second chance had been granted Jamaica; it was a time when all the products of our history's mistakes had reached a truce with each other. Black and white and brown and yellow, rich and poor, working, middle and upper classes, oligarchy, vested interests, professionals, farmers, fishermen, business people, craftspeople, artists, religious denominations, even opposing political parties were joined in optimism about the future, and prepared to make, to varying degrees, a contribution and sacrifice. This was my father's dream: the politics of participation.

In our life of valleys and peaks, the seventies would be both the pinnacle and the trough for which my father became widely known. His ascent was as abrupt as a sudden change of mind. The early momentum, a groundswell begun by centuries-old slave rebellions, urged on by our black nationalist prophet Marcus Garvey, by Pardi and Bustamante and all the heroes of 1938, found its stride and its voice in reggae, and now bore my father along on a tumult of conviction. He had always liked to challenge the outer edges of things — to push boundaries further. He appreciated this in art, in dance, in music. Now in politics he was like a surfer, a player at the edge of a stretch, every moment of his life a balancing act. Joshua and the seventies belonged to each other.

He seemed to have pulled together all the elements of his life: the frustrated artist, architect and choreographer, the general of toy armies, the defender of the underdog, the lighter-up of rooms, the visionary and inspiration, sounder-offer and orator. The island was living his personality. His restlessness, his rapture, his rash impetuousness — his causes and carings, his sudden concepts — seemed to be no different from the nation's. There was a sense of endless movement, as though the only imperative was change.

There was such a sense of hope.

If this was my father's highest pinnacle to date, though, it was *my* deepest trough. My old feeling of abandonment returned. Of all the mistresses of his heart, I would discover that Jamaica was the most powerful.

Mardi and I became rather as my great aunts had been in Pardi's life: proud, but somehow unessential, always present but in our attendance like the fading trail behind a comet. On special occasions — the official opening of Parliament, or budget debates — we would sit together in the tiny ribbon of balcony above the floor of the House of Representatives, Gordon House. In the first sessions the men still wore suits and the women sometimes wore hats, but my father soon changed the official dress code to the kariba, a short-sleeved version of a suit that men wore without a shirt and tie, far more sensible in our warm climate. Mardi said she missed three-piece suits, but she probably missed Pardi. I regretted the change only because I thought my father looked more stunning in conservative attire.

It was strange the first time I looked down from the balcony at my father as our prime minister, at the opening of Parliament in 1972. I had been a child when my grandfather had led the country before independence, a familiar old man amongst other old men and a handful of women in the ancient wooden building that had housed the legislative body. The stairs and banisters there had been like those at Drumblair, and the floor had creaked under Pardi's old leather shoes, and everywhere there had been polished wood and cracked upholstery, high ceilings and elaborate carpentry. Pardi in the government had seemed little different from Pardi at home.

But this was a youthful Parliament with a younger leader and with many more women, and a modern building that bore little evidence of our history. I looked down on the tight, immaculate waves of dark brown and grey that commanded the roof of my father's head, as though I were back in Drumblair, seeing him arrive at the foot of the stairs. I almost expected him to lift his head and look up and smile, to establish our connection. But everyone else needed his attention now. His entrance had been flanked by party supporters and the curious, and we could hear the clamour of the crowds in the streets outside. The press had circled him as though this was America or some other star-struck country. Even the tiny new opposition party led by Edward Seaga, who had replaced Hugh Shearer after the election, seemed remarkably cordial.

"River come down from bank to bank," said my father, delighted with the landslide victory. The PNP had won by fifty-six percent of the popular vote. Carpenters had to be brought in to reorganize the legislative seating to accommodate the majority of thirty-seven on one side and only sixteen on the other. Douglas was there as well, in one of the rows behind my father. He had been named minister of youth and community development. He looked up at us and grinned several times, and most of the new ministers waved at Mardi, nodding their heads as though, with both sons there, this was her accomplishment.

On Labour Day my father invited Jamaica, a country entrenched in a view of manual or domestic labour as menial and inferior, to shed centuries of bias. Would people join him to pick up a broom or a paintbrush, a hammer or a hoe, to clean up a street or fix a schoolhouse or paint a community centre or plant a tree? "I do not believe I have a right to lead this country if I am unwilling to show that I respect the dignity of every Jamaican worker," he said. Thousands all over the island responded to the idea, and many middle-class people — almost euphorically — joined in helping on Labour Day projects, as they were also helping to teach in literacy and skill-training drives.

The government, in an effort to ease the immediate problem of unemployment, started a street-cleaning program. The beneficiaries became known as crash program workers. But soon many of the people who had supported my father reverted to criticizing his initiatives. They laughed at their new government, which had created this presence of "crash program" workers "cooling out" at the side of the street, and mocked the ignorance and inexperience of those who needed their help; mocked the dialect they spoke, mocked their enthusiasm at being offered hope.

"We get that cruelty of class consciousness straight from the British," Mardi observed.

She was right, of course. We had inherited a country with its undoing engraved in the grain of who we had become: a people trained to be economically dependent and socially insecure.

"They mock, they laugh, they treat life as a joke, while people out there are suffering," my father would say. "While they are laughing, let them remember that the television cameras are upon them and the sufferers are watching them."

My father had become lean and athletic. For many years he had played tennis, but now he became militaristic about exercise and ran several miles each morning. He remained a non-smoker. He abstained from all alcohol, drinking endless tonic water with bitters instead. He cut down on starches and anything sweet but guava cheese, forgoing his favourite dark chocolate, and every day his dinner was the same: a serving of grilled meat, with pale green squash-like cho-cho, boiled, punctuated by diagonally sliced carrots. He seemed always intense and aware, his edges more sharply defined. His jaw was adversarial, his eyes somehow darker, his ears more protruding, like wide-ranging antennae. It was if he had narrowed his life down to certainties, reduced it to a concentrate, as though he were in training for a race.

I had known his new wife, Beverley, for many years. She was a friend of mine, in that loose-knit Caribbean way in which one meets someone for five minutes and greets her with the exuberance of a deep connection thereafter. After Barbara's death, I invited her a couple of times to come to tea, to meet my father, but she never accepted.

"Does your father drink tea?" she asked incredulously, and laughed. She laughed a lot. My efforts to act as matchmaker for my father had become an obsession with me. Every woman I met, I met as though for him; saw her as though through his eyes. I longed to be able to present them to him as my gifts — I suppose, subconsciously, as extensions of myself. I used them as bait. I wanted a way into his light, wanted to cross into the orbit of his interests.

"Stop offering your father out, Ra," Mardi warned me. "You know the day he falls in love, he'll marry again! Your father doesn't date, he marries. You'll have a third stepmother and you'll be sorry!"

Beverley was tall, and had the haste of someone who suspects she may only get where she's going via a gauntlet. Her naturally assertive posture gave her an aura of regal confidence that masked many insecurities. In her face lay all her contradictions. Her mouth revealed her spontaneous generosity and her courage, but the guarded vulnerability of doubt in her eyes betrayed her uncertainty.

She was only a few years older than me. She had a restless, driven energy, a sense of purpose about anything she did, as if she needed to fill some emptiness, or make up for lost time. I noticed that she easily became bored. She would laugh joyously whenever we met, but I felt that I had to keep the jokes rolling, interest her with stories about my father, amuse her with my craziness. I became chatty, indiscreet, irreverent, making nonsense of everything. I donned this demeanour like a suit of armour, and the distance between that suit and an inner self with whom I felt no ease was the width of my moat. More and more I became a parasite, my father's reflection, an excitable flicker distorted by the intensity of his glow and my own disingenuous invention.

Beverley finally did meet my father while I was in England. I only discovered they were dating after my return when I ran into them at a nightclub. She was crouched in the seat beside him, trying in vain to hide among the shadows of jazz, or amid the distraction of her companion's inescapable aura.

By the time the 1972 elections were held, the two of them were involved in what seemed to be an uncomplicated relationship. Beverley never nagged and they seldom quarrelled. There were none of the signs of tension that attended "high dramas" of the previous reigns. They shared a good-natured ease as he engrossed himself in his work, and she accompanied him on his long campaign trail. Then they got married, quite unexpectedly, shortly after the PNP victory, in a discreet ceremony at Regardless in the presence of a handful of family members.

Beverley's father was an Anglican lay preacher and had worked as a stationmaster with the Jamaican railway company. Always a member of the PNP, he used to take his daughter along with him to political meetings. He had been transferred to Port Antonio when his daughter was ten. Beverley had spent much of her youth in that lush, wild easterly region of the island, which not even tourism has managed to tame or corrupt. She never lost the common sense she learned from rural experience, nor her early fascination with politics.

When I met her, she was an announcer at the JBC. She was a hard-working, down-to-earth, debunking, no-time-for-pretences sort of person who could smell a fraud a mile off. Though middle-class herself, she had not grown up with the pretensions of Kingston life, and had little patience with what she considered urban middle-class squeamishness. She was unequivocal about her commitments. She added a street-smart, grassroots consciousness to the often ethereal nature of our family, spoke her mind freely with little thought for diplomacy; would place a bottle of water from the refrigerator straight onto the dining table, as Daddy despairingly asked where the jug was; spent lavishly on the things she liked, would give away anything she had and saved little; was generous and volatile, funny and irreverent. I tried to ingratiate myself with her by laughing at our own middle-class family hang-ups, from the daintiness of our linen table napkins to our formality over making appointments, even with each other. My own pretensions I kept carefully hidden.

For all our dedication to the oppressed and the working classes, our family was quaintly British middle-class in our habits, even in our choice of food. Our conversation — how we spoke and what we spoke about — tended to be middle-class, even if our sympathies lay somewhere else. My father had spent his adult life representing a world with which he shared very little social intimacy. He never went into a rum bar or cruised the constituency the way Douglas did. He would go to a little rural home on the campaign trail, where someone had painted the house for his visit, and when he was offered a drink he'd ask politely for a glass of white wine, or his tonic water, and then try to hide his annoyance when the perplexed host would present him with some Wincarnis, a local "tonic wine." But this made no difference to most Jamaicans. That was who he was, and that was the way they loved him. They knew he could represent their case anywhere in the world. This was their bond.

It's funny the things one remembers. My most vivid recollection of my father's fourth marriage is Beverley telling me that he didn't like milk in his scrambled eggs. "He hates them all milky and runny. I don't know why he doesn't *tell* you!" she said. I had always made his eggs with milk.

My own first marriage, a long-distance arrangement, had felt unreal to me from the beginning, and had ended amicably by this time. I had moved into an apartment building with my young son, where I was surrounded by supportive friends who helped me with the baby, and found me a job in a real estate office across the road. There was serious pay and

a company car. I hated the job and missed teaching, but needed the bigger salary.

I was forever tracking down my father, to quarrel with
him for not giving me his time, to ask him in vain for grandfatherly favours, to pin him down. It was strange that as a
daughter I always sought control of him; as a father he never
sought control of me, seldom told me what to do or what, in
retrospect, I should have done, though sometimes I wished he
had. He was unnecessarily democratic with his children.

"I have a country to run," he would say in exasperation.
"I have a people to serve."

Beverley noticed that, in making any decision, my father
always wondered what his mother would think. Like Mardi, he
believed the best of everyone. Although unwavering hatred of
injustice lay at the base of her husband's thoughts, Beverley
recognized that he could be swayed in making some decisions.
He could change his mind overnight, and sometimes he did.
Some people felt he tended to listen only to the last person he
had spoken to, which could be confusing for people working
with him. One thing I knew: he always believed in innocence.
When there was more than one side to a story, he often found
himself straddling conflicting views.

He would come hurtling into Regardless to see his
mother on his way to or from changing the world. It was
strange to see this familiar figure accompanied by security like
shadows always trailing him; in my grandfather's day, security had meant two unarmed blue-stripe constables who
watched the home at night (the bane of Mardi's existence
became the nightly provision of coffee) and an allowance for
a chauffeur. Independence had apparently made the leader's
needs more complicated.

"Oh dear, sometimes they all take themselves terribly
seriously," observed Mardi, but she never said who "they all"

were. I had already decided that I preferred my old father, the one with the cigarettes and drinks and sense of humour. He had become so lean and ardent now, so down to the nitty-gritty bone of everything.

There was a special branch of the force to keep government officials safe. My father moved like lightning, as though wishing he could leave his minders behind. When he jogged in the morning, they would become exhausted trying to keep up with him. He would send them on errands, as though hoping they might forget to come back. He seemed to be constantly taut, on the verge of exploding. My grandmother said this was a Sagittarian arching his bow.

My father's first year in office started as a honeymoon with Jamaica. Even skeptics were prepared to give him a chance. He was finally in a position to make a difference nationally, and he didn't begin at a single point; he began everywhere. It was as though he took the tree of state and shook it and shook it. He created jobs for the perennially unemployed, and established skill training and a national literacy program and a workers' bank. He lowered the voting age to eighteen, set up local community health initiatives and changed the emphasis in agriculture to attracting and assisting small farmers. He began declassifying the civil service and embarked on public housing schemes. Internationally, along with other world leaders, he promoted the New International Economic Order, designed to reduce the gap between northern and southern countries of the world.

In his first budget speech, as he outlined a brave new world, producing generous gifts from each ministry, he seemed like a runaway train. Mardi and I had the feeling he was getting carried away.

"Poor David," said Mardi, watching the minister of finance, David Coore, who was his oldest friend. With a look of resignation on his face, he was holding onto the sides of his head.

Then the government starting taxing wealth in addition to income, levying taxes on idle land, and began a national youth service.

The middle class grew uneasy with these reforms, and the way my father was aligning Jamaica with Third World struggles. Their concern grew when he accepted a ride to a foreign conference on Fidel Castro's plane. This would be the beginning of a close and genuine friendship between the two leaders, a friendship that would return to haunt my father's political life. Two years later, US hostility would crystallize around his support for Cuba's involvement in the war in Angola. My father always felt that it was his refusal to oblige Washington and remain neutral on this issue which earned him the enmity of senior American policy makers, not only jeopardizing any hope of aid, but triggering the CIA's destabilization tactics on the island.

His political enemies would eventually weave all this into a threat that played on middle-class fears. Manley favoured Communist and terrorist regimes abroad, they said. He would force middle-class children to mix with peasant and ghetto children, at school and in the proposed national youth service. He would take over idle lands. Despite repeated government assurance to the contrary, American companies became afraid he would expropriate their large holdings of unused bauxite lands. Was he taking Jamaica into Castroism? The hysteria had begun. My father soon found himself on the defensive against growing opposition at home, and a hostile American government.

As early as Christmas of 1973, family gatherings had begun to feel huddled and besieged. Beverley was now pregnant. Mardi always said that the sea was for the young and foolish, and the hills were for those ready to grow wise. My father may have taken this seriously, for he built an embryonic house on a couple of acres of Nomdmi land, a gift from his parents before Pardi died, and started retreating to the mountains.

My father translated *Nyumbani*, the Swahili name he gave the house, as "peace in my home." Joseph said it actually meant "welcome to my home," but the house was built with the opposite objective. It was to be my father's escape, and very few people were ever welcome. Like his parents, he needed to retreat as far from civilization and people as he could; unlike his parents, having got there, he tried to domesticate a wilderness feral since the beginning of time.

There, under the rise of oblivious mountains, he steadied himself and refuelled his spirit when he could. Only at that distance was he able to regain perspective. He started writing a book, dictating it into a tape recorder at Beverley's suggestion. It explained his philosophy of change; it was a summary of everything he had thought about between his time at the London School of Economics and the present. The approach it presented was as near as one could get to democratic socialism, caught between Puerto Rico's dependent economic relationship with America, and Cuba's revolutionary socialism allied to the Soviet Union. He called the book *The Politics of Change: A Jamaican Testament*, though in fact the testament was his own. He dedicated it to Beverley.

Nyumbani had a puzzling effect on me. I wasn't told about the initial decision or the plans to build the house, so it added to my sense of exclusion from my father's world. Our personal calls and meetings were fewer, and most things I knew about him I read in the newspaper, or heard from my friends or Mardi. I have never liked change, so I felt sad when I first saw the immaculate lawn that had replaced Nomdmi's ungroomed apple grove, with its barren fruit trees undressed to bony branches and twigs with fringes of scratchy grey old man's beard.

"But surely you'd rather see your poor overworked father have a little peace?" Mardi reprimanded me when I complained about the colonization of the hilltop.

But Nyumbani became a source of tension between my father and Mardi, too. It was all about perception. My father, who was trying to encourage austerity and self-reliance, decided to build his home out of bagasse board, a particleboard made from the compressed residue of sugar cane. The house was his yearly summer madness all over again, the scratching of his architectural itch. He asked an architect friend to design a fireplace out of stones from the Hope River below. But when bagasse board is sealed and painted, it looks no different from cement, so my grandmother, seeing what she considered to be a fancy modern house with the added luxury of a fireplace, decided he was trying to show up the more simple and austere Nomdmi. I thought at first that it must be a joke between them, for the house was cheaply built with a mortgage my father had secured by his freehold of gifted land, but Mardi's resentment grew.

She noted with further irritation that her son had mown the lawns and slopes, and had planted cottage flowers, neat beds and hedges and vines. He began growing roses as Pardi had done, but dozens and dozens, on a specially cultivated hill — varieties from all over the world. The final injury came when he extended Pardi's coffee farm and stored his fertilizers in Mardi's sacred study, Mini, since she wasn't using it.

Mardi was furious. She felt that Mini, Pardi and herself had been disrespected. But when a ridiculous rumour claimed that trenches dug for the roses were really mass graves for the PNP's political enemies, Mardi was so appalled that she hurriedly returned to her defence of her son.

Mardi developed an ambivalence towards my father that swung between pride and a shadow of resentment. Sometimes I wondered if she worried that as her son's stature grew, it might overshadow the memory of his father. There he was, at the head of her husband's party, at the head of the government her husband had led. Internationally he was making a more famous name for himself. Even when he was criticized and cursed, the cries were louder than were ever heard against Pardi. The prouder she was of her son's achievements, the more protective she seemed to become of his father's memory. No matter how he honoured his father, praised his vision of the country, he was in danger of obliterating him.

If the government had enjoyed a honeymoon, 1974 marked the end of it. The impact of the Organization of the Petroleum Exporting Countries (OPEC) price increases hit the economy, and the government was forced to announce a bauxite levy. This was regarded as a declaration of war against the capitalist world. Everywhere I went, people grumbled about my father's policies in front of me. They couldn't complain about the minimum wage, a sugar cooperative, a national insurance scheme, increases in welfare relief, a mental health act, establishment of a family court or free uniforms for primary school children; they were silent on all those issues. But as the essential utilities began to be acquired by the government, I heard the mutterings. "What, your father is taking over Jamaica?" they joked, but behind their smiles lurked uncertainty, a need for reassurance. As soon as anything failed to run smoothly, they would round on him.

Crime had gripped the city of Kingston by the throat; it was no longer confined to the ghettos, but was moving into the more prosperous areas. Violence had escalated to an alarming extent. Women were terrified in their homes, as more and more people knew others who had been affected by crime. At night the rattling of gunfire became as familiar as the pounding of reggae in nearby towns. People who would never have left because of economics or politics were leaving because of crime. Jamaica was in turmoil, and the government had to take control. After two young, progressive business-men were murdered, the penalty for possession of an illegal gun became automatic imprisonment without chance of parole — a draconian measure planned to be only temporary. The country was relieved, yet the extremity of the new laws seemed too much for some people.

My father was caught in a series of crises — economic, social, moral and legal. I can only imagine what went on in his head as he fought battles on every front — nipping and tuck-ing to outwit Babluck.

The journey of life was not always smooth, nor the out-come perfect, but its texture with all its twists and turns, its moody meandering, seemed to my grandmother, nearest of us to its far horizon, to be narrowing down to some indestruc-tible scaffolding of family. On Valentine's Day, 1974, Beverley gave birth to a daughter, Natasha. To my son's amusement, the newborn was his aunt. In a break with tradition suggestive of the times, my new sister's name was taken not from the Bible but from *War and Peace*.

T E N

THE PASSAGE OUTSIDE my father's bedroom, a carpeted walkway that led from the top of the staircase to the four bedrooms, was protected on one side by a white rail. Beneath it fell a hollow, open shaft the height of the house, an inexplicable feature that we called "the well." We would drop unbreakable items down it when we were too lazy to descend the stairs. Other times voices would rise from it, reminding us of what seemed like a former world.

The family often retreated to the passage when the nurse sent us out of the room, or when our patient was sleeping. Sometimes we talked to the doctors there, often in whispers, aware that his hospital bed lay just beyond the window facing us. We'd hold our small conferences there. It was like a waiting room whose neutrality made it common to everyone, a joint between directions, a conjunction between phrases.

From there I could hear the mumble of visitors, my father's laughter or his enthusiastic sports statistics, the strumming of Della's guitar when my father helped his daughter-in-law with her music. She wrote her own songs, and he'd spend hours making her repeat a bar over and over for phrasing and pitch and even diction, correcting every detail and nuance. Della had married Joseph in 1979, and she had become one of us, an essential part of our family. When she'd leave the room, a small figure bearing her comparatively giant guitar, I'd still hear my father de-dumming her phrases.

The broad white rail provided support and strength to my father's beleaguered army. It was where his generals discussed strategy and made their decisions.

"What are we going to do about this Carter visit?"

"Stop worrying over it. Only *he* can decide." Joseph indicated my father by lifting his chin towards the window. His face was a composition of tensions.

In late January former US president Jimmy Carter requested a visit to see our patient; his presidency had coincided with our father's stewardship of Jamaica in the seventies. We knew that our father, always a private man, wouldn't want to be thought of as bedridden; wouldn't want to be prayed over or pitied. We also sensed Glynne's opposition to the visit. But I had received phone calls from friends and government officials who were anxious the meeting take place.

"Tell Dad," Joseph said. He felt it all depended on whether the decision was to be based on health or on history. "And that's *his* decision to make," he said.

As Joseph left, I could hear his barely audible rubber-soft footsteps crossing the tiles downstairs and going out the front door. His thick mat of short black hair had suddenly revealed a small bald patch which the doctors said was caused by stress. I wasn't surprised. Like most men, he bore emotional weight without releasing the tension. "If only I were on estrogen like dad, then I too could cry!" he had joked ruefully.

If he was alone, my father would signal when he needed something. I don't remember if it was the sound of faintly clapping hands that caught my attention, or movement in my peripheral vision, but when I looked at his window I saw his

hands held aloft, meeting slowly at their fingertips, then parting like the fronds of some ferny plant caught in a draft. They
looked like eerily ominous messengers.

We had offered to place a bell beside the bed so that he
could ring for asistance, but a bell happened to be the symbol
of the JLP. It had come to represent two generations of political hostility. He was probably joking when he rolled his eyes
at the suggestion, but we dropped the idea. It would indeed be
strange to think of it as his instrument of rescue.

I hurried to his door. Seeing me, he left his hands in their
last clap for a moment, leaning on each other as though in
prayer, then brought them back to their home on his chest.
Although he was turned to his right side, he was propped by
so many pillows under his left shoulder that he appeared to be
lying almost flat on his back.

"I wondered where you were," he said. He was frowning,
and looked like a small child with a problem.

"We were out there talking. Joseph has left. We were wondering about this Carter visit." I crossed over to the foot of his
bed. It's funny how I assumed that, because he couldn't see us
in the passage outside, he also couldn't hear us. "Maybe it
would be a vindication of your policies in the seventies?
Setting some record straight for history?"

He looked wearily away from me.

"History is history," he said tonelessly. Then he assumed a
mocking tone of slow gravitas. "History is always there, silent-
ly looking down. The endless contemplative. God's ledger."

He sniffed deliberately a couple of times, so slowly — all
of his movements had now become slow — and looked carefully around the room, his mouth slightly open whilst he
made some little futile bites on one side of his bottom lip. He
seemed to be calming a fear.

"What's the matter?" I asked.

"Do me a favour. I know it sounds silly, but I thought I smelled something burning."

I didn't smell anything, but I went downstairs and checked the stove. Nothing was amiss. I returned and reassured him, suggesting that someone might be burning rubbish down the road.

"Thank you," he said. "You won't go without checking, will you?"

"No, I'm not going."

He looked relieved. "I like when I know you're there in the next room. Glynne and you here. Feels like family."

Despite all his marriages, there had been so few years in which he could have felt that comfort. The longest period had been his span with Beverley, before she left. Although they had been the busiest years of his life, he had made a concerted effort to give as much time as he could to his new children. I remembered him telling me that he had discovered, with Natasha, that continuity was the secret to parenting.

"Do you ever feel bitterness about the seventies?"

"Never," he said. I believed him, for I knew he seldom harboured resentments. "More disappointment, I guess. That there was such an opportunity, and we couldn't get it to work . . . everything, *everything* . . . ," and his hands mimed irritable circles to illustrate his point: "the economy, the IMF, the Americans, the moderates, the left, the right . . . ." Now he smoothed the sheet on his chest with a slow, painstaking gesture. "God knows we tried. But we were like Chicken Little with the sky falling down on our heads!" He gave a short, heraldic toot of a laugh. "I hadn't yet learned to be content within the limits of the possible. It's strange, really, both PNP governments were premature, each in its own way. But maybe some periods in history are there to show you what *could* happen. Like Pardi's federation, a dream deferred. We'll yet revisit the seventies . . . mark my words."

I watched the brief flare of inner light, amazed at the energy he could still summon. After giving that last sentence its required posture of defiance, he looked exhausted. His eyes appeared uncomfortable, as though needing to blink. I passed him his glass of water. As he held it his hand trembled, and he asked for one of his "rescue" pills, small yellow capsules that provided short-term relief from the pain and could be used between his doses of morphine. I gave him one and with a sinking movement, one that made me realize how much of his strength was used to hold his skull upright, he let go, settled into the pillow and closed his eyes. They moved restlessly under his lids.

We were biding time till the gentle night nurse came. She arrived exactly on time at ten, and gave him his morphine. Soon it started working. I sat quietly and watched him. He peeped at me and waved, and then he seemed to fall asleep, so I was surprised when I heard him speak again.

"I don't think the house can quite cope with a president's visit," he said.

"Rex called me today. His feeling is that to decline the visit would be to deny history a chance to properly recognize you." I had rehearsed that sentence all day.

"I hear him!" he said, lifting his voice on the second word, and smiled. "But history can't come to me here . . . now . . . ." He became vague, as though he had got lost in the thought, and each look was long and punctuated by the occasional eked-out blink, as if the interim were the light and not the darkness. "Nor I to it, even if I could move these old bones!"

Short as his life must now be, the room had no immediacy but pain. When we had taken care of the physical needs that distracted him, my father had only his spirit left with which to deal, and the wide-open spaces of thought in which to wander — as though life were bringing the avowed activist to final contemplation, turning his perspective to hindsight.

I was still agitated about the question of President Carter's visit. I wondered if I owed it to my father to strengthen my resolve against my sympathy for him, for what I thought was the greater need of his legacy. When he got no agreement from me on the point, he said, a little disapprovingly, "Truth is, I'm not sure *I* can cope with the visit."

"But your legacy . . . ," I said uncertainly.

He focused his eyes on me, as if trying to remember something, and then they drifted to some distant outpost of his consciousness.

"My legacy!" he said some time later. He looked sweetly surprised, maybe a little modest or flattered, but I knew he was only being charming. "You kids are my legacy!"

Douglas came soon after, when his brother was sleeping. Whenever he arrived, he'd meander through the house looking for the orchids that Rennie nurtured. He'd find them beyond the patio, hanging from a tree or mothered by a couple of old logs, and he'd eye them suspiciously. Douglas thought they got too much water. "They don't like a lot of attention," he'd say. "That's why I like them." He would offer to take them home when my father "was finished with them," as though for my father they were merely a fad. My uncle took orchids seriously.

I heard his sandal buckles jingle as tonight he headed straight up the stairs, perusing the flowers in the passage as he passed them. We leaned on the rail together and stared at the window as though at my father's fate. I remembered how Douglas had reacted when I had called him to my flat to tell him that his brother would not be able to walk again. I had been surprised by his vehemence. He had turned round and punched the cushions on my sofa, and sobbed uncontrollably, saying over and over, "Why him? I am older, it should have been me."

"Don't you think Dad should see Carter?" I asked him now.

"Only if he wants to."

"But his legacy," I pressed.

"What's Carter got to do with his legacy?"

"Well, the seventies . . . ."

"Look," said my uncle turning abruptly to face me, and gripping the rail as though to keep things straight. "The seventies are nothing to do with the United States. The seventies are about Jamaica, plain and simple. You want to know about Michael's legacy?" He stared at me with the intense certainty that absent-minded people get when they decide to focus their attention. "He freed Jamaicans from what Marley called 'mental slavery' . . . what Garvey was all about. And he was the only person who could do it. People will tell you, oh, he should have done it more slowly, people should have been prepared for socialism; they weren't ready. Well, that may all be true; they may not be ready yet to make the best of it. But the fact is, by correcting basic social injustice, he made poor black people — the vast majority of Jamaicans — know they were as good as anyone else."

"Was he your hero for that?" I asked, amazed at the pride with which he now spoke of his brother.

"No!" he snapped. "He is my younger brother. But he did it, and he was right." He stared at me through his square, wire-rimmed glasses. "Because without a revolution, someone has to unlock the door."

I frowned.

"He had the key; he let the genie out of the bottle."

∼

I am one of the thousands of Jamaicans who abandoned my island during the seventies. I will always be. No going home now will ever lift that burden from me.

I left in late 1975. I never knew what my father felt about my leaving. Knowing him, he may well have taken me at my word. I told him that my second husband, a building contractor, had plans for extending his business to Barbados. This was true, but it was a contingency plan, not a reason. Barbados was acceptable to my conscience; the Caribbean was not America or Canada, was not the First World, to which most deserting Jamaicans flocked. And Kik was there.

But at my centre I knew that, in leaving Jamaica when I did, I had let my father down. Even if he didn't know why I'd gone. Even if nobody said anything. Though I believed in the country he was trying to build, I left because of him — because I couldn't face another trough, one that seemed twice as wide and twice as deep as those before.

Before leaving, I was remarried at Jamaica House. My father gave me away. Sarah was my only attendant. I was several months pregnant with my second child, and Beverley took me to her designer, who created a pale pink dress like a multi-layered cake that disguised the considerable size of my belly. A matching hat with a flounced brim created a further distraction. Sarah wore a darker shade of pink, her long black hair pulled back from her face, falling into ringlets behind her. She was only eight, still marginally chubby, but already her mother's woman-face was looking back at us, with her intense, dark eyes, and the way they lit up a second before her mouth did, like lightning heralding her peal of laughter. She was unusually restrained for a Manley child, though Mardi said that that wouldn't last, for she was all Swithenbank, Mardi's paternal tribe, "and Swithenbanks . . . ." She left the thought there, suspended in mid-air.

I was out of touch with Sarah, for she lived far away and in a different world. I was out of touch with Joseph too; when he was home from boarding school, he lived in Jamaica House.

He was sixteen, rebellious, loved Aretha Franklin, ignored me, tormented Sarah whenever she came to stay and was learning karate. He was put in charge of the music for the wedding. My father and Beverley planned a late-afternoon ceremony for eighty guests, to be held in the oblong courtyard between the two wings of the building. I would descend the staircase on my father's arm to "Forever My Love," by Carly Simon.

The morning of the wedding, my father blocked off an hour to practise the choreography. Over and over, with me draped on his arm, we slow-stepped the stairs, pausing after each one, with me doing a little shuffle to keep up — even though I was on the shorter inside curve — which, at the wedding, would be concealed by my gown. Over and over, because my father and I couldn't stop giggling. The procession had reminded him of a scene in *Stalag 17*, an old Second World War movie he loved, in which two male prisoners painting a white line decide to veer off their prescribed course to peep at some Russian female prisoners in the women's shower, their white line trailing unevenly behind them.

Sarah followed two steps behind us, so the guests would be able to see her above her father's head as the procession descended. Each time we fell into disarray, she would wait behind, solemn-faced, then patiently climb to the top again. She practised carrying a bouquet, clasping a bud vase with one of my father's Nyumbani roses.

"From the top," shouted my father over and over to Joseph in the living room below, where he was manning the stereo, till he deemed our performance perfect.

I walked proudly down the circular stairway that afternoon on my father's arm. The reception was held on the lawn. The evening became a good-natured window of truce between the guests and the Manleys. I dearly loved my husband and his family. His friends were mostly cheerful, emotionally stable, middle-class Jamaican families, worried about the government's policies, the increasingly noisy rhetoric of some left-wing members of the party, and most of all probably worried about the marriage of their friend to me.

With the recent sharp increase in oil prices throwing our balance of payments into crisis, the government had introduced austerity measures. Foreign items like cornflakes and imported saltfish were banned as unessential. (For some illogical reason, housewives became vitriolic about Beverley, feeling that as a woman she should know these items were essential.) It was so like Jamaica to have as its national dish saltfish and ackee — a fish that came salted from Newfoundland and had nothing at all to do with Jamaica, and a vegetable from a tree originally transplanted from Africa. And it was so like middle-class Jamaicans to be appalled at the notion of producing home-grown cassava flakes for cereal. Instead, housewives travelled to Miami and returned with boxes of the banned stuff, along with bathroom fixtures, soap powders and anything else they needed, even if a local brand was available.

Years of importation were all we knew, and a colonial economy designed to get us to spend on the empire's products whatever little we earned. Never was our desire to import, our disinclination to live within our means, so defiantly evident. The centuries had bred so much dependence in us that we railed at what we saw as an erosion of our freedom; few of us saw the irony in this or recognized the wisdom of what the government was attempting.

Naturally the guests at my wedding examined the buffet table for anything that was banned. Some of them complained about the locally produced whisky, which was a far cry from their habitual Scotch — but had they seen a bottle of forbidden Dewar's, the outcry would have been far worse.

As though making sure that his years of work would endure the roller-coaster of public emotion, my father continued setting his thoughts down in a second book. In *Voice at the Workplace* he offered his "reflections on colonialism and the Jamaican worker." Inspired by the years of his favourite job working with the union, this book, which he dedicated to those workers, would be his favourite.

In the months leading up to my wedding, I'd seen little of him. He was working like ten men, according to my grandmother. Beverley was studying political science at the university, was active in the party and had been elected president of its all-island Women's Movement. As first lady she was more concerned about improving the lot of Jamaica's women and children than about cutting ribbons; she would have had an easier time if she'd stuck to the latter. I knew these things from the newspapers, and I knew some of what my father felt and thought through Mardi, but for the most part all I heard was his name, and sometimes hers, in irritable mutterings.

People became extreme. Some who had been caught up in the heady dreams of a new society grew disenchanted when they felt their comfortable way of life might be threatened. One day, a bank teller who had once been my student told me sadly he was leaving. I tried without success to convince him that he was one of the people who stood to benefit most from the government's progressive policies, for now he would live in a society where a poor black child could dream of one day being promoted to the position of bank manager. But he was not prepared to weather the storm and resettled his life in America.

While many prepared to emigrate, professional people sometimes embraced the cause of socialism in symbolic ways. A public relations writer took the air conditioner out of her car to share the lot of the masses, and to avoid appearing bourgeois. An architect building his home cemented his passport into the foundations of the building. Those who threw their lot in with Jamaica decided that this was where they had been born, and this was where, through thick or thin, they chose to remain.

My baby sister, Natasha, was featured in the news, in photographs everywhere, even on calendars. She had become like a national toy. I even saw her picture in a bar. Natasha was the best-known baby in Jamaica, the first baby to grow up in Jamaica House, the first child of independence. Jamaicans love children, and here was a child that they felt belonged to them in a special way.

As times became more difficult, though, the attention was less flattering. Joseph and Sarah suffered verbal attacks on our father at school. There were endless jokes circulating about him, funny but sometimes cruel. As a small child Natasha sometimes saw approving crowds cheering, but more often she was left puzzled by angry demonstrations outside what were, after all, the gates of her home.

"How come the rest of us never had this attention?" I asked my grandmother.

"Be glad you didn't," she said. "She may never forgive Jamaica for all this fuss."

Natasha had a narrow face like my grandmother's, and when she puckered it up in a rare smile her mother said she smiled like me. In temperament she already reminded me of Uncle Douglas; she was quiet and introverted, with an instinctive reserve. Like Douglas, she would stiffen slightly if you came too near. She had a reticence that always left my father guessing.

My second son was born in Kingston in February 1975. An easy birth, a beautiful child. I named him Michael Luke, for his grandfather, and in the vain hope that his middle name might provide the family with a physician like his biblical namesake. Although I knew that my husband and I were planning to leave Jamaica with our two kids before the year was out, I didn't tell my father till the last minute, and then I described our exodus as temporary.

There was more trouble on the horizon. In July 1975 Joseph, Sarah, Natasha and I accompanied our father and Beverley on their first state visit to Cuba. During the five-day trip we were all impressed by how well the Cubans were thriving, and by the thoughtful sincerity of Fidel Castro.

On the way home we talked about the obvious progress of Fidel's revolution, his remarkable efforts to build a society in which everybody's needs would eventually be met and the admirable premise of his dream: that every life was to be equally valued and nurtured from birth. We also recognized that the discipline, the military order, the massive organization and regulation of life that had been vital in accommodating these changes would be anathema to Jamaica.

Soon after we came back, my father addressed a crowd and said some spur-of-the-moment words he would have to explain for the rest of his life, words that in his monologue changed from dialectic to polemic as they passed from his mind to his mouth. Euphoric from the trip, inspired by what he had witnessed and facing increasing opposition at home, he tried to explain that people must not be motivated only by the selfish desire to become a millionaire overnight; that they had an obligation of service to Jamaican society. No one is quite sure what his exact words were, but it is claimed that he said that for those who wanted to go, "There are five flights a day to Miami," and that this phrase caused the middle class to flee. It seems certain that he did suggest that whoever couldn't live with his politics was free to leave.

The words were repeated in the media for days. Jamaica was in an uproar.

"Bev says I shouldn't have said that," he confided later, looking hopefully at me, his last bastion of unquestioning, sycophantic support. "But to tell you the truth, Ra . . . each time I lay down the gauntlet to the forces of reaction . . . the status quo . . . or take even one small step to the left, I feel a portion of some invisible weight lifted off my shoulders." He looked up as though towards one of the flights of departure.

"I don't think you should have said it either," I told him, dreading his disapproval but trying to be honest about how I felt. "It's like looking at your children and saying, 'If you don't like the rules, get out!'"

"How can it be comparable?" He was petulant. "I've been taken out of context," he insisted, and this phrase too came to be associated with him. "Taken out of context" — he said it whenever he believed that he had been misunderstood. But some of us worried that he was prone to getting carried away; that sometimes he was a victim of his own soaring rhetoric.

He raged about the fact that people twisted everything he did, twisted his purpose, that if he made an infinitesimal mistake, all his headway went straight down the drain. Public scorn was always waiting to bait him, to break him, when all he cared about were the sufferers — the victims of a cruel history — the tentacles of capitalism; like wood-ants eating down a house, chewing at us from the inside.

We were used to his occasional storming and ranting. We knew this wasn't real temper, for the minute he got his way he'd stop, and he'd be all smiles and a little sheepish. He merely lost his patience when he felt that something was unjust, when he knew he had said something reckless for which he would have to pay dearly. For neither my father's charm, nor anything anyone else could say, was going to make this problem go away.

In the meantime, despite the stringent measures taken, crime had reached terrifying proportions, and there were confrontations with the security forces and widespread arson. In June 1976 the government declared a state of emergency. General elections were called for December 1976. As the campaign got under way, the atmosphere felt like a civil war. Society was being torn apart. Battle lines were drawn up. Each side felt it was in the right. The PNP felt it was defending the cause of the majority, in the tradition of our early slave martyrs, of Marcus Garvey, of the architects of our independence, in the spirit of the African liberation struggle and Fidel Castro, who had sent his troops into Angola, and against the entrenched interests of the oligarchy at home, British imperialistic thought and now the CIA.

For the JLP it was the reverse. For them the enemy was the threat of Communism at home and abroad; the possible ill effects of all this change. They each were fighting for the country's soul, they thought. And all the time, egged on by the polarities of the Cold War, we were only fighting ourselves.

But while the privileged were deriding him, while almost every organized group had turned against him, when even a daughter had abandoned the country, my father still had support. The mass of Jamaican people — the poor who had listened to Joshua as their prophet and poet and philosopher, the disenfranchised who had waited for centuries to see the walls of Jericho come down — welcomed his words, no matter what ideological label was slapped on them.

By now, though, the economic situation was getting desperate. The social policies needed funding if the system was to have any credibility. Although it had been necessary to put out initial feelers to the International Monetary Fund (IMF), the PNP went into the general election still believing they could survive without that assistance. They ran their campaign on the slogan "We Are Not For Sale." They saw in IMF conditions that the price of help was Jamaica's sovereignty. And in December 1976 they won the election by an even larger majority than the one before.

My father repeated this defiant commitment in Parliament in January 1977. But despite every effort to avert the crisis, he was forced to accept IMF help and conditions later that year. The drastic economic measures required of Jamaica by the IMF added to the already unbearable burden of economic hardship on the poor. They demanded reductions in social spending, adjustments in the exchange rate and the removal of subsidies for basic consumption items. In the next election the IMF would come to haunt him again when the opposition humorously used the initials in graffiti for the slogan "Is Manley Fault."

So began the government's undoing. Michael had flinched. Joshua had chanted down Babylon, but Babylon had chanted right back.

ELEVEN

THE TENS MACHINE — for transcutaneous electrical nerve stimulation — applies small electrical currents across muscles or nerve junctions, cancelling pain impulses by overloading the nerve with a random impulse that numbs it. Joseph could explain this to me without searching for words, without blinking. Like his father, he only had to read a thing to know it.

The machine, on loan from one of the doctors, was introduced to my father's medical regimen by his physiotherapist. It was part of a renewed effort at rehabilitating him. Rehabilitation meant something different to each of us: to the doctors, maybe the chance to offer us a little hope as we tried to keep abreast of this marathon of pain; to Joseph and me, the possibility of his using a wheelchair; to the nurses, a healthier daily routine — improving his circulation and quality of life. I think my father just welcomed the distraction of the physiotherapist's cheerful company, or anything else that added interest to the monotonous plane of each day stretched out before him.

Although we were shown how to place the four small pads on my father's back, he insisted that only Joseph knew how to configure them. No matter how intense the pain, he visibly relaxed when Joseph came, lying back in relief and waiting like a shipwrecked passenger afloat in dangerous seas. Joseph would wipe down the rubber squares with cotton and sterile water — or perhaps alcohol, for I remember a rummy smell. He would apply globs of a pale blue substance that looked like hair gel, secure the tiny devices with tape and finally turn on the pulse of the TENS. A soft whirr would tremble reassuringly through the hospital bed.

"How's that, then," Joseph would more announce than ask, surveying the completed setup, which lay before him like an aerial view of a baseball diamond. By the time his thin, powerful fingers had completed the arrangement, my father had often let go emotionally, and was either resting or already asleep.

One afternoon my father was expecting a visit from David, his youngest child, Beverley's son. He was excited, but his pleasure was tempered with concern that David, who had not seen him since summer, might be upset by his deterioration. And I knew he was wondering just how obvious that deterioration was, knowing he probably couldn't trust us to tell him. He asked for my small lipstick mirror, and seemed relieved that his face remained little affected by the ravages of the disease.

David was at boarding school in England, but had managed to come for a visit. He was brought straight from the airport by Rosie, his godmother, a police officer who had been the head of my father's security staff and was now our emotional ally and friend. David was sixteen. He was already well over six feet — taller than my father, taller than my own two full-grown sons. With his recently stretched bones he gave off the echoey feeling of a new building. He had the easy, unpretentious self-assurance of a last-born and favoured child.

David was both old for his years, and touchingly young. He'd smile and you'd see the child come out; he'd shake his head disapprovingly and walk away from a game with the neighbour's kids, somehow always the leader, and you'd feel he'd grown up too fast. If there was one feature that distinguished him from the rest of us, it was the absence of any apparent nervousness.

David was born to Beverley in 1980, shortly before the general election which swept my father's government out of power, along with the politically gruelling decade. In all the turmoil and violence of that time, he was born slightly over two months premature, weighing less than three pounds, no bigger than one of my father's long hands, each of which could hold him separately. He came like the peace and promise of a washed sky after a storm.

I had been away for most of the years when David was growing up. My relationship with him was slight but precious, based on my brief visits to my father when he was a little boy and shared his bedroom with me.

Now, for the first time, his face reminded me of someone, but I couldn't think whom.

"Grizelda," came his nickname from above my head, as he leaned down to kiss me.

"Dad," he said, his face filled with the joy and expectation he always saved for his father. Without the slightest hesitation he strode over to the bed and placed his long arms gently around the back of his father's neck; weak though he was, he had raised his head to greet his son. David rested his cheek on the top of his father's head long enough for them both to close their eyes, to share and yet contain the unspoken pain.

"I see you're turned on," David said dryly, observing the electrical paraphernalia as he sat down on the chair beside the bed.

Clearly relieved to have a pathway out of their private moment, my father said brightly, "One could say I'm plugged in!"

David threw himself into schoolboy news, and then they turned to sport, exchanging scores, agreeing on the heroics of their heroes. I kept trying to think who it was he reminded me of.

David had brought his guitar along. After a while he picked it up and said quietly, to no one but his father, "I'll play you a song I learned for you."

Rosie led me gently out of the room.

"When did he lose all this weight, Ra?" she asked.

I felt guilty for not calling her. "Over the last few weeks he's been throwing up all the time," I explained, and kept looking at her, hoping she would find some way to dispel my fear, to once again fix what needed fixing. We all relied on Rosie, even though she had stopped working with my father a couple of years before. In our disjointed lives she had been a twenty-year continuity, and she was now as much family as family. I knew we were both thinking that we were near the end of a long road.

"Why didn't you call me?"

I had no doubt that she was remembering her brother, also in the police force, who'd lost a long struggle with cancer; she would be making comparisons to him like the ones I reluctantly made to Barbara.

"We're doing our best," I said, "but it's unrelenting." This decline had been so swift that sometimes it was difficult to keep abreast of the news in my own head.

Through the window we could hear David punctuating the words of his song, which he spoke more than sang in between chords. My father seemed to nod his head more in rhythm to his own emotions than David's words.

"But you must call me," Rosie insisted. "Any time, day or night, if you need me . . . someone to stay, something to fetch, anything you want, Ra. Anything at all. *Anything* at all for Mr. Mike. He's like my own father." Tears slid down the sides of her long, dark, beautiful face.

David's voice was now silent, his fingers plucking the final notes of his offered refrain. My mind went back to the puzzle of his face. And then it came to me, time passing through birth and death, victory and defeat. Proof of the generations. He had the face of my grandmother's angel — the one she had drawn around its initial frown, the furrow made by charcoal damp from her widow's tears, eleven years before David was born.

Barbados was my exile, my island of Elba. It stands apart from the sweep of its archipelago with its capital, Bridgetown, and its future, both facing the Caribbean. Its back — its wild east coast — is like a blind spot in the island's psyche, turned firmly in defiance of the cruel Atlantic and the ghosts of Africa that lie beyond, or below.

Islands in an archipelago are like siblings: capable of loyalty, of intense feeling, but not always getting along. Their rivalry is locked into their geography, their proximity; into their psychology and their history. In the Anglo-Caribbean, the greatest source of argument between the islands is their respective size. Jamaica, the farthest west, is the largest island of Britain's ex-colonies, and possibly the most extensively beautiful, with its body rising into mountains, its meandering intimacy of gullies and riverbeds, its lush but often inhospitable contours. When Columbus first tried to draw the mountainous island for Queen Isabella of Spain, it is said that he instead resorted to crumpling the piece of paper, which he offered as his description.

But Barbados was never owned by the Spanish. It was, from the start of European colonialism, an English possession. It is the most easterly and the most solitary isle. It is almost completely flat, and the trade winds slam across its body, quarrelling in a perpetual, irritable howl. There is salt everywhere. Cars rust, wood warps and paint peels. Leafy things become fringes.

The brief time from 1958 to 1962, when the islands were joined in the federation, only turned long-term mutterings into loud disputes. The big islands were afraid of having to support the smaller, poorer ones, which they considered backward. Like selfish older, bigger siblings, they bullied. It was all a matter of who would have to get what from whom, what would be more and what would be less, and what would be equitable. Their diverse histories made them like step-siblings. Jealousy and unfamiliarity made the islands unable to rise to the concept of family.

Barbados is not lush, and it has none of the illusions of magic, or the mystic secrets, of a hidden interior. It stretches in rolling plains as far as the eye can see, or till the eye beholds only the sea. Flat land can be a great equalizer. The Barbadians had no hilltops on which to perch as a sign of superiority, no interior into which runaway slaves could disappear, establish viability as free people, and then re-emerge as peasantry. Democracy seems to have evolved naturally there. Barbadians argue most of the time, about anything at all, but though they differ — sometimes profoundly so — and are often accused of being the most racially prejudiced islanders, towards both black and white, they manage to live side by side and get along with their lives.

It is said that because Barbados is the most easterly

island, it was the first port of call when the ships of the middle passage came over the Atlantic from Africa. Plantation owners met the ships and hand-picked the most docile, well-behaved, healthy bodies for their labour force, separating what they considered to be the human wheat from the chaff. By the time the ship reached Jamaica, its last port of call, there was no cargo left except rebels and mavericks and unsubdueable spirits who had been passed over on previous islands.

It's interesting that both Jamaicans and Barbadians tell this same story with an equal note of pride. If the story is accurate it may explain the difference in national temperaments, and if it isn't, the difference is there in the telling.

"Like dogs and cats," my godfather would say, laughing in his heavy Barbadian accent, "and I ain't saying who is the dog, and who the cat!"

My godfather was the man Barbadians called Dipper Barrow. He had become my father's friend when they were students in London. At the time there was a whole slew of future political leaders studying there, including Forbes "Odo" Burnham from Guyana, Eugenia Charles from Dominica and Pierre Trudeau from Canada. Although Barrow had been prime minister of Barbados for fifteen years, and was now leader of the opposition, he always found time for me. To me he was simply Uncle Errol.

He was down-to-earth and unpretentious, each week shopping for himself at a nearby supermarket — something I had never seen my father do. You'd pass Uncle Errol in an aisle, squeezing a fruit or a vegetable, pondering the ingredients of some bottle or can. He loved food in the way good chefs do, making a science of understanding each ingredient, knowing that care is as important in the purchase as in the ultimate presentation.

My godfather sometimes invited me to his seaside home, Kampala, for Sunday lunch. He would prepare the food himself, a short and overweight figure dressed in green hospital scrubs. He had a deliberateness in all his gestures, as though he had a single speed, and when he spoke his voice was flat and his utterings were cryptic, leaving you to fill in the outline created by his dots. I remember him scaling a freshly caught fish he had picked in the market. "See this snapper?" he said, with a huge smile on his face, and I waited as he moved on to whatever was next — stuffing the belly, seasoning some meat. "Last time I saw your Uncle Odo, he was wearing gloves" — slice and dice vegetables, muttering his Barbadian good sense as he went. "I know you ain't able with pepperpot" — never missing a beat in his preparations or his conversation, sweat pouring down his face.

"Why was he wearing gloves?" I asked.

"Man, nearly two hours . . . last time I saw him . . . never took those gloves off . . . ."

"Leather gloves?" I was mystified, as he clearly knew exactly what the gloves implied.

"Man, *gloves* . . . ," and he reached for a colander and started piling in pieces of cut-up vegetables, as though they had to go on getting ready no matter what happened with these gloves of Odo Burnham.

I enjoyed being with him. I found that, against the void of anonymity in my new life, these visits were like markers. Each left a trail, a familiarity I felt I could always retrieve if I needed to find my way back to myself. He would tell me incomplete stories about my father, brief glimpses of their years as students, his daughter, Lesley, and I being pushed by our fathers in our prams, my mother cooking, my father pawning his typewriter.

I knew that he and Odo Burnham had been my god-fathers in London, but my mother disputed this, pointing out that they were "ungodly" fathers who had gathered at the house for a mock ceremony, she and my father being confirmed agnostics. Uncle Errol never mentioned this. He just dropped his slivers of commentary: "Barbadians don't understand arches . . . build them anywhere, arches and more arches . . . upside down, sideways . . . ." He'd talk about me and my father: "apple of his eye," "changing your nappies," "walk up and down with you, singing — man, talking to you about history." Turning a huge spoonful of stuffing onto my plate, he laughed at the incongruity of that, as I did; "History! Long before you could walk or talk!"

I would call him about all my most minuscule problems: how long to bake a chicken, where to find a cobbler to fix my suitcase strap. Once I called to complain about a cruel article written about my father.

"Bring it on down," he commanded. And there in his small leader-of-the-opposition office, amongst a forest of papers that cluttered his ancient desk, he produced a fountain pen and some ink and proceeded to dribble the pen over the offending page, blotting out the article.

Sometimes he said to me, "You're pining for your daddy. Why you don't go home?" I was on a peninsula that stretched out aimlessly to nowhere, and the longer I walked along it, the longer I knew it would take me to come back. But I would go into lengthy explanations about the violence, the endless criticism of my father, the future of my children. If he was listening, he never said much, until one day he interrupted me and made the longest contribution to our dialogue he would ever make.

"You Manleys all too sensitive. *How* your family end up in politics? Got to have a real thick skin for politics." He shook his head. "Man, they does cuss you, whatever you do and whatever you don't do, and they does cuss the next man too. At the end of the day all you really got to know is, you done your job the best you can. That is it. The problem with your father, he's always explaining. Wants everybody to love him. Everybody can't love you." And he laughed bitterly, his own humiliation of defeat obviously nudging him. "Better you do a thing, and leave it at that. The act speaks for itself. All those regular Christian decent sensible things your father doing, we done here long ago, but we never called it any 'ism' . . . socialism or this or that. These terms just set everyone off on a lotta red herrings. Complicate things. Rhetoric!" He tossed the word out above the freshly stuffed fish, as though giving me a better look at it. Perhaps the word reminded him of his impatience with long-windedness, because he returned to the reticence of monosyllables.

Exile is the counting of compensations. It is nothing to do with the country one has left or the country to which one migrates. It is a state inside oneself. The fact that I chose to become an exile tells me more about myself than it does about my country. An elderly aunt once told me that someone who is unfaithful to a country will be unfaithful to anything. She was a Jamaican, but was speaking, fervently, from England.

My exile was a break of faith with something inside myself that was as basic as balance. From the moment I left Jamaica — knowing that I had turned my back on my family's history, on my island's pain and argument, on its efforts to survive and its fury to self-destruct; turned my back on my struggling father, knowing in my heart that what he was attempting was noble and necessary, and that what was changed, even what got broken, had long needed changing and breaking — from that moment I carried exile in my heart like a stone.

Islands have to know your smell from young to claim you. They will not adopt in the way that continents do. I remained a stranger. My second marriage, which could have succeeded, ended — the fault entirely mine — and little but obstinacy kept me away from Jamaica. For a long time I had no job, little money and two small children.

I replaced remorse with anger. My father was the object of that anger, yet while I hated him I longed for him, and though I pined I hated him still. He was the enemy I could no longer point to, a presence I could not shout at. He was just a silence as I waited for the telephone to ring, a daily absence more present than all the envelopes of hope the postman brought. A blameless silence. A soundless, gnawing cavity within.

I saw little of him during the years I lived in Barbados. There was a plan for him to come with Beverley and Natasha to spend one Christmas with me, my second in Barbados. From the moment I heard that my father was coming, although I had no money to spare, I painted my rented home and planned a special dinner. I called my godfather and we discussed the guests and chose the menu, most of which he offered to cook. I protested.

"Who going cook, then?" he laughed. He knew I couldn't cook, for I had told him the story of the only thing I prepared, my father's scrambled eggs. "And all I got for my trouble was Beverley telling me he didn't like them made with milk," I grumbled. He stared at me incredulously. "Girl! Instead of recognizing the sweetness of his forbearance," he said.

I bought a tree and lights, borrowed crockery and cutlery and lamps for the evening, and bed linen, rugs and blankets for their three-night holiday.

My father called the morning of the flight, with abject apologies, to say he couldn't come. He might as well have stuck a stake through my heart. I blamed him for disappointing my children, and hurting and humiliating me. I never considered for a moment how desperate his political life at home had become. The deeper in trouble he was, the more I focused on what I saw as proof that life was punishing him. For his ego, and his audacity in fighting on and fighting back. For what I saw as the years of his neglect of me, for replacing me with wives and children, for always being able to move on without me. I became my own small, embittered island with my own ghosts gnawing at my shores.

Most Jamaicans emigrating in those years kept it a secret, mainly because they were afraid of the stringent penalties if they were caught taking money out of the country. Mardi began to recognize when friends were saying goodbye. There would be wistful visits, lines blurring between regret and disappointment, anger and sympathy, and embarrassment if she mentioned her son or daughter-in-law in even a light-hearted or incidental way.

Afterwards she would phone or write me to say that she knew So-and-so was leaving, that she recognized the tone, that it was all so sad. My father was trying to do everything at once; he cared so much, she'd say, "but he doesn't trust time, your father . . . and he's probably right." She felt that he was trying to carry the nation along with him, but that some people — good people, people the country needed — were lagging behind and no one was being patient, waiting for them to catch up. She knew it was dangerous to lock horns with the United States, and despaired at this widening gulf of misunderstanding. She felt everybody needed to calm down and be a bit less zealous about everything. "They're not likely to have a man like him again in a hurry," said the defensive mother, "so let Jamaica think it can throw him way! Anyway, when all is said and done, the heart is always on the left."

When I learned of my father's defeat in 1980, I was alone in my flat in Barbados. I was expecting the phone to ring and it did, but earlier than I expected, which I knew was a bad sign, for my father was too careful in these things to rush to assume good news.

"Babluck," my father said. No greeting. No Beverley, no secretary, no Rosie to put him on when she had got me on the line. I felt sadness but also relief. I was prepared for this, not just because of the cyclical ten-year swing in voting that was then peculiar to our history, but because I knew that Jamaican society was being torn apart. My guru godfather had reminded me of an old Jamaican proverb, "What gone bad a'morning, can't come good a'evening."

"Beaten by a landslide," my father said. Nothing in small measures.

I think I only said, "Daddy," on a sigh, but he was at his briefest, just little lip-deep words he raced through: he was okay; things had a way of working out; we must all be brave; and before I hung up, for he would always wait for me to hang up first, "You must come up soon. Mother needs you." Then quietly, after I said goodbye, as I was about to replace the receiver, "And so do I."

A dream deferred or a dream destroyed was a question my father and Beverley would ponder for many years — ponder to what extent they may have damaged that dream themselves.

I have no firsthand knowledge of my father's pain, nor any sense of the embattled years that led to that election; no sense of the horror of carnage — seven hundred and fifty dead Jamaicans, victims of the long months of tribal war now becoming a way of life; no sense of Beverley's anguish under a neverending barrage of abuse aimed at my father; no understanding of the fury of America's State Department, enraged by my father's foreign policy; no knowledge of suspected sabotage, an army helicopter spinning out of control with my father and my brother Joseph on board.

All I know of the rest of that long night, as the votes came in unseating much of the People's National Party, as warnings were received that there might be retribution, is what Joseph and Beverley told me much later. Joseph described my father and Beverley in their bedroom at Washington Drive, lying flat on their backs on their king-size bed, looking up at Beverley's canopy — hoisted there to protect them from the possibility of falling lizards.

They were facing the fear that they might be about to die. My father wanted her to go somewhere safe with the children, but she told him that the two of them had been through everything together, and they must stay together now. He called a friend with a pre-arranged signal — "I am sending over the champagne" — which meant "I am sending the nurse with the two children." David was still fragile from his premature birth, so Beverley expressed breast-milk to send with him. My father had no money, but Beverley had five hundred Jamaican dollars in her wallet, which she retrieved and sent with the nurse. When she said goodbye to Natasha and David, she thought she might never see them again. Let it be over, she thought. Let them come and get us now.

When time passed and no one came, their lying there became funny. Beverley sat up and said, "Come, let us go for a drive." And out they went, into the unknown night to meet their fate. At first they were prepared for the worst, but then they saw that people were hailing them from the sides of the street, commiserating, cheering, waving. Some told them that they had voted him out to save his life.

From the moment I heard that he had lost, I knew that I had touched the bottom of the valley, and this was the beginning of my next ascent. As I walked slowly up and down the long, echoing room of my apartment in Barbados, whatever concept I had of home flickered in me, for the first time in a long while. Home, however shattered, would still be home.

I went to have an operation in Jamaica after the 1980 election. Mardi and I had decided that I should stay with my father. She was having a hard time with bronchial asthma, and seemed frail. When I got to the house my father took me onto the patio, pulled out his handkerchief and dusted off my seat where huge white flowers had yellowed and stuck to the wrought iron chairs.

"This is a disgrace," he shouted at no one in particular, but someone came from the kitchen. "You mean you don't clean the place for my daughter's homecoming!" I was taken aback. It was the first time in twenty years he'd called his home my home.

My father's life was again in hiatus. His marriage was rocky and he was very sad. His nameless house at the bottom of Ebony Hill, originally a small bungalow built for his aunt, had already acquired the customary series of extensions. Rosie seemed to be holding the household together, juggling all the agendas, acting as everyone's organizer and confidante. Natasha, at seven, already had the unsettled look of a child whose parameters are changing too profoundly around her. David, a cheerful baby only a few months old, seemed impervious to all sorrows. Whatever confusion he had been born into was simply the world as he knew it. He beamed at the people around him as though his were the only eyes that could see in our dark.

Beverley and Sarah took me to the hospital and settled me in, the day before my surgery. My father was preparing for a meeting of Socialist International in Geneva, but he promised to visit me the next day, before he left. Sarah went wandering down the ward and found a young girl who had been crying softly in pain, and read the Bible to her. "I'll read to you again tomorrow when I come," she promised. The girl was eighteen. She died that night.

The following day I had the surgery. When I was wheeled out afterwards, and was lying on a gurney in the recovery room, I remember my father leaning over me. I was still in the stage of grasping at figments, trying to stay lit, trying to join the world again. There he was, my beloved father, coming and going, going and coming, in and out of my mind, to and from sight, like a road running round a mountain, like a sun ducking behind clouds. "Daddy," I must have said five or six times, as each time he dawned on me as though for the first time, and I remembered all over again that I loved him.

"Don't go." I was holding onto his hand. "Stay with me," I said.

"I have to go to Geneva," he kept saying. "The op went well, pet . . . everything's okay. I'll be back in a week. Rosie will look after you. What can I bring for you?" he asked.

"Shoes," I whispered.

"Shoes? Sure. What size are you again?"

I couldn't yet feel anything in my body. I must have remembered that I had had the operation, for I reached down to feel if I still had my stomach, if this was still what I had known as me.

"I need to know your size, pet," I heard him say again, and through the net of sleep I could see from his hovering — from the way he asked gently and slowly, as though trying to keep any urgency from me — that he was really in a hurry.

Half asleep, I was still a child in my heart. I was a little girl whose feet were too big, whose stepmothers were always taller and prettier and more sophisticated and perfectly proportioned, and from my habitual hankering — for approval, for love — came that same sad deception.

"Size eight," I said.

TWELVE

HOW TO GET MICHAEL ENORMOUS down the stairs? That was our recurring problem. In the earlier days of his illness, when my father had to be taken to a downtown hospital for radiation to two painful spots in his spine, someone had suggested Plan A, a stretcher. But the stairwell was narrow and steep, with two corners.

"That plan could only work *without* the patient," remarked Rennie, and he devised Plan B — the wheelchair. The logistics were painstakingly worked out in rehearsals with Rosie in the wheelchair instead of my father. When the time came, Rennie carried his seated charge down the stairs with the help of Mousey, a member of my father's security team, my father enjoying the ride and delivering instructions along the way — "Back up, man!" and "Easy does it, easy round the corner" — and noting that it was a good thing he'd lost so much weight.

But now my father had developed a problem with his stomach, and at first the doctor thought it might be an intestinal block. He needed X-rays. We realized that he was too weak to be sitting up for a car drive through the slow Kingston traffic, as he had been on previous occasions, so the

doctor arranged for an ambulance. But we still had the difficult task of getting him down the stairs. Again we turned the
matter over to Rennie.

"What happen now, Mass' Mike?"

"Thwarted again." My father shrugged with resignation.
"The gods not smiling on me."

"Never mind that," said Rennie, "they can't smile all the
time." Rennie had been born under the sign of Taurus, and his
calm philosophical bent was always a comfort to my father.

"We'll need a crane to get me down from here," my father
told him.

"We resort to Plan B," Rennie said resolutely.

This time, all by himself, Rennie gathered my father up
into his arms like a delicate plant and lifted him into the
wheelchair. Then, with the help of security and Rosie's
instructions, he carried him down the stairs, releasing him in
a single smooth movement so as not to shake his roots, and
placing him on the ambulance stretcher.

"Not the first time I doing this, you know," he explained
to my father as he settled him lovingly onto the metal con-
traption, my father's limbs limply cooperating as though
anaesthetized by trust. "I grew up with my grandfather. From
as long as I know, he was in a wheelchair."

"Ah, Rennie," was all my father said, but he made a little
humph sound that meant he had processed what he'd heard.

When we reached the clinic, the two sullen ambulance
attendants wheeled my father's stretcher into the radiology
building and parked it against the wall of the narrow corridor,
where an air conditioner irritated the leftover decorative holiday streamers pitching about overhead. My father watched
the men intently and thanked them profusely, apologizing for
being a nuisance. Given his union background, it was unusual for workers to ignore him, but these two just nodded

briefly, looked at each other pointedly and left him there. Definitely Labourites, I decided. Soon after that, the driver, who was laughing raucously with the attendants outside the corridor and only wiped the grin off his face when he was certain we could see him doing it, leaned round the door to say that they had another call and would return for my father later. We guessed that they were off to have supper and a drink, but we hoped our patient wouldn't notice.

There was so little space at the clinic that we had to wait outside the building, taking turns to check on my father till a nurse wheeled him into the chilly X-ray room. Over the years my father had paid numerous visits to this radiologist, and the jocular, efficient doctor had become a familiar presence. My father liked him. On first seeing his patient's pronounced loss of weight, the doctor tried to retrieve his spontaneous reaction of shock, and hide his despair.

"What's up, brother Mike?" He leaned over my father with his great arms holding either side of the stretcher, his face close enough to resuscitate him, as if willing him on by his own life and strength.

"Ah, it's been a bitch," my father said, more gently than the words deserved.

The radiologist X-rayed his spine, but said he needed no pictures to tell him what was what.

"Not a thing wrong with your gut, you hear . . . it's your mighty bladder that's full!"

We all sagged with relief, and I remembered that, after one of his many operations, a urologist had told my father that he had the biggest bladder he had ever seen. David, then only about six and processing life through a series of cartoon characters, had nicknamed his father "Bladder Man."

A straightforward problem with a straightforward solution was the first bit of good news in a long time. We were clutching at straws that were already utterly tattered, glad for a useless bladder, only because it was a lesser evil than stomach surgery. Life was in a horrible balance between bad and worse.

My father was wheeled back into the corridor, where he lay alone and embryonic on his comfortable side, facing the wall. Life came and went, full-blooded, sauntering or hurrying — voices above him, footsteps to and fro, a careless emancipation beyond his reach. Here we were, in the process of falling, watching crepe-paper streamers shuddering in the cold gust of some invisible system, my father's face-to-the-wall as a curious shrug, and the rest of us waiting to see if the spine of our family would snap now or later.

We waited for the ambulance for over an hour, taking turns standing beside the stretcher in the narrow corridor. Where he lay, the cold air was trained on him. I covered him with an extra blanket that Rennie had insisted we take. My father made no effort to connect with what was going on behind him; he just looked at that wall, occasionally blinking. What was he thinking? It brought to mind the decade of the eighties, when for a long time his country had simply ignored him, and he had picked up the pieces of his life with his usual quiet dignity. Maybe he could only relate to a world when he was its centre, when he was needed.

I placed my hand on his shoulder to reassure him that he was still at the heart of somebody's world.

~

In the remote heart of winter, in a faraway city circling a hill that Montrealers proudly call their "mountain," I received the news that I had been running from my whole life.

It was just before six o'clock on the morning of February 10, 1987. It was a Tuesday.

The phone rang. I was alone in my bed under a huge eiderdown, in a city whose landmarks meant nothing to me, whose language I didn't understand. The night was a heaviness of nothing, a nothing without shape or density; just a suspension of time around me, and an inevitability that I'd grasp whether I wanted to or not, the approach of an emotional landslide as the telephone rang and rang.

It was as though my grief had always been incomplete since the day of my grandfather's death, when Mardi came out of the room hovering at the door uncertainly, and said tearlessly, "It's all over." As though, through all those eighteen years, my loss had been searching for its other half, searching to make sense of itself, searching for its boundary. Nothing to be seen but the digital glare of time on the clock radio, one of those digital clocks my grandmother hated, with a red glow like an exit sign in an eclipsed theatre. Grief is an animal who already knows the dark. I moved slowly across my bed to the persistence of the phone, knowing it would never stop — it had rung too long.

"It's Norman. I'm sorry, I have bad news. Mar's dead."

Whole again, tight shut together. Mardi to Pardi.

My father had continued his jogging all through the eighties, unless he was away or not well. With the exception of drinking white wine, he kept up his healthy habits. No smoking, and whenever he was home in Jamaica he'd be up at quarter to five, reversing his car past the sleeping guards at the gatehouse and the embankment of bougainvillea, heading for the Mona Dam where he'd jog.

During the early eighties he was often invited on the American college lecture circuit, and for the first time in his life he was paid very good money for his thoughts. He remarked to me dryly that he was one of the few people who had been able to make a living by his mistakes.

The family had returned to survival mode after his defeat. Again the homes of both generations lay next door to each other, separated by the same old fence. Douglas and his younger son, Roy, were living with Mardi at Regardless. Not much money, not many visitors, no one married to anyone, but of course there were more children. It reminded me of my school days on Washington Drive, after Pardi's defeats. Here again was the family, in between jobs, in some great space littered with aftermath, as though it were the night after a party.

Except for me. By now a nomadic pattern had become part of my character. I had not returned to live in Jamaica. In Barbados, during a trip when I planned to resign my job and pack my things, I had met a Canadian whom I subsequently married in 1986. I moved to Montreal, and my life remained a kaleidoscope of dispelling or returning shapes and colours, as one picture faded and another assembled.

After three marriages I should have noticed that my personal life resembled my father's. But if my father was still searching for some circling orb of brilliance in his life, for partnership in some state that would be all-inclusively self-fulfilling, my reasons were different. I was an emotional refugee seeking asylum. It wasn't someone else I was in search of, but myself.

When I arrived for my March wedding in Jamaica, David — whom I remembered as a chubby, cheerful baby I'd glimpsed only briefly — was at the house. He was five years old. He had become a small person. I felt we were meeting each other for the first time.

"This is Rachel," said our father when I arrived.

He looked at me, with my long hennaed hair scraped back in a ponytail. He was a little boy puzzled.

"Your sister," prompted our father.

No, he said. I wasn't his sister Rachel.

He was very courteous, and took my hand and led me down the long corridor to my father's bedroom at the end, where he showed me a cluster of five framed photographs hanging on the wall opposite my father's bed. The canopy had gone.

They were my father's five children in order of age, two above and three below. He pointed to a photograph of a younger me, my hair dyed jet black and trimmed like a poodle's above my face. "That's my sister Rachel," he said. So I suggested he call me Grizelda instead, and he said okay, and he kept that name for me.

As though not to omit one of his two small children from the intimate reunion, my father proudly produced a sheet of foolscap paper from his desk drawer. With a red felt pen he had carefully recorded Natasha's words: "*The waves looked like blinding, white canoes sailing across the dark sea.* Feb. 22, 1982, Natasha looking at the breakers rolling in to shore at Rosehall Intercontinental Hotel at 9:15 p.m."

My father was busy abroad, busy at home. Apart from reorganizing the party, which he felt he had a duty to rebuild, he was farming with expansive fury in the hills. He had amassed many surrounding acres, so that he could cultivate his father's coffee on a much grander scale and extend his flower farm to produce enough for export. Down the hillsides he planted coffee; along the hilltops anthuriums, statice, chrysanthemums and long-stemmed roses. The farm should pay, everyone agreed; the world price was high for Blue Mountain coffee, and there was a great demand for flowers.

But although my father came from a line of Manleys who declared themselves mountain men, they had never been able to keep their farms solvent, much less make them profitable. He installed sprinkling systems, but the limited tank-and-drum water supply was not sufficient. A source farther down the hill could be accessed by pumps that were either inadequate or kept breaking down. The latest one was delivered by his old friend Eli, the "sheriff" of Kingston, an ex-mayor and the ex-minister of justice who'd initiated the draconian gun laws. Eli now had a flower farm in Florida.

The pump arrived with instructions in Japanese. "We can manage," insisted the Jamaican workforce. Puzzling over the instructions, they assembled the pump, which promptly flooded the farm. The apparatus was back to front. Later, when the plants were attacked by insects, the "sheriff" sent a pesticide and gave my father careful instructions: "One teaspoon for so many thousand gallons of water, over so many acres of ground." My father, always enthusiastic, figured he had a big bag, so why economize? He administered half the bag and nearly lost the entire farm.

As for labour relations, it appeared to Joseph, who was one of the farm's directors, that his father ran the enterprise as a commune, with all the workers living there and growing their own little plots of marketable produce. Even if a farmer was fired for stealing coffee or some other petty larceny, he would be retired onto the land, still there every day, growing his vegetables or ganja, just off the official payroll. One of the headmen who insisted on playing his boom-box at full throttle was simply shifted down the valley to where the throb of his reggae felt less immediate. My Uncle Douglas, who now ran a more sophisticated farm that grew unflowering decorative plants for export, observed that, like most things economic under my father, the farm lacked cohesive management. It was a little like the way he fathered us all, in that he saw life as a process of trial and error, an accommodation of enthusiasms — life unhindered, as a licence to grow.

Her grandson Roy was a comforting presence in Mardi's life. A quiet person always beset by health problems, Douglas's younger son would sit and watch her feed the birds, listen to her interpretations of their calls and of the family's predicaments, fetch the newspaper, answer the door; or he'd refill her prescriptions, wander down the road to buy something she needed from Mr. Chai's corner store, or bring her coffee with two dollops of condensed milk in the mornings.

"Who do you think will write the family memoir?" Mardi asked one evening when some of us were gathered at Regardless for our usually vociferous dinner.

"I will," said Roy in his slow, deliberate voice.

We looked up at him in surprise.

"Good for you, dear," said Mardi encouragingly. Then, after a moment, "Now tell me, why?"

"Because I am the only Manley who listens," he said, smiling at his audience, who fell silent for the first time that evening.

It was good that Douglas and Roy were staying there, and my father next door with some more grandchildren, for there was less and less of what we knew as the physical Mardi. She had narrowed and shrunk, though she was never stooped; a dissipating mist, lace at the edge of a wave. Sometimes I thought she wasn't really smaller, only farther away, as if we saw her from a great distance. The air around her seemed to move with her, as if the quiet cobwebs draping her time had been disturbed. She spoke less, and in shorter phrases. "Dust everywhere," she'd say, when she was coughing with the emphysema that was her legacy from working in fibreglass. But she was every bit aware of everything, taking in her family, taking in a world that was changing so quickly both around and beyond her.

"I've grown a black rose," my father announced one day.

"A black rose?" Mardi said, mystified, repeating the phrase as though nudging a horse into a stable, nudging herself into a world where roses were black, or her son would want to grow a rose of no colour. When it won him a prize, she said, "One son with a flower farm that hasn't any flowers, the other one growing black flowers that win prizes. Oh my" — she shook her head — "I haven't lived in vain!"

Out of defeat and divorce and loneliness, the eighties had also brought the family a kind of relief. We were out of the glare of the public eye, an eye that now mostly averted its gaze to make us feel its pointed disapproval.

"Your father's back is to the wall," Mardi wrote to me, in 1986. She wanted me to come home. My father had returned from a lecture tour where he had fallen ill. He had found himself in a strange country, in a strange hospital, with strange doctors and strange equipment, on a rotating table that moved every so often to swill more barium through him for pictures of his stomach. He needed an operation for his diverticulitis, and he said he wasn't having it anywhere but home.

I came for ten days and stayed with him at the hospital every day. He looked daunted by my permanence there, though I didn't realize it then. I thought I was doing my duty, and I wanted to be there. One day, trying to help prop him up on his pillows, for his stomach hurt with its wound, I managed to drop him. I was in a terrible state when Joseph and Della arrived with Sarah and Natasha. They cheered me up, teasing me and calling me a paranoid old "Suck-Up," but my father had to be given a dose of painkiller due to this mishap.

My father lay there on the bed, doped up with pethidine, his face a smiling, sleepy Humpty Dumpty who had had a great fall, and there we were, all the king's horses and all the king's men, crowding the room and driving the nurses crazy and practising being one, to put Humpty Dumpty together again.

Something gentle and simple and normal happened to us in that room, with the five of us beside my father's bed, together for the first time in years. A doctor who came by looked in and smiled. "Oh, I see you're with your family," he said, and my father indicated the group around him with a wave of his hand and a smile, and he wasn't too busy and we didn't have to leave and this memory we would have for all time, like a snapshot in an album that we could take out whenever we needed it.

"This is how it should have been," said Sarah thoughtfully when we left that evening.

Mardi, ever more spectre-like, now had a single remedy for all her worries: she worked. She worked through each breath — these days a hard-earned and valuable commodity, a resistance in her throat that she fought while we looked on helplessly — while my father arranged for her to see doctors, or sent for oxygen or hearing aids or new glasses. She worked while Douglas collected her *Newsweek* magazine, selected books and classic videos for her, while Roy replaced the oxygen canister or passed her the puffer. In age her body had succeeded in finding many more voices. Her work moved deftly between life and memory, between an island's victimization, its green time of innocence and this battlefield that had triumphed as the Jamaican psyche.

She created a guileless world in bronze — a stylized garden beneath overhanging trees, with the simple grace of children meeting goats, a crèche of hope. "Once upon a time . . . ," said David, who'd come to visit sometimes, pull up a chair and sit in the very middle of a circle of guests on the patio (she'd say, "Just like his father.") Goat upon goat emerged from her kiln, souls who walked the mountainside alone because only by themselves could each one find balance. "Baaaaa," she would announce to me over the phone. She sculpted joyous drummers and dancers. Orpheus lost in his harp — "He's not playing, Mardi. He's listening," said the thoughtful Natasha at just nine years old.

And then abruptly, as though the seventies would not be still, came the heart-wrenching sculpture "Ghetto Mother," a massive, wounded piece of history. A woman protecting her terrified children, who were huddled around her. Two out-stretched arms, all she had to protect them from the guns of the ghetto and the politics of Jamaica's sons; an island trying to save her children from herself. Even in bronze I can still see the clay, the tops of her fingers forever inverted in its mass, each hollowed print a mouth bearing its worn-out cry to the mob beyond, to the chaos that betrayed the ghetto mother, to the past, to the future, each a sound in the wounds of the clay, a sound from the failing lungs of my withering grandmother.

In November 1986 my father wrote to me. "Mardi. Very courageous. Starting a magnificent new drawing — a Lazarus conceived with astonishing directness and intellectual clarity. It can be a masterpiece. But also, inevitably, weaker these days. I say this because you must be *very cheerful*, and to do this must expect a much more frail person. But the spirit remains undaunted. Thus: *prenez garde* — just be natural and supportive — and don't share this analysis with *anyone*."

I knew he was right about her frailty. I could hear it in the threadiness of her voice over the phone, I could see it in the scratchy handwriting in her letters. When I saw her again, she was metamorphosing into a ghost. We all spoke softly around her, as though she were some ancient painting whose preservation even the air threatened.

"Am I getting more deaf," she asked me one day, "or is everyone speaking more softly?" And she was right, though it made no sense.

The gate between the houses was usually open, and nearly every day someone "popped over" to see her. I already felt nostalgic for her, sorry I wasn't near, sensing how little time she had left. I took comfort from the fact that Douglas and Roy were there, that her family was close. Rosie came often to help her. And my father was there, like a rock to everyone. "And you know," said a friend, "when you're not there, Beverley always does the little things you would do for Mardi."

On my last visit with her, Christmas 1986, we walked to her larger studio, and there on the bench was the model, in clay, of an earlier wood carving, "Tomorrow" — the bust of a figure whose hands opened beneath its face like a trusting flower facing the midday sun. "Pardi's favourite carving. Now there'll be a bronze. My last one. I've started drawing," she said. Each phrase came out like a separate, considered breath.

Leaning against the wall was a life-sized picture, all blue water and sky and surrounding light, and a brown woman ascending from the sea towards heaven with her uplifted arms entangled in clouds. The clouds, wisps of white and hollows surrounding her, diverged into the heads of three horses.

The woman with horses in her hair. Her work, instead of being scaled down, was getting larger. "My eyes!" she explained, amused. I hadn't thought of it. Growing older must be like moving to a new country.

I also saw her sketches for Lazarus, laid out as though in instalments over the studio. Standing to the left, on an easel, was a swaddled, mummified figure of Lazarus waiting to be raised from the dead. The studio had been extended when she was creating a monument that couldn't fit in the original room, and now, on the newer cement walls at the back, huge figures swirled as though she had run out of paper or time.

"I have a problem," she said. "For the life of me . . . can't get Jesus to raise . . . Lazarus from the dead! And d'you know why?"

Resurrection was now too close to the bone for me.

"Why?" I said. "Maybe Lazarus isn't really dead!"

"Oh he's dead all right," she said. "But . . . I can't find the *power* in Jesus to raise him."

"I hope you're not planning to die and leave me," I said, and couldn't believe I'd said it.

"But I can't stay forever." She seemed relieved to have the subject come up. "You have to let me go sometime. I'm tired, you know."

I could feel her effort as she pulled in enough air to recover what she'd expelled. I thought of the expense to her of every word, the exhaustion of simply breathing.

"I couldn't tell you goodbye for the last time," I said.

And the woman with horses in her hair told me a final story. The last time she had seen her mother, Ellie Swithenbank had been living in a little house in Neasden, feeding the birds on the windowsill as she always did. Mardi was returning home the next day. She kissed her mother goodbye, and when she got to the gate she suddenly felt that she would never see her again. So she stopped and turned round. Her mother was sitting rocking in her chair. "Go on, Edna," she said, "it's late." And my grandmother said she knew that she mustn't look back, that the gate was an opening to a different way of knowing her mother. Boundaries do not kill, they contain.

When I was leaving to go to the airport, Rosie was waiting in the car for me. I kissed Mardi goodbye at the door of Regardless, for the first time holding her shoulders instead of her holding mine, and I went straight to the car. As I was about to get in, I realized why she had told me that story. In horror I turned to go back to her, but she was waiting for that, already looking at me from many worlds away, and held her hands in a wide-open "weh fe do?" gesture. She shrugged. Just a little that's it then, can't help, kind of shrug. And I got in the car and wept all the way to airport.

It was the coldest February night anyone in Kingston could remember. My grandmother sent Sarah for her stole. My sister had brought over some crude forgeries of Mardi's work, which an astounded friend had come across and thought best to show the family.

"Oh, my," said Mardi, quite unbothered, "now I've really arrived!"

She had spent the day with her friend Easton, an impish jack of all creative trades, who had brought in a camera to take pictures as she worked on her raising of Lazarus. He had also brought her a recording of music she'd heard on the radio and admired. She was scraping the charcoal furiously over the canvas, an old agnostic once again peeping at faith, invoking the Old Testament God who so often had sent her, as a child, to hide under the dining table from His wrath. His eyes were like thunder, lightning and fire. She was leaving Lazarus the means for his resurrection.

That night Mardi got into bed with her Walkman, my father's Christmas present to her. Roy filled her nebulizer and brought her a hot cup of Milo. He gave her an extra blanket. She went to sleep playing her new recording of Quincy Jones' "Amazing Grace."

Douglas came in late from a party executive meeting, and went to sleep in the next room. Roaming the dawn, which he usually shared with Mardi, Roy wondered where she was and peered round her door. That was when he found her.

My father, who sang only when he was joking or joyous or softly cajoling, was singing as he circled the Mona Dam on his morning jog. He was flanked by two friends. He lifted his head to the greenly precise early mountains, who were already awake, misty shawls over their shoulders in the cool February air. The wind was so sharp that it seemed to blow through his mind. Having reached rock bottom, he could only go up. He sensed that a new era had dawned with the year. The government was losing popularity, and his party had won a huge victory in the local elections, which were seen as a referendum on the JLP's policies. He had survived a serious operation for diverticulitis, he had been doused under a wave of humiliating defeat and had come up on the other side, his children were closer to him than ever, friends were drifting back, and though he was on his own, and missed the passion, love was gentle to him now.

"Amazing grace, how sweet the sound," he sang.

"Why all this singing?" asked a friend beside him, for he usually talked as he ran. But he went on singing against the wind, singing a song he didn't particularly like, and he didn't know why he sang it.

He drove home still singing, and there was Joseph in the doorway as he got out of the car.

"Dad, I'm so sorry," he said. The little boy named after the man with the coat of many colours, who'd spent his youth far away, was here now, in the strange way that destiny returns all things to where they belong. "Mardi died."

My father stood looking towards the brow of the hill where she'd been, and still was. Then he turned slowly round from her to the very beginning, looking over towards the ghost of Drumblair as though to the source of a river, for long enough to clear a path through the trees of his memory, for long enough to hear her car drive up the gravel and hear the car door slam, to hear her heels clicking across the wooden floor and over the muffled area of the lily mat, maybe twirling in joy twice under the light, her dress swirling on the fullness of life as she recounted the evening, and then the hope of her steps — lighter and faster than anyone else's — climbing the stairs, the stairs to his world. Just once more. Just for long enough.

THIRTEEN

THE PHONE RANG. Vita, who had brought up the juice, took the call. Her eyes widened and she straightened as if she intended to salute. She held the receiver out as though to the room itself. "It's Nelson Mandela," she whispered in awe.

"Mandela for me?" said my father, and frowned for a second at the phone, as if the instrument might be mistaken. Then he appeared to gather himself for the call. Vita and I tiptoed out of the room.

My father shook his head as I came in to replace the receiver when the call was over. He suddenly covered his face with his hands and sobbed into them, pulling in a breath when he needed to, with a hoarse cry that sounded as if it had been tugged out, and that for a moment made me wonder if he was laughing. I knew his tears were happy-sad. Mandela had heard that my father was gravely ill, and had wanted to wish him Godspeed and get-well; to acknowledge once more his contribution on behalf of Jamaica in the struggle to free South Africa from apartheid.

I was tempted to say something soothing, but realized it was simply a time to cry. Mardi would tell me that this was the end of a drought, and that the coming of tears was like the coming of rain, a necessary thing. Vita had faded as a shadow does when a cloud moves over the sun.

Tears that will not rescue us from physical pain will come for emotional anguish. I suppose the man who'd spent his life trying to end the bullying of cane-cutters and banana workers and bauxite workers, trying to stop the bullying of the Third World by the First World, of black men by white men — the man who had won the United Nations Gold Medal for work against apartheid — still needed to hear whatever Mandela told him.

"I'm sorry. It's easy to cry nowadays. It must be the estrogen." He smiled meekly and his face looked like a garden after rain, cleansed and vulnerable, renewed and restfully hopeful. "Sometimes I feel it may all have been in vain," he added very softly.

"Pardi used to feel like that," I reminded him. "But *you* once told me that in politics everything has a time when you have to let history catch up."

He smiled at the return of his words. "Just to know it mattered," he said.

He was calm now, his hands content as they rested, laced on his chest. He seemed to have found the salve he needed: just to know it mattered.

The call came after dinner. It was in the spring of 1990 and all the windows were open. I picked the receiver up carelessly; felt the familiar no-greater-joy at hearing my father's voice and sat down on the edge of the bed to chat with him. The same bed I'd been asleep in the morning I'd heard about Mardi. The same bed from which, a few weeks before, as I watched Nelson Mandela on television leaving prison, I received my father's triumphant phone call: "Ra, Africa is pushing up the Alps!" This time he began aimlessly, talking long enough about little enough for me to know he had something more specific to say. Then he gave me the news, but my mind did not at first settle on the fleeting word *cancer* — maybe because he said it in passing, as though for lack of a better word.

"Cancer!" I said finally, aghast.

"Well, yes, sort of, but the thing, really, is this . . . ."

He had received the news at a happy time. Things in his life were coming together again. He was in love, the PNP was back on its feet, his children were emotionally closer to him. As he spoke to me I had the feeling that he didn't have time for this illness. His intention was to finesse it; to use the same tactics he'd used with his hearing aids. He'd simply "go public." He had issued a statement, and was writing an article to inform people of the dangers of the illness, how to ensure early detection and how to handle treatment.

He was excited about the prospect of estrogen, joking about at last being able to see the world from its other perspective. A cancer centre in New York had confirmed the diagnosis of prostate cancer, and was offering state-of-the-art this and cutting-edge that, and he was going to begin banking his own blood in case it was needed during surgery. By the time he was finished outlining his strategies, he had almost made the bad news another challenge, another of his epic, massively over-organized processes to bring together people and things and allow everyone to feel like a contributor to the greater good of the entire human race — whether we had tracked down the latest Plácido Domingo production, or the most recent surgical procedure.

My father's life had already changed considerably, again. Shortly before the 1989 election for which he was campaigning, he had come to visit me in Berne, where my husband had been temporarily transferred. There he had told me that he felt like an old bone rattling around in his still nameless, grown-to-sprawling Washington Drive house. He wanted to get a small townhouse, and keep Nyumbani as his home in the hills. One day he would live up there, write his books and grow his roses. There was also much more he wanted to do. He said he felt a duty — to Pardi, to himself, to the party, to Jamaica — to put the PNP back on its feet, to leave things in good order, and then, after a few years, he would retire from public life. I knew his early political ardour was over — he didn't seem as driven any more — but, as he said, "One still hopes for a better world." As far as I was concerned, he had planted the seeds for that better world already. Given time, they would grow.

It was clear to me that the copious phone calls he had been taking in his room were not about politics. I realized he was in love again, and I guessed that the woman was Glynne. When I asked him bluntly he seemed relieved, and for the rest of his visit he was delighted to share what had become a great happiness for him.

Part of me was glad to be there on the ground floor of my father's next high-rise relationship. But soon I was paying the price for insider information. From Gruyère to Davos, through cheese fondues and strawberries buried in clotted cream, he talked of little but the wonder of who she was. Soon he was eliciting my help to encourage her to dance, to paint, to write, to realize all the dreams he was having on her behalf.

My father would say, with some pride, that he never did things in small measures. His adorations were extreme, his election results — winning or losing — were landslides. His final election was a landslide victory in 1989. Again prime minister, this time he declined to move to Jamaica House, using it as his office, and Vale Royal for official entertaining. His overwhelmed new townhouse — which struck me as a pastel doll's house the first time I saw it — had become the prime minister's residence.

By the time the surgery was due, my husband and I had

moved to Toronto. I went to Jamaica to accompany my father to New York. But he developed pneumonia before he could go. It had been coming on for days, like a hurricane tracked at sea: a cough and aches and pains that were first diagnosed as bronchitis. For some reason my father, usually a cooperative patient, delayed getting an X-ray. He said that he'd had too many in his life, that his concern was prompted by knowing he had cancer. But he was taking antibiotics and not responding, and the bronchitis accelerated into pneumonia, with its telltale harbingers of spiking fever, chills and ague.

The day he left for the Kingston hospital, he looked like a waking version of his own dying father twenty years before. His face was grey; his eyes were sunken and dark, their whites yellowing. He had hollowed like one of his mother's carvings. His expression was deliberate and watchful, seeming to come from that gulf where the dangerously sick can see another side. After he'd left, I stood in the living room with Rennie, thinking how dazed and empty the little place felt without him; knowing he was in grave danger.

It was decided that evening to move him from Kingston by air ambulance to a Miami hospital. He was reluctant to go, but the doctors explained that with his various allergies he would need access to a wide variety of antibiotics, some of which were not available at home. The infection was spreading fast, his oxygen saturation level was sinking, and once he needed a respirator he would no longer be able to travel. Despite the stormy weather, he was flown out that night, with the help of doctors, government members and friends. He left on a stretcher but in Miami, at five in the morning, he insisted on walking onto the tarmac. He said that his disembarkation on foreign soil must be perpendicular.

For a week no one knew if he could be saved. He had a pseudomonas infection, caused by a common bacteria that most healthy people have in their bodies, but he wasn't most people; he was like an old car that had lost parts from time to time. He had no spleen, no large intestine, only part of a thyroid, and he'd been diligently giving blood for the coming operation, so his platelet count was dangerously low. It took a week to track down an antibiotic to which his pseudomonas wasn't resistant.

I stayed with him, always wanting to help, always wanting to be near him, although I knew my presence was creating tension with Glynne. It was my daughterly duty to stay but, to be honest, it was also irresistible. Even when he was sick, my father's bedside was exciting. Doctors congregated to plan strategy, nurses stayed longer than they needed to, family and friends, visitors and VIPs poured in, groups congregated in the passageways.

He had the American Secret Service next door, in addition to Rosie; he had a press secretary and numerous Jamaicans visiting him; but most of all he had Glynne, his new reason to live.

He returned home three weeks later. The doctors in New York told him to stay on his estrogen injections, and to wait until his lungs were healed before flying up there for the cancer operation.

If this life is only the tributary of a big river, then it seems to me, an islander, that New York is the tallest, roughest waterfall. There is a persistence that keeps the city what it is: a great port of transient souls, a restless, palpitating heart whose rhythm one cannot know in the confusion of its fads and immediacy; one has to step back far enough and long enough to understand it. At a distance its torrent takes on a concise predictability; its enduring truth becomes the accommodation of anything.

The hospital reminded me of the city to which it belonged. The building seemed taller and busier than the hospital in Miami, its rooms smaller. I had the impression of vertical motion, like those toys with Swiss hill-climbers going up and down attached to a rope. I stood on the escalator and wondered how many of the people being swept along on that liquid staircase lived under a death sentence. I could not believe it was my father who was here. Our family was not a cancer family. My grandmother had said we died of "lungs and heart." Cancer, she had said, was caused by holding in hurts. Apparently it was not in our family disposition to have this disease.

So for my father I thought all the positive things one is tempted to think. Prostate cancer was different, I had heard. One could live for many, many years, and end up dying of something quite unrelated. And in any case this was somehow less malevolent, something tropical and quirky belonging to our region, which I told myself had been overstated as cancer, in the way skin cancer is often mistakenly considered no more than an unpleasant foible of skin exposed to sun.

This, after all, was my father. He didn't always come out unscathed, but he always came out. One thing I knew from the very beginning of life, one presumption that remained through everything: there would always be Michael.

He was in surgery for four hours, and then Joseph and I were there in the recovery room, a surreal blueness of light, and our father's face was swollen with the relocated blood, like a blown-up balloon whose greetings have stretched and blurred. His eyes were just slits, and made Joseph and me giggle. We hovered over his head on either side of the rails, leaning over him as he lay there like an abandoned puppet, attached to bottles and monitors overhead. His was the third bed in a long row, the room just one stage of some giant assembly line that repaired the product at the so-many-thousand-mile check, and I wondered how many operating rooms they must have for so many patients to be recovering at one time.

We hugged him with our words; he translated us through

our hovering; we reassured him. He felt warm to us in that cold room. His voice sounded hoarse after the airway used in surgery: soft and deep and grandfatherly. "I love you both," he kept saying. "I love you both." We could feel that he did. We were a small archipelago, the Atolls of Michael, for just a bit. It was the morning after a hurricane, and we had survived, and we looked across whatever devastation lay above the infinite and connected soul of us, the invisible, underwater mountain range from which each of us emerged, separate yet indestructibly joined to each other.

The surgeons in their greens and gumboots assured us — as much as anyone could with this disease, they said — that their patient *should* now be free of his cancer. They reminded us of all the good reasons he could continue his life normally, even walk later that day. I knew he was okay. I should have left, but Natasha and David were expected and my father had asked me to stay on.

When I arrived at the hospital the following morning, Glynne and I started scrapping, getting on each other's nerves.

"It's nice of you to want to keep me company," she said, "but I knew your staying on was a mistake." She left to get herself a sandwich.

But staying hadn't been my idea. My father must have told her this. Why did she think I was staying for her? My father lay there and said nothing about having asked me to stay. I felt he had let me down.

My father had a helpless look on his face. I knew this was wrong, all this tension and quarrelling around his sick bed.

"It would mean so much to me if you two could get along," he said.

I felt the old nettle of injustice welling up in me.

"No!" I said, trying to stand my ground. "Don't ask me this. I beg of you, Dad, don't ask me this again."

"Again?" he asked. He looked bewildered. But how could he not understand? I'd been wanting to tell him this for years. Now here was my big moment of courage or rebellion and he didn't know what I was talking about! He couldn't be that insensitive. He wasn't. He was being a coward, and I was furious. No matter how sick he was — even if he was lying there with tubes attached to him — I needed him to know that, from here on, our relationship had to be one on one. All my life there had been somebody interfering, changing our rules and our routines and our habits, redefining his relationships with his children. I had the old sense of my family skin being invaded, my rights infringed. Someone was ripping the delicate thread of our weave. It was happening all over again. It was selfish, but I felt I *had* to say something; we were running out of time.

"All my life I have had to love whoever you ask me to love, and to accommodate the people *you* love in *my* life. I don't want to do this any more, Dad. It doesn't matter who she is — Glynne's not the issue — it's the principle of the thing. I want to be able to feel my own feelings. I want to be able *not* to like her if I don't want to, and to know that I won't lose you." I took my first breath. "At fifty, I want no more mothers!"

"I hear you," he said, and he looked resigned.

I had never spoken so boldly to my father. I was weak, I felt I was falling apart. I had no idea what my life would be like after this. I got up to go.

"Are you leaving?" he said gently, his arm extended towards me like an offered truce that, unacknowledged, he then withdrew and placed on his chest again. "Sorry, pet." As easy as that.

I gave a little wave — I remember it because it matched the trembly feeling of the lump in my throat — and I left, packed my bags and flew home.

FOURTEEN

IN LATE FEBRUARY 1997, a friend I had gone to school with forty years before, who hardly knew my father and who came from a family politically opposed to ours, gave my father a pair of blue pyjamas. She didn't ask to see him, simply left them at the house. I gave them to him. He was touched. She had made them herself, with snaps down the sides so the shirt wouldn't have to go over his head. When I arrived the following day he was modelling them. He lay without the customary sheet, displaying yards of blue material much larger than his shape. His feet stuck out underneath, their extra-long toes like fingers, like supplicants mated side by side in prayer.

I was leaving later that day for a week in Toronto. I had many good reasons for the brief visit north — a husband; my publisher, for whom I had written a memoir called *Drumblair* — but it was breaking my heart to leave my father as he was.

A tremendous tension was deepening around him; not his tension, but the inevitable pressure building up among all who cared for him. It was caused by the endless waiting, the hoping against hope, the hopelessness of hope, the PSA-test roller-coaster of a few falls after Jinxy's serum and then numerous risings, the blood transfusion that had flushed his cheeks and given him two weeks of Indian summer, the commencement of a mild form of chemotherapy personally administered at home by a compassionate oncologist who had recently lost her own father.

All of us were doing our best, whether it was as fiddly as bending the straw in the middle without blocking it so that he could drink lying down, as personal as taking a blood test as we searched for a match for his rare blood type, as imaginative as finding a video that made him laugh and caused his unused stomach muscles to ache the next day. We were all doing what we could, although we were not all getting along; someone would frown on someone else's effort as it failed or got in the way. We were fighting each other because we couldn't fight destiny and we couldn't fight God. And I was the most over-wrought of all, and I still had not learned that useless care is a hovering and a burden.

I tickled the insteps of his feet and he didn't move, for he couldn't feel them. "Still fooling me!" I was reminding him of a childhood ritual, his old ploy that had tricked me into thinking that his calves were ticklish, not his feet. Now his feet really were indifferent, and he had to look down to see what I meant. He smiled, and I said, "No, now is when you *mustn't* laugh."

An envelope of photographs taken at Nyumbani about a year before had just arrived. One of them showed my father amidst a bed of lupins in the garden. The blooms were purple, like a cluster of enthusiastic constituents surrounding him, each with its own unique expression. My father looked like a huge red flower among the lupins, an odd plant out, as if a seed had accidentally strayed into the wrong package. He stood there in his big red shirt, arms akimbo, paused between gardening and gladness, smiling under a white floppy hat.

I sat down. I was biding time till I had to leave for the airport. "You know, if you want me to stay, I'll cancel this trip in a minute," I said, leaning down to peep at him sideways through the rails of his cage.

"I know that," he said. "Of course I want you to stay. But I can't ask you that. If you gotta go you just gotta go." And he smiled and recited, "Birds gots to do it, bees gots to do it, even the ratsbats gots to do it . . . ," something silly that somebody in his school used to say, another of the small treasures that would burst upon him at odd moments. He was making light of the situation because he knew it was dense with foreboding for me.

Suppose, I thought, suppose. And I looked down at my lap so he wouldn't see me cry.

"Ra," he said. I wouldn't look up. "Ra, look at me."

His finger would probably be there at my cheek to "catch" me. I moved my hand to touch his but nothing was there, so I looked across at him and smiled as he clicked his tongue and pointed a finger at me, for I had forgotten he couldn't reach me from there.

"I don't want you to leave me," I said, though it was a grim thing to say.

"I'll try not to," he said politely, but with a prim-cornered smile at the edge of his irony. "Listen to me. You know what would make me *most* happy?"

"What?" I bent over and fished in my bag for a tissue. He waited till I sat up again.

"I want you to get on with your life. Go and see your husband. Go and see your publisher. I want you to start your writing again. You have a future there, Ra. Don't be obsessed with the past. Use it as fodder! As you did in *Drumblair*, if you want to. But *use* it. Don't let it rule you or defeat you."

I looked away, unable to speak, to find words.

"Come here," he said, and he reached out both hands as best he could. I leaned over and placed my head against the rails next to his hands.

"Let me tell you about me. In a sense my whole life has been the story of being caught up, as if in the current of air created by two giant propellers. It's called the slipstream. It's powerful, but it's only a wake of something else. What I chose to do with my life only made it more difficult to define who I was and what my life was about. Somehow I was always fighting that exterior momentum while desperately trying to create my own. If you're not careful, you end up doing nothing else. You're forever tethered. And there is an emotional slipstream as well. You kids have to break free of an even stronger current: the slipstream of a slipstream."

He was telling me something that was as important for him to know as it was for me.

"Cry a big cry, and then get out a nice big hanky and move on. In the end that's all we have, you know. Life. Only on loan. You've been a trooper looking after me, but you've established your own life now. Use it up. You know, even here, locked up in this bed like an old fowl in a coop, I am happy to be here. Happy to have Glynne wandering in after work or her dance classes to give me her news and call me a big dummy, happy to see my children busy and getting on with their lives. Sad about Jamaica, its insurmountable problems" — he stopped to shake his head and look up at the ceiling and make a mime with his open mouth that looked like "Oh God!" — "and every now and then I think, what the hell is happening? Then I say to myself, well, maybe the country needs to break free of the slipstream as well. Maybe it has to find its own path. After all, two generations of Manleys was a lot. And for all that, I'm happy I can give an opinion now and then and think I'm helping. Happy to be alive, even *barely!*"

Okay, I tried to say, but my voice kept tumbling back down my throat. Thank God Sarah came in. When she'd called to say she was coming, my father had asked Rosie to go to the bakery and get patties for her.

"What will Daddy do for a week without his old Suck-Up?" she asked affectionately, laughing.

"He'll have to make do with *you!*" I said.

Rosie arrived at the door, bearing a box of patties and plantain tarts, and held it out towards Sarah. "From your dad," she said.

"For me?" she asked in surprise as she opened it. "Patties! Daddy, you're giving me patties! Isn't this uncharacteristic?"

It certainly was. Our father would dig us out of any trouble, pave our way, inspire us, believe in us, give advice, give money, rage at us once in a while, forgive us anything, but it was odd that he had thought of patties.

Sarah looked at Rosie. "Don't you find this uncharacteristic?"

"*Me?*" Rosie said, pulling her shoulders up, and herself out of the line of fire.

"It must be the estrogen," he said mildly.

Sarah offered him a patty but he turned it down — "Not for me, Sass . . . the damned chemotherapy" — so she gave him a little piece of plantain tart.

"Have a patty, Ra. Didn't he bring them for both of us? You know she'll get jealous," she warned him, with mock sincerity.

"Our Ra *never* gets jealous!" he assured her, though there was a tentative note to his joking.

"Oh, not of the siblings today? Just of the stepmothers!" said Sarah. "You know she thinks she's your *only* child, *and* your wife, don't you, Daddy? Isn't that true, Rosie?"

Rosie laughed, scrambling to her feet and hurrying for the door, leaving us a piece of Jamaican wisdom. "Me come here fi' drink milk, me no come here fi' count cow!"

At that moment, I wished Barbara could see us, for with

our unfamiliar, awkward effort at banter, the three of us were the closest that we had ever been.

I promised I'd bring back some drinking straws designed to bend in the middle, and I left them sitting there — Sarah ravenously eating her patties, with her daddy like a chipmunk, the mouthful of plantain tart lodged in his cheek.

At the top of the mountain, both the air and the earth are thin. The valleys may be low but they have an immediacy, a richness of blood nearer the heart. Things grow there. Maybe the greater the height to which the earth aspires, the thinner the substance. By the time the mountain has reached its peak, the earth is a brittle thing, the air but a breath, and there is little but spirit left.

My father's third and final term in office lasted only two years. By April 1992 he had left politics. Every step he made caused him to huff and puff. His lungs had been seriously impaired by pneumonia. This forced his heart to work harder, which — combined with the stress of the job — caused it to become enlarged. His doctors advised him to retire.

The PNP did not want him to retire. His friends didn't either, or most of his family. Apart from his political foes, most of Jamaica didn't want him to retire, despite the fact that he was nearly seventy. Only Glynne did. Only Glynne and my father.

Why did we all want him to stay? Was it because we felt an era would be ending? Were the party and Jamaica itself just used to having him there? Or did we sense something elusive in his nature? Did we fear that, without a tangible responsibility to us, he might desert us? Were politics, his leadership, even the constraints of his sickness, the only holds we had to keep him within the limits of our frame? Would he disappear from our lives? Vanish beyond some new horizon with Glynne? When he inquired about a house to rent in Henley on Thames for the summer, ridiculous rumours began that he was buying a house in England with the intention of emigrating. I've always suspected that Jamaicans spin pre-emptive rumours when they want to prevent something from happening.

In his last brief period as prime minister, my father made no effort to re-create the landscape of the seventies. In a world that had careened defiantly and unapologetically towards the right, Jamaica had easily returned to many of the familiar patterns of its past. "The country has evolved, the world has evolved and we must evolve with it," he said.

Some people wondered how an ardent socialist who had always decried capitalism as evil and exploitative could now champion the free enterprise system. But he designed life around reality; he was not a man to live in the past. He could abandon what became irrelevant and never look back. Whatever it took, one had to move on.

"Socialism in my case was more structural than personal," he said to me one day; that is, it had been a means to an end. I think social justice was that end, and it was that, more than socialism, that excited his ardour.

But an old socialist's instinct still guided my father's point of view, often revealing itself like a slip beneath the hem of a skirt. Although his government and the private sector were cooperating, my father's quest was now to find ways in which the free market system could work to improve the lot of Jamaica's poor. He called it *empowerment*, and said the word with the grit of his passionate seventies' defiance. Some proceeds from privatization helped establish and fund an investment agency to assist the poorest youth, who had no collateral. He negotiated substantial debt relief from First World governments. By the time he resigned, he had ordered the liberalization of the Jamaica dollar, floating it against world currency.

The two tides that had always pulled my father away from any other imperative were youth and freedom. If he had achieved nothing else in the seventies, he wanted to believe that he had rescued the majority of our youth from the shattering effect of colonialism on the Jamaican psyche. Now he would have to entrust life to the consequences of freedom, trust that, after the immediate carnival of self-interest, the youth who were the beneficiaries of the seventies would be the keepers of a flame that was now just a flickering hope.

His leadership had become much more low-key. But as he steered our somewhat leaky ship through a rough economy, what did return of the seventies was a sense that, whatever was happening and by whatever means, behind it all, somebody *cared*.

Any weekend his work could afford, he'd go up to Nyumbani with Glynne. They'd garden in their floppy hats, she in overalls and he in pants that weren't meant to look baggy but did, and bunched at his heels — which reminded me of the lovably rumpled old age of Pardi.

Up there, he was Planter and Glynne was Dancer. Those were their code names on the farm radios. Rosie was Blue, and the children were numbers one to five in order of age. I was the only one who liked that. It was proof of an unspoken family pecking order that otherwise only established itself within a car. In the absence of a wife or girlfriend, the eldest offspring present always took the front seat beside our father. If I was there, the seat was mine.

In the mornings my father would establish himself on the lawn as farm director, and the supervisor and a workforce of two would be there like stagehands, the flower beds their actors, rehearsing. My father scaled back flower production when Joseph summed up the farm economy as a hemorrhage. Joseph said that, as fast as the money flowed in from the coffee, it flowed out through the flowers. My father's response to his mounting farm debt was merely a determination to keep track of his own folly.

Glynne would be at her seed boxes down at Natasha's doll's house, the little bamboo cabin already ghosted with memory. Or she'd be bent in half in the sack of her overall jeans, her hat a giant white butterfly bobbing near the ground in the distance, tugging up weeds, down and up like an oil rig on a Texan horizon. Every week we'd get sweet peppers and tomatoes, asparagus and various herbs. As far as I was concerned she was the only one who'd ever done anything useful with that land. It brought home to me not so much the fact that she was practical, but how impractical two generations of our family farmers had been.

How can I describe Glynne? She had a gaiety that was irresistible. Glynne loved to dance. She had danced since she was a child. When she talked about her youth in Scotland, she always talked about either her Communist grandfather, whom she had loved, or her dancing. Her youth had been surrounded by illness, and for a considerable period of time she had been confined with her mother in a convalescent home. As a result, she had a natural and at times unattractive impatience with sickness, even her own.

"Ra, I am the wrong person for this," she conceded in despair during one of my father's many bouts with illness. But I think most of time she tried her best.

Glynne made my father happy. A doctor had told him that cancer was often associated with guilt, and the site of the cancer often indicated the source of the guilt. Well, Glynne unguiltied him; no question about that. After a life in which he'd carried the burden and responsibility of his name and other people's expectations, and the guilt that we, his children, made him feel — intentionally or not — about us, about his broken marriages, along she came and helped him slip this intricately woven net. Here was someone who encouraged him to face what was left of his life as though it were all a new day, as though nothing called for regret. Although she had a strong work ethic, she had in many ways a hedonist approach to life: eat well, make life fun, live every minute. She had an irreverence for much that my father felt duty-bound to take seriously, and an obvious bewilderment at his need to cure every ill, solve every problem, put everything right.

For the first time my father was comfortable doing things he'd always either done defiantly or regretted not doing. They travelled a lot, and planned long holidays with the children coming and going. For the first time I'd see my father wearing sandals and pushing an overstuffed shopping cart in a supermarket in Henley, worrying about the bill without letting Glynne know, or self-consciously trailing behind David through a sports club in New England, anonymity somehow never suiting him. He'd stay in fine places, eat in the best restaurants, buy expensive clothes, spend what he couldn't really afford. He wouldn't host the family Christmas dinner, wouldn't buy gifts for people merely out of courtesy, wouldn't go to places he didn't want to go to or make speeches he didn't want to make. He wouldn't give his children permission to do things merely because he felt bad about something unrelated; she convinced him that he'd done everything he could and should have done for us. He'd done enough for his family, for his party, for his country. Life couldn't keep demanding its pound of flesh. It was his turn to demand more of life.

Nyumbani had always been intended as my father's eventual retreat, his finale. One day, he'd say, one day. He wasn't going to die of a broken heart or of boredom as his father had. "I didn't only leave politics because I was tired," he'd said one day. "I left because I had taken politics as far as I could take it, intellectually." He would reclaim this spiritual home like a composer knotting the truths of his life into a last great symphony.

As if in declaration of that intent, immediately after he retired, my father and Glynne were married at Nyumbani. The simple ceremony was held in 1992 on April 12, Sarah's birthday, in the long-gone apple grove, on the grassy circle of lawn below the verandah, the house stretching up proudly behind the gathering like a dog pricking its ears at the echoes of mountains. My father's neatly pruned cupressus trees, the three wise men, stood there — tall, witnessing presences as detached in temperament as the mountains behind them.

The bride and groom arrived from different directions, coming across the immaculate lawns to an invisible altar. The bride was escorted by her three daughters, all of them dressed in combinations of white and yellow. Our father was accompanied by four of us loping along in no visible formation — Sarah and myself in lilac, each on one of his arms, with Joseph, his best man, and David behind us. (Natasha had stayed in London to sit exams.) I'd drunk too much wine and I had an attack of arrhythmia, which my siblings teased was probably heartbreak, given the occasion.

"Call me Chanel Number Five," Glynne quipped, and though it is difficult to take a fifth marriage seriously, there was something sad — a conclusion foregone — about that wedding. A small group of close friends witnessed a moment that in retrospect seems fleeting, a moment that would be outlasted even by the ebullience of the cottage flowers surrounding the ceremony. Rosie proposed the toast. Not even the distraction of the unexpected wail of bagpipes, chosen by Mardi's friend Easton for the wedding march (perplexing even to the bride, who, unbeknownst to most guests, was half Scottish) in honour of Glynne's roots, could take away some underlying sigh whose slow completion was like a gravity compelling us all.

For their honeymoon they travelled on a cruise ship up the fjords of Norway, where Glynne managed to persuade her self-conscious husband to join the aerobics class. But Babluck was there at his side. The telltale symptoms of his disease knocked on his door to remind him that he was living on borrowed time. Passing through England on his way back home, he visited an oncologist. He was told bluntly that his cancer had spread from soft tissue to bone. For two years, while he governed a country and divided his heart between competing commitments, his own cells had mutinied like vandals ravaging an unguarded house.

Glynne sat beside my father as the doctor pointed out the evidence of "hot spots" on a small lit screen. The graffiti were etched all the way up my father's spine to his skull. He was advised to resume monthly injections of estrogen, but warned that this would work only for a limited time.

I was in Toronto writing a book. After I'd left New York, after our quarrel in the hospital, I wouldn't speak to my father for six months — wouldn't answer his calls or his letters. I started having a recurring dream:

I am sitting in a movie theatre, almost at the front, and that's odd for I don't like sitting so near the screen, because everything is too close and I can't see clearly. It's dark, and everything's in fractions in and out of the flickering light from the screen, but I don't remember the movie. All of a sudden I feel the unmistakable weight of a cat that has jumped on my lap. Its front paws knead at my arms, and it's got my thin forearm in its jaws and is relentlessly biting me, and I can feel that bite in my own jaws, which

are clutched together, and my saliva is oozing lemons and burn-
ing the inside of my cheeks, and I scream, "Call a doctor, call a
doctor," for I know I must get a tetanus shot, and the lights go on
in the theatre, and the cat lets go of my arm and powers himself
off my lap with his strong hind legs. I can see a precise bite, with
what look more like the marks of human teeth, around a wound
like a mouth, and there's an outline of red like the jam streak in a
layered vanilla cake, but there in its well is my bone, dead white.
The cat is khaki-coloured. I see his rump disappear like that of a
large rat bumping over the tops of the seats, row by row, behind
me, and I know that when he reaches the back he will return to
me, running under the seats to jump onto my lap again. I know it
will happen over and over . . . .

The cat looked like Percy, the source of so many early argu-
ments with my father. And since I had been told that each part
of a dream is part of the dreamer, my forearm, the weakest
part of me, was clearly my vulnerability. I asked a friend who
studied dreams, and she laughed and said the dream was
probably about my fear of recurring stepmothers. Whatever it
meant, I went on dreaming it.

After six months of ignoring my father's messages and letters — while family and friends reminded me that life was too
short for this, and his life in particular — I relented, as always,
and went home to see him. By now I had a hundred pages of
a manuscript to show him. And I told him about what I
believed was my worry dream, about sitting in the theatre
with the cat biting my forearm.

He frowned. "You don't remember the name of the
movie?"

"No. That doesn't matter," I said with a shrug.

"But I don't agree. Surely the most telling part of your
dream *is* the movie," he said.

The movie? "Why does that matter?"

"The movie is the reason you've gone to the theatre! It passes before you on the screen and you can't remember it. You see, you keep looking at your arm. But your arm represents the past, and you're looking back at it, so its ghosts eat away at you. The theatre is opportunity. Now, the movie — the movie is the future. The movie is the rest of your life."

We went on to talk about my manuscript. My father said he loved the start of it. So did Glynne. His experience was invaluable to me, and he helped me frame the vital political context of the story. Glynne helped with the editing. She was good at that; she treated it like pruning. It reminded me of the speed with which she would clear away plates from a table, hardly able to wait for us to finish a meal — as though she were restoring some state of equilibrium by re-creating a symmetry she had temporarily had to forfeit.

Between Glynne and me there was an unspoken pact, or at least a truce. It was a tactical alliance, with ulterior motives on both sides. We both needed each other. I had made up my mind not to be estranged from my father again, at any cost. I knew by then that, in dealing with my father's wives, I could never win, and I hoped to avoid another trough in my life. She needed me less, but I provided a supportive entrée into a family that was tired of changes, and skeptical of this fifth marriage. Underlying our tacit conspiracy was the fact that we both wanted to spring-clean his life of the past, and to ensure a future with him. My father was our common goal.

But the truth was, under it all, there were times I really liked her. She took me along to her dancing, wrote me long newsy letters, gave me unpretentious, thoughtful gifts, always wrote thank-you notes. She liked to analyze life and people's motives, to scheme and wonder why and puzzle about things; she was emotionally competitive, insecure and shrewd and even sometimes sly — all traits frighteningly similar to my own. She was fine as long as she controlled things, as long as things went her way. Aren't we all? "Two peas in a pod," said my father, though I suspect he knew it was more like Greek meeting Greek. The truth was, I would have loved my father's wives much more if they hadn't been my father's wives. They were, all of them, exciting and a little crazy and neurotic, in some way or other that interested me. But they were trespassing on what I wished were my territory.

At least with Glynne I had the satisfaction that she was, though she hotly denied it, shorter than I am.

Anyway, whatever the reason, we managed to get along. Maybe life was really as simple as Rosie said — just a matter of knowing whether you were here to drink milk or count cows.

A journey to the mountains is always a decision. It's an old-fashioned packing up and going, and one might as well be making the trip on the back of a mule, with laden hampers on stout-hearted donkeys. It means taking a total break from one thing, and committing oneself to another.

Whenever I arrived at Nyumbani, even when I came in the car with them, I knew that my father had to brace himself to share a place he cherished for its silence, its autonomous seclusion, its unequivocal terms: limitations in return for perfection, cultivation in return for beauty, observance for inspiration. Nyumbani kept its secrets, in return for keeping his — the ultimate privacy. We would spend weekends there with our projects; they helped me, they helped each other, and like a middle-aged baby I loved the sense, however tenuous or conditional, of belonging. This was their sanctuary. Only family members or very close friends were ever invited up that hill.

Sometimes David would come. When David's interest moved from tennis to basketball, a hoop was erected on the tennis court. My father had spent a life of lumbering grace, being strong and fast and well shaped, making up for what he couldn't achieve through dexterity with his imagination and memory and enthusiasm. Now, not really an old man but a sick one, he was reduced to dignity in diminishment. He would walk quietly behind David, who always thumped his ball more slowly when his dad was with him, and off they would go to be sportsmen. He assumed the role of his son's coach, and the two of them practised out there in the sunlight, the elder sitting on a bench above the court as though watching a miracle, the younger leaping over and over, like a porpoise, to the ring overhead — tapping, swinging, foiling his imaginary competitors, with his coach ho-hoing from his seat on the sideline.

Sitting there, already sick and in pain, my father was watching youth and its infinite possibility. Perhaps he was back in his own youth, but this time free of the ever defining past, unbridled by the legacy of his own father, free from a country's assumptions or praising or blaming, just that great bounding horse his mother had seen in the sky — a moment of promise as his son hung there mid-air, the ball held at the tips of long pincer-like fingers. They would return in their queue of two, David a gentle teenager who had generously foregone any temptation to natural rebellion against his father because there simply wasn't enough time.

Often it was just my father, Glynne and me. That was the nearest I could ever get to him. Down to three people, and the third was someone who was now prepared, for the time being, to include me. I was aware how sheer the precipice was, should I fall, and how carefully I must tread. Loving my father was always hazardous for me, and experience had taught me that I was never indispensable.

It didn't matter how early you got up; the hills, like young children, always rose before you. The sky would start at innocence, building strength all morning through its muscle of cloud. By afternoon it would be sulky and overcast, as though daylight revealed a world not sufficiently respectful. The morning loved what she saw in her lens, and captured things in a way we who shared the landscape had never grouped them in our minds before. Two stone benches side by side, with a table between whose grey would be lost in older light, the wide, clean angle revealing the land sloping away to Natasha's doll's house, no more than a tiny pagoda of memory shrouded in faraway mist.

Without morning we might not have known that Blue Mountain and Lady Peak were there behind the valley and the house, between the dark shoulders of the trees. Their curtains would close later. It didn't matter. "You don't always have to see the highest peak," my grandmother had said with irritation to visitors who complained when they didn't, as though the visit were therefore in vain.

My father used to say you had to envy the height of a mountain to want to climb it. He was not a man who envied mountains. He just liked to live with them. I suppose all peaks have a strong sense of their own stature, and I believe that my father was also a peak.

He had planted a Jacuzzi at the edge of the valley, and surrounded it with a hibiscus hedge. When he and Glynne were alone, they would immerse themselves there under the moonlight, they told me, with their wine for the evening, and their selection of music pounding over the hill from the latest Apogee speakers, the notes clearer, as all things are, in the open silences of hills.

But sometimes my father would have the Jacuzzi cleaned and filled for me, and I would sit in the tub after lunch in icy sunlight, the hot water churning, the noise of the motor shouting for attention. I'd look up at the reclining island, its blue breasts slung from its torso, aware but unaware of me as any mother is of the attachment of its nursling. I would compose poetry in my head that I thought I could never lose, and I'd lose it by the time I emerged from the water. It was a far cry from Nomdmi's Washingtub, the old-time bath named after my grandfather's middle name, which Mardi had painted black to absorb sunlight. We used to haul Washingtub onto the grass outside Mini, and sit in it and look up at the tall trees, under which Pardi assured us we would think noble thoughts. But in the Jacuzzi I would lie watching small clouds coming home in the sky above me, moving back into their rooms, and the hills were like housewives waiting as they watched for the gate, listened for the door; nothing was homeless in the hills. I'd think about my mother and Thelma, Barbara and Beverley and Glynne; Joseph and Sarah, Natasha and David; and how we'd all helped and taken turns to keep the good ship Michael Enormous afloat. And I'd think about how life comes full circle, how old tubs become new tubs, how little farms become big farms; how the things one feared become things one has learned to handle. How mountains give second chances.

On weekends my father and I, the surviviing ghosts of Drumblair, would sit on the high verandah at Nyumbani, overlooking the circle of lawn, and work on my book.

"Find out the dates of the Red Army's consolidation of everything Churchill and Eisenhower agreed should be Russia's sphere of influence. Find out when the Marshall Plan was . . . I think it was '48. It was an epic time, all the stars were out and the planets were in balance. Venus was around, Mars was around, Jupiter, everybody was bubbling up in the sky. Now, in Jamaica what is fascinating is how far the country is dividing into Busta and Dad's personalities . . . how those two diametric personalities were polarizing a natural constituency."

I would turn on a little tape recorder he had given me, the tiny cassettes labelled MNM/RM — CONTEXT. The recorder captured his voice, so full and immediate, gravel and threads, a tenor whose texture was that of a baritone.

There were so many weekends and so many tapes, and each afternoon the mist curled over us like history. It would float in over the garden and hover with the gentle rawness of a child's breath. I could smell the land after rain, baby clean and explicit, giving expression to the scope of nature by granting each element its own syllable: separating the earth from the grass, the conservative asters from the lurid anthuriums, the wet lily leaves — rain-splayed children seeking attention after a fall — from the dogged ferns, the nasturtiums that should have been insects, from the long-legged, resilient begonias; even Planter's beloved statice, content to act as ushers, from the exhausted petals of the vivid azaleas.

I never stayed a night at Nomdmi after Mardi died. I thought of it as a place that was interrupted, still waiting for my grandparents. After they'd both gone, it was like a private conversation into which they had withdrawn. One had no business listening. Each thing was raw with the tender state of living it was left in: the blanket over the chair, the calabash swinging on a rope from the eaves in the ceiling, the sweaters smelling like Manleys. Nomdmi hadn't changed after Pardi's death, or after Mardi's. Its wandering mist welled up like sorrow, drifting over to us at Nyumbani.

My father was unable to understand my reaction. Nomdmi was misty-eyed by nature and geography, he said. History and its occupancy were joys to be celebrated. He never misses anything, I remembered. So I kept to his side of the tennis court that formed the boundary between the generations, and watched the roof of Nomdmi at arm's length, thinking one small thought at a time, measuring memory as intermittently as a parent measures the height of a child.

"Nomdmi belongs to the spirits who found them," I told him once. "And they're gone. And the place makes me sad."

He cleared his throat and looked towards a cluster of far chairs that shared a common footstool. I wondered if he was remembering a more rewarding conversation he had had with someone over there. "That is the otherness of this world," he said philosophically.

"But growing up has proved to be a loss of places and people," I grumbled.

"Life is life." He shrugged, shifting his chin upwards to one side as though clearing a hurdle, or maybe sidestepping the prospect of my obstacles. "As I see it, you or I — anyone, for that matter — each person is only one soul; no matter the terms of life, we have only this one time to connect. All the fullness, even the part-times, this is what we've got. Mother and Dad knew that."

He looked across at the sky where he considered a pair of white clouds drifting along in obedient single file, stuffing and unstuffing, adjusting themselves separately. "You know what? Think of Mother and Dad as a single complete piece of art, a work of art that you were able to watch for at least the last part of its creation. It is there in the sculpture of the stone, or spread gloriously over the canvas. You look at it and celebrate it for what it says in being complete. Loss is always an immediate moment of sorrow; loss of the old to time is like nature growing over the connection of a leaf to a stem. The leaf withers and falls. It is time." He paused and frowned, seeming to remember a painful aspect. "Early loss is wrenching. You bleed like hell for a while. But eventually we must all pick up the pieces and leave the masterpiece there on the wall or on the plinth. Cuss like hell for Babluck. We are still here to serve our own time."

"A benediction from Pardi and Mardi," I said, running my fingers through the mist, its impact slight as his thoughts against my gloomy certainties.

He sighed a heavy, hard-jawed sigh.

"You know, you must be careful not to romanticize so much. Don't make plaster saints out of them. They were very human and very real. That's the trouble. Dad has become a fixed symbol to Jamaica. He is no longer flesh and bone, one can't feel the struggle of life in his memory any more, and that struggle makes people real and makes other people care. Busta is flesh and blood and, for all Dad's splendour and nobility of purpose, Busta is much more memorable because people *care*."

"But Pardi *was* almost a saint," I said, somewhat indignant.

"The hell he was," he snapped. "He was no more a saint than . . . " — he had to shake his head and collect his patience — "and that was what was so incredible about him, that he was as imperfect as any of us, as prone to mistakes and temptations. You know, I live my whole life being compared to my father. I'm the first one to tell you he was the greatest Jamaican who ever lived, and as far as I am concerned just the *sweetest* man I ever knew. But he wasn't always right and he wasn't always perfect. He was too wonderfully alive to be a saint — he had too much damn texture for that! You think Mother would have stayed with a saint? She would have got bored. She was no saint herself. If you're going to write about somebody, tell the truth or don't bother to write."

But while he spoke he was looking at me, and I wondered if it was himself, not his father, whom he was trying to realign in my focus.

"You don't know how hard it's been all these years, with this towering statue of a man."

"I thought you adored your father. I didn't know he was a problem for you," I said.

"Of course I adored him, I loved him to death. He was my hero and my friend. But you think it's easy when, from the first day you walk into school, his name is up there on every wall? Best hundred-yards runner, best hurdler, best high jumper, best long jumper, Rhodes scholar, war hero, King's Counsel, party leader, premier, national hero? Every day you are compared, by the party and by the country and by your friends and by your mother." He looked sadly but frankly across at me. "Even by your daughter."

I looked away at the three thick, carefully pruned trees in front of us.

"It's a pity you can't enjoy Nomdmi. Mother would have wanted you to. Next week I plan to cover those trees with twinkling Christmas lights for all the gods to see!"

He was pulling me back from the past to the present, pulling me away from the precipice with its sharp breakaway. I looked at the three wise men standing stock-still, earthly opinions against the blue thoughts of the sky. I was always touched by the reverence of his sudden enthusiasms, the infinite care with which he attempted to relate them. My father always gave intangible truths a shape.

"Are you afraid of dying?" I asked.

He disliked my questions about likes and dislikes, fears or fancies. He couldn't understand my need to feed the endless lists in my head, which I excused as necessary exercises in logic and memory. He probably knew they were a nervous tic I had developed to make sure I was in everything, like punctuation marks.

"Of course I am," he indulged me. "I have offered myself no religious comforts. And I have a vivid imagination!" He laughed theatrically but then shuddered, dropping his shoulders.

"When I see all this, I know there's a God," I said.

He smiled. "Lucky are they who know."

Leaving this thought safely behind, he got up from his rocker and walked slowly towards the edge of the verandah, his hands braced to support the base of his back. He searched the lawn for some lingering thought, and *ummed* in a searching way till he came up with what he'd been looking for. "Do I see the majesty, the magnificence of all this? Of course I do. I marvel at it. Do I think it all happened by chance? I doubt it. But I am not arrogant enough to believe I have the answers."

"No, I didn't mean . . . ."

"I rather like the mystery, tell the truth. But I won't let man interpret all this for me. I have my own relationship," and he swept his hand in continuation of the abandoned sentence, displaying the landscape as though he were a magician's proud assistant.

"Aren't you afraid there's nothing more after this?"

He looked around for Glynne, but she was not in sight. He returned sadly to the chair.

"I don't know if that's what I fear. I suppose I fear dying, as we all do. But isn't it just like man to believe he has a right to conjure up more for himself? Not for any other creature, mark you, just for himself, alone in the universe? He invents eternity so that his own mortality may not be in vain! I think it's a piece of cheek on the part of man to believe there is more than this — more than this one stab at it all. I think, if we were meant to know everything, nature would have given us the imagination and the brains to figure it all out. Let there be mystery, I say!"

Glynne was back in sight. He stroked the arms of the chair under his bent elbows, watching his wife as she pruned or picked or weeded, filling a flat basket that hung on her arm.

It was midday, and Glynne crossed the lawn and climbed the steps to join us. It was time for music and a bottle of white

wine. The elegant lawn stretched before us, and two women
rose in generations from one of my grandmother's works,
which sat on a tree stump still sticky with resin. A tall tree
with pruned limbs centred a flower bed. Nothing towered,
nothing diminished, nothing concealed. There was balance
between all the elements of this landscape. There was mute
green everywhere, like time.

They looked at their garden, and I wondered how come
people look at their own creations as though seeing them for
the first time.

"What more can you do?" I asked. The garden was orches-
trated to perfection. It was art at that point when we'd tell my
grandmother now stop, anything more and she'd spoil it.

"Oh, there's always something," he said.

Of the time left to my father, these were special days.
Their garden was set like a table before them, and the sky was
full of mountains who had lent them this place for a generation. A wind blew over the interruption of the forest, making
everything dip and tremble just a little, while Nyumbani
turned the other cheek, and small clay wind chimes chanted
as though answering my grandmother's calls of "coo-eee,"
made so many times over the valleys. Perhaps her calls would
ring across the hills forever, with only the potter's earthen
pieces to reply.

My insides went still. This garden was perfectly emblematic, breath-held, an indent. My father knew a garden, unlike
a country, will repay any show of attention with blooms. This
was his creation of that perfect world he imagined as he stood
there holding his father in a promise at their last party conference together; but that world was political, and he knew by
now he would be leaving it far from perfect.

But here now, within reach, was this stage upon which for
a fleeting moment of eternity my father's choreography would

play. It had all the elements and energy of his life — the intellectual artistry, the meticulous negotiation that draws diverse elements towards common cause, the manipulation and delegation of skill to work in his favour, the harnessing of the strong, the protection and encouragement of the weak and unrealized, the breaking of centuries of laws and accepted mores right there in front of the very gods his mother had found.

And here was the mist, slowly taking it all away.

FIFTEEN

I RETURNED FROM TORONTO on the Monday before my father died, and came straight to the house to find him almost defeated. He had developed pneumonia again. He seemed to be down to some last accumulation of strength, which was no more than the ability to be that stillness I saw in the bed before me. His hand, a thing I was always borrowing and returning, was as weightless and ethereal as sunlight through the flesh of a leaf — a leaf he hadn't the strength to hand to me, though, when I took it in mine, it responded with the lightness of helium.

There were so many quiet concentrations around the room, I don't remember each, but I remember a sense of betrayed attention, and the underlying preparation, like feet approaching the end of an escalator — sentences no longer whispered but frank and flat and grim against the thick hush of this cocoon. There were bustles of action now and again, but these soon settled into the lateness of the room.

I noticed that the puzzles were all neatly stacked in their boxes, and for the first time no one had bothered to open another. A nurse spoke on the phone about the possibility of a new job. The TENS machine was boxed to be returned to the doctor. I was reminded of a hotel room that housekeeping knows is about to be vacated.

But the more fate threatened, the more constricted our emotional space, the more doggedly the room itself remained the same. Each corner came to its just conclusion. No mystery, no madness here, simply function. It could have been a padded cell. And that was when I discovered that long, narrow rooms are never more than that. They remain long, narrow rooms, regardless of how much one tries to create areas or moods. We didn't matter to the room, and the room might as well not matter to us. It didn't give a damn that we were waiting for death.

"We have stopped the chemotherapy," he had told me when he phoned me in Toronto. His voice sounded hoarse, but he was matter-of-fact and clear-minded. He wanted to know what I thought, and that was the only time his tone had lifted as if to question. I told him he should only take what he felt up to taking.

Entering his room felt like stumbling into a play. I entered a world that neither saw me nor heard me. Like an automatic pilot, rigid logic was guiding every move.

"Something's wrong," I said to Joseph.

He took me aside and tried to explain that nothing more could be done. There had even been talk of persuading me to stay in Canada, but our father had said no, he couldn't do that to me. Either I was thought to be cracking under the overwhelming strain, or my presence was thought to be overwhelming; I didn't clearly understand which, for I was hardly listening. My insides tightened with indignation at the thought that at a time like this — or at any time — anyone could question my place at my father's side. Even him.

A million wraths opened their eyes from a million unanswered hurts, and I felt like my grandmother's old horse, Gay Lady, when she climbed up the sky with her forelegs. I don't remember what I said as I railed at my father from another room, but I blew from that anguish straight to his bedside, and the presence of death so close had no power to dissuade me, nor grief to shroud my anger.

"Michael," I said, recalling that day so many years ago when he had forbidden me to address him in this way. Until now I had obeyed him.

"Michael," I said, "look at me. *Look* at me!" He was already looking at me when I said it. "You are seeing me for the last time. I am going away, and though I love you dearly I am not coming back. Do you hear me?"

I was showing him myself with my hands, indicating the length and breadth of me with incoherent gestures, and the room for the first time seemed small and destructible, frozen meanly around me. The basic premise on which I had based my life had been removed. I was at the end of possession, with nothing further to lose, nothing more to fear; I was at what felt to me like the point of ultimate injustice, the point where oblivion would be easier. I did not care what I struck, or what I might leave in my wake. This was a last stand, my only way to end being invisible.

I was desperate. He was leaving again, and this time he wasn't going to say goodbye and he wasn't going to return. No tantrums would bring him back. It was every trip, every exile, every absence all over again. Helpless, I was threatening to take away the only thing I had to take away — myself. To see if the threat of my absence would keep him; to see if my absence mattered. To see if *I* mattered. To see if I *existed*. As though all I would ever add up to was the extent to which he'd notice me.

"Ra, stop!" My brother tried to hold me as I was leaving. "Don't do this to yourself. Can't you see? Your heart's clenched on a vacuum. You are not abandoned, Ra. He can't help this one. This is death."

I left nonetheless, going back to my rented flat. There, the tears I shed made no case for anything at all.

Life had to go on, so the next morning, for the first time in months, I put on leotards that Glynne had given me, and went to dance class — the sound of music unexpected, unwelcome, this world not a place I wished to rejoin.

When I returned there was a message on the machine. The nurse had been trying to reach me. My father wanted to see me.

"I am never going back," I told Joseph.

"But that's silly, Ra. He wants to talk to you. He's completely confused. He isn't getting things straight any more. He asked for you, and when I told him you were back in Jamaica and he'd seen you, he said he thought so. He said it was strange, he thought he'd seen you at the other end of the room, waving a flag. He said you were saying, "Woo-woo," like an owl, and he couldn't figure out why. I told him that you were angry, that you were very upset because you had heard what had been discussed in your absence. He asked, what could he do now? How could he put things right? Should we all discuss it together? He hates these confrontations, and anyway he hasn't the strength, and probably hasn't the time — he's not going to make it, you know — so I told him, you want to put everything right with Ra, just tell her you love her. That's all she wants to hear. And then I guess he tried to find you."

I knew I would never be free. My heart would never disengage. I would never get away. Nothing would entirely break, nor would anything really mend. My father was dying as he had lived, with everything compelled by his gravity circling him — wars being fought for or against him, whether he knew it or not. How could I face his death when I was still trying to assemble the pieces of his life that were mine?

Maybe the truth was, I felt that as long as I kept fighting, how could our story end?

He asked the nurse to phone me again on Tuesday night. She talked to me first, and I felt consolation hearing her voice. But her words should not have consoled me. She told me that my father felt he needed help, and said he didn't know what to do next. What could I tell him? I couldn't promise more when there was no more, and I wondered again about whether he had accepted the doctor's prognosis; I wondered why whatever elephant-to-the-hill instinct should kick in wasn't kicking in, why he couldn't feel at peace with his death so near. Or was it not near? Should we be doing more?

It seemed to me that dying was not within his possibilities. A force of nature will do what it has to do. It never gives up, it cannot. It can only propel or blow or erupt or burn or flow. It has no capacity to stop.

The nurse must have given him the phone. "I don't know what to do," I thought I heard him say, but I couldn't be sure. And he said more but the words were like the creaking limb of a tree, or a wooden house settling, shrinking back to itself after a day of sun.

"Tomorrow I'll call the professor of internal medicine," I told him. "I'm going to talk to him and ask him to come and see you." He was someone we all trusted.

I told him I was coming to see him soon, and I said the same to the nurse, who came back on the phone to say he couldn't sleep, and could I come. But I was afraid to go over there. I told the nurse to remind him that I would call the specialist in the morning.

On Wednesday morning Sarah arrived at my door, the last grim chance of rescue, the fluke of fate that may save when the certainties of planning and preparation have come up short.

"Come. I'm taking you to see Daddy."

The house was quiet. It was nearly two o'clock, the end of the morning shift. Vita was by the foot of the bed when we entered, and looked pleased to see me. "Mr. Manley, look who has come to visit you," she said brightly.

I waited by the door, and Sarah's strong fingers, full of rallying confidence, cupped the back of my neck as if I were a ball she was going to pitch at our father.

"Here's Ra. I have brought her to see you."

There comes a time in illness when one can no longer be appalled; when one has learned to look for the flicker of light that is the expression of life, and the wounds and the losses of this or that are simply expressions of fate. It is the time when, from the floods, we treasure a small twig of green that we see as an olive branch, and we say that cities have perished, and that civilizations will have to be built from memory and from this.

He opened his mouth and a ghost lifted his hands — or they didn't lift, but from the shuffle of air I knew they wanted to lift — and I knew he was saying, "Ra," somewhere through the unintentional separation of his jaws.

Sarah talked over our heads. I can't remember what she was saying, but I know she was telling us to sort it all out. I never sat down, I felt there wasn't time. I wanted to stay but I wanted to go. I leaned over, and his fingers are still to this day holding me above my elbows as he gurgles something in my ear. I could not hear what he said.

"I can't hear him," I told Sarah, and he was looking up at me where I had pulled back and straightened, and he was saying something to me again.

Sarah was smiling at me. "I can hear him! He says he *loves* you. 'Ra, I love you,' he said!" This she repeated with certainty, and widened her eyes at me as though to emphasize the value of my gift.

And my father lifted the flat flap of his thumb straight up and towards Sarah while looking steadily at me, as though waiting for some vital confirmation.

"I love you too, Daddy."

And we left.

"That's all you ever wanted to know, Ra, and when he tells you, you can't hear him!" Sarah said this shaking her head, with her arm round my shoulder. And that arm was a branch of our father, one of five branches — restless, questioning, always knocking, like the old man still fighting death in the bed upstairs.

What would become of us all after our father? What green would each branch live to be?

"Shut up, Sarah!" I said.

~

My father had come to Toronto for the launch of my book *Drumblair* in September of 1996; had come when he shouldn't have. He had come with Glynne, for two days.

"He insists," she said over the phone before they left.

"I'm coming if it's the last thing I do," he said, and in fact it was the last trip he made. He could be on his feet for only seven minutes and then he would have to sit down, so we made sure, as the evening progressed, that he moved from one reserved chair to another.

He had spent evenings coaching me to read extracts before I returned to Toronto. Put the emphasis here, drop your voice there, run this into that, put hyphens to remember to glide . . . "old-shawls-full-of-sorrow" so you don't fill up the "full," don't pull the sense out of shape. Stop for the laugh. No, no, give them time — aha . . . there you are, ripple of applause . . . sip your water . . . okay, sip your wine.

Rex, who had collected my grandfather's speeches, who'd been the other voice of a special conversation with my father for so many years, introduced my book. It felt right that someone who had layered my family's life in so many ways, through each of the generations, was there to introduce me. When he finished his speech, my father clapped, nodded his head and muttered, "I hear you!"

When it was my turn to speak, I held onto the podium, my hands trembling a little, and looked across at my father. Though he was failing, his strength was all around me; it was there, invisible but irresistible, in the large crowd of Jamaicans who'd turned out that rainy Toronto evening.

I looked at him for a moment before I spoke. I knew that, deeper than all the currents his life had created in me, lay my own fate — the fate of my genes, the fate of who I was and who I would become. No longer an eddy in the flow behind him, I could feel his resolve pushing me forward, charging me to go on, to pull away from the slipstream, now that I'd got far enough to start my own engines.

I looked down at the page, which bore his pencilled promptings, and I started to read. Started to read the stories of my family, from Pardi to Mardi to Douglas to him. It was my book but it was their story and, no matter the flow or the oceans we yearned for, at the source we were one.

When my reading was finished, he turned to speak to my husband. "She's her own Manley now," he said softly.

SIXTEEN

OUR FATHER LOOKED HOPEFUL when he saw Joseph and me come round the door. It was hope that lifted his eyes towards us; everything borrowed for his journey had been returned but this.

"He has difficulty clearing his throat. We need a suction machine; one will come from the hospital at ten this evening," said the afternoon nurse.

"Babluck," my father muttered through some deep drain.

"Babluck," I agreed, and I asked the nurse if we should go and fetch the aspirator.

"Yes," she said, as though handing a letter to a waiting porter, her eyebrows lifting as if to make room below for her private thoughts. She would fight to ensure my father's last struggling breath.

I took two stairs down at a time; Joseph probably took three. This Saab would be my father's last car, as beloved and troublesome as his children, and now it seemed almost human; it was making its final ride for him. It took heart, and maintained a passion all the way through the early evening streets, passing the upcoming dead slow of rush-hour traffic on the opposite side, fled a speed trap. Joseph and I were accomplices to a fugitive, and we suspended time and laws and safety and probably common sense. We were one lean, taut contraction of intent.

A wrong turn, then the right one. We ended up in Emergency, where the usually comforting presence of my father's gentle night nurse, here in her regular hospital job, I now found disquieting. "Go on — take it — but you *must* bring it back," she said conspiratorially, pointing to the squat iron machine. She handed us a tube wrapped in plastic as she looked furtively at the confusion that surrounded her.

"We are counting breaths here," said Joseph in the car going back.

And there we were, mounting the steps one at a time. I brought the plastic attachments, and Joseph had the heavy machine, which he carried like a bassinet.

The room had changed. Two doctors were there now. The nurse pointed at the machine and at the bedside table. Her movements were calm and certain as she attached a tube that ended in a spout.

My father had seen us arrive. I stood at the foot of the bed and answered his anxious eyes: we are here, Dad, we begin again.

He was looking at me as though he were floating on water. He was looking over his feet, and I was something that he located on the line of horizon, a point of assurance against the possibility of drifting.

His eyes moved to the nurse at his side. She was cajoling him gently, respectfully: open your mouth, open your throat for me. He was gurgling, yet his eyes steadily, methodically, sought the information he needed for combat. I was terrified. I went to the other side of the bed and held his hand in both of mine. It was more tense than bone that day; it was down to will and courage.

"Mouth wide open, tongue out of the way, dear," the nurse explained almost affectionately. He did, and she aspirated, every time congratulating him, encouraging him. Then she gave him a rest. I was still holding his hand, and I stroked it. It was beautiful still, with a fragile elegance.

"You know, if I could just clear this throat, I could get on with my life."

It was such a funny thing to say, such a juxtaposition of one footstep with eternity, of the incidental with the sublime; so perverse that clearing one's throat like Percy the cat should be the last weapon in the arsenal, the final challenge of an epic legend, the ultimate key to this kingdom. Yet those would be the last words I'd hear him say.

The nurse prepared him to try again. I assisted with a thereness of hands and eyes. Twice I felt Joseph at my elbow. He was calling me to come, to come to the other side of the world. "I cannot come, Joseph." I felt as if I were trying to thread a needle and someone was standing in the path of the light. "You must come, Ra," and I knew I must. He took me to the top of the stairs, but I didn't want to go down.

"You just want to smoke," I said.

His "come" was terrible, though, and I knew again that I must. I called for wine, in this house that was somehow hobbling but at full speed, and the wine came. When you look back at times like these, things do come from the nowhere of everyday.

The patio was the gentlest place in my father's home. Night chorused around it, prepared to follow whichever liturgy we chose.

"I don't know how to say what I have to say now," Joseph told me.

I was letting the wine in wildly, letting it in like blood — like my brother's nicotine, which left behind only a saunter of smoke.

"This is it."

He looked at me, a child showing me some precious broken thing that cannot be fixed.

"This is it, Ra." And he wanted me to make it better, and knew, with the emptiness of that wanting, that this was the time we first would look at life from the other side.

"His pressure is sixty over forty."

I could feel our father with us. He was a huge trunk of a tree. Too big to disappear because the sap had dried up, and these were the last leaves.

The far wall with its ceiling-high shelves displayed a lifetime of objects, each stranded in its own space: a ceramic vase with four handleless cups, a mother and child swirled into a slice of mahoe, an aluminum bird fat as a wide-bodied airplane, a Turkish coffee pot with tiny cups on a brass tray, a torso of a man who had never had any expression and — standing in front, as baffled by us as we were by him — an example of cultivated north-coast primitivism, a laughing giraffe with tiger stripes.

"They say that if he doesn't sleep it will be an awful death," Joseph warned me.

"But we are clearing his throat . . . ," I said, as my own was shutting down.

"He will *drown*." At forty, Joseph still retained that maddening certainty of very bright children.

I suggested that we phone the professor of internal medicine again. Joseph called. The doctor was not surprised; he said that this free fall of pressure was Michael's impending death. We should encourage him to sleep.

He would never wake up.

By the time I returned to the room, my father was no more than a decision that had been made. I told Joseph to call whoever needed to be called. My father was tired. Sleep now,

Daddy, try to go to sleep.
  Go to sleep.
  My beloved father.
  Go to sleep.

It is winter in the mountains, and there is a fire in Nyumbani's drawing room. I watch it licking at the edge of a well-burnt log, like a dog finding some sweetness in an old bone, some ultimate solace where it is not reasonable to expect any to be found. I am not sure which is the lip of flame and which is the charred heart. But it is sunset, and the peaks are wild stallions beyond the confining reins of my father or the spirit of his mother or the soul of his father. Three trees stand on the edge of his lawn, and I watch their darkness gathering in defence; watch them pulling the greenness into shadow like serious thought. "They are the three wise men," I hear my father explain, "who approach the mountains in twilight because they come all the way from the east."

As I look at them, I am looking at my ancestors, each life a single peak in a range, each day a rock on that peak, the minutes small indentations on the rocks, surfaces on which to place but a single step. Each life, each rock, each step is now inextricably bound to this one day, the only day. The final page. This Thursday.

"There will be peace," I say, more for myself than for him, for I know that whatever peace death may bring, it is still the last thing he wishes for.

The night nurse has come, and we're all around the bed. A doctor is listening to his heart with a stethoscope. I am saying the Lord's Prayer for him — let him in, be good to him. I am saying "Our Father" because its familiarity has overwhelmed me. It has chosen to be said.

Joseph is holding our father's long feet, abrupt ghosts under the sheet. Joseph is like a pot of earth at the base of Michael. He says the words with me. We all say the words. Except my father. He is almost straight on his back. I am holding onto his hand as though once again he will lift me over all this.

Though his eyes are now closed, he looks guarded — until suddenly he opens them and appears to be gently surprised. He is looking straight in front of him, at Mardi's drawing of that young girl pencilled in red, with her hand on her heart, on an aqua page. He looks pleased, as though he sees someone he recognizes. "Have you seen Mardi in the path?" I ask him, knowing there will be no answer.

Then he closes his eyes again. He has fallen asleep impeccably.

You stand at the end of a story, quite unable to turn the last page. You have read too much and you have not read enough. Too late, you realize that all the parts you skipped over and dismissed should have been cherished. So much time was spent on sentences that were only details. You would like to read it all over again, but in the living time of the first read, of the first writing.

I am lying at the centre of darkness. I know my eyes are open because I witness an abundance of falling stars. They tumble like acrobats out of the dark, each brilliant spark the end of its own eternity of burning; the end of some long shout whose final echo is right here in the brief plenum of my imagining. Though they are on fire, they cannot bite the dark; each brittle selfishness shares neither shadow nor light. They are their own stark companions, moments of terrifying activity within dense blackness, within the water-thick silence of ever or never.

I am still in the room. My father is sleeping above sleep, like the black notes lying halfway up the white keys of a piano. He is flat and noble, strung at the perfect tuning of all his consequences. I am sitting beside him, for the long wall stretches to my left and to my right. I am brought to some Africa of my longings, the deep, sad, bruised pit of all stomachs, the aching outline of a hollow that has no tears.

My father is perfect and proud, and his light has accumulated into a journey-line. His flesh is unselving like a chrysalis, weaving cobwebs for its thready soul. I am already part of a world that has nothing to offer him. He needs nothing here, no air, no heat, no glass of water — no light if I move the blinds.

It was that, Daddy. It was just that.

ACKNOWLEDGMENTS

My heartfelt thanks to:

The Canada Council for the Arts; The Norman Manley Foundation; The Bunting Institute of Radcliffe College, the Fellows of 1999, and my sister writer Christina Shea; The Virginia Centre for the Creative Arts; the medical professionals and friends who helped my father during his illness; and especially Prime Minister P.J. Patterson, and Ministers Omar Davies and Peter Phillips, for their constant support and assistance; Tony Bursey, David Coore, Neta Crawford, Gena Gorrell, Natalie Grow, Ainsley Henriques, John Hoad, Tracy Isaacs, Deborah Kelly-Rousseau, Sheila Kennedy, Cookie Kinkead, Rose McFarlane, Brian Meeks, Trevor Meldrum, Marsha Moses, Rex Nettleford, Jeanne Nightingale, Dorothy Prosser, Ian Randle; Gordon Robinson; Israel, Drum and Luke; the devoted Noelle Zitzer; and Louise Dennys, godmother to all my words.

Rachel Manley is the author of the memoir *Drumblair: Memories of a Jamaican Childhood*, which won the Governor General's Award for Non-fiction in 1997. She has also published three books of poetry and edited *Edna Manley: The Diaries*, a collection of her grandmother's journals. A former Bunting Fellow for Literature at Radcliffe College, she divides her time between Toronto and Jamaica. She has two sons, Drum and Luke.